THE ACCORDION FAMILY

Other books by Katherine S. Newman

Taxing the Poor: Doing Damage to the Truly Disadvantaged
(with Rourke L. O'Brien)

*Who Cares? Public Ambivalence and Government Activism from
the New Deal to the Second Gilded Age* (with Elisabeth Jacobs)

The Missing Class: Portraits of the Near Poor in America
(with Victor Tan Chen)

Chutes and Ladders: Navigating the Low Wage Labor Market

Rampage: The Social Roots of School Shootings (with Cybelle Fox,
David Harding, Jal Mehta, and Wendy Roth)

A Different Shade of Gray: Mid-Life and Beyond in the Inner City

No Shame in My Game: The Working Poor in the Inner City

Declining Fortunes: The Withering of the American Dream

Falling from Grace: Downward Mobility in the Age of Affluence

The Accordion Family

BOOMERANG KIDS, ANXIOUS PARENTS,
AND THE PRIVATE TOLL OF GLOBAL COMPETITION

Katherine S. Newman

BEACON PRESS · BOSTON

Beacon Press
25 Beacon Street
Boston, Massachusetts 02108–2892
www.beacon.org

Beacon Press books
are published under the auspices of
the Unitarian Universalist Association of Congregations.

15 14 13 12   8 7 6 5 4 3 2 1

This book is printed on acid-free paper that meets the uncoated paper
ANSI/NISO specifications for permanence as revised in 1992.

Text design and composition by Wilsted & Taylor Publishing Services

Many names and identifying characteristics of people mentioned in this work
have been changed to protect their identities.

Library of Congress Cataloging-in-Publication Data

Newman, Katherine S.
The accordion family : boomerang kids, anxious parents,
and the private toll of global competition / Katherine S. Newman.
p. cm.
Includes bibliographical references and index.
ISBN 978-0-8070-0743-3 (hardcover : alk. paper)
1. Parent and adult child. 2. Adult children—Family relations.
3. Competition, International. I. Title.
HQ755.86.N4888 2012
306.874084'6—dc23   2011027846

For Kathleen McDermott,
friend and fellow student of the
human condition for thirty-five years

CONTENTS

MARIA TERMINA AND HER HUSBAND, Alberto, live in the northwestern city of Bra in the Piedmont region of Italy. The people of Bra are traditionalists who struggle to hold the modern world at arm's length. Proud to be the hometown of Carlo Petrini, the founder of the Slow Food Movement, Bra hosts a biennial festival that celebrates artisanal cheeses from around the world. This tiny, leafy, quiet town of less than thirty thousand people swells to more than one hundred fifty thousand when the cheese connoisseurs show up in full force.

Alberto Termina, now sixty-seven, has lived in Bra almost all his life and worked for the same firm as an engineer for about forty of those years. His wife, Maria, is fifty-seven. They have three children, and Maria has been a stay-at-home mother, taking care of the family since her daughter, Laura, was born. The Terminas' youngest child, thirty-year-old Giovanni, has always lived with them and shows no signs of moving on. Giovanni graduated from the local high school but went no farther than that and is content with his steady blue-collar job as an electrician. He works on construction sites and picks up odd jobs on the side. It's a living, barely. His wages are modest, the building trades go up and down, and—in all honesty—his tastes in motorcycles are a bit extravagant. Though he is a skilled worker, Giovanni knows he could not enjoy himself with his friends as he does if he had to support himself entirely on his own earnings. But since he pays no rent and can eat well at his mother's table, his living expenses are low, leaving money for recreation.

Maria cooks for the family, cleans Giovanni's room, and provides advice when he asks for it, leaving the not-so-young man free to enjoy his passions, especially that motorcycle. "The biggest expenses I have to take care of are for going out . . . during the weekend, in the night, going out for dinner . . . or travels and holidays," Giovanni explains. Life is sweet.

Laura, the Terminas' oldest daughter, has also recently returned to the nest. Newly divorced, she and her five-year-old daughter moved home so that Grandma Maria could watch over her granddaughter while Laura goes out to work every day as an accountant. Resting in the bosom of her parents was a balm to Laura after the collapse of her marriage, and for now she sees no reason to plan for a future on her own.

Of the three children born to Maria and Alberto, only Giorgio— Giovanni's twin brother—lives on his own. Giorgio went further in school, completing a degree in economics at a local university and moving to Turin, where he works in marketing and statistics. He is the odd man out, not only in his family but among many of his family's neighbors. More than a third of Italian men Giovanni's age have never left home; the pattern of "delayed departure" has become the norm in Italy. This has made the country an international butt of jokes about *bambini* who will not cut the apron strings, the so-called "cult of *mammismo*" or mamma's boys.

It is no laughing matter in Italy, particularly in government circles where the economic consequences are adding up. Prime Minister Silvio Berlusconi came out in support of the campaign against *mammismo*, having been elected on the promise of doing away with "those hidebound aspects of Italian life which 'inhibit dynamism and growth.'"[1] In January 2010, Italian cabinet minister Renato Brunetta proposed making it illegal for anyone over eighteen to live with his or her parents. He made the suggestion on a radio show where he also admitted that his mother made his bed until he was thirty, when he left home.[2]

Why should government officials—including those whose own family lives are hardly worthy of admiration—care one way or the other where adult children make their home? The fact is that those private choices have serious public consequences. The longer these aging *bambini* live with their parents, the fewer new families are formed, and the evaporation of a whole generation of Italian children is knocking the social policies of the country for a loop. Plummeting fertility translates into fewer workers to fuel the retirement accounts in an aging society. The private calculations of families like the Terminas, who wonder how long they can support Giovanni, are becoming the public problem of prime ministers like the famously cavalier Berlusconi.

Are parents like Maria and Alberto listening to his advice? Surprisingly, no. Giovanni's dependence once would have been seen as aberrant, even shocking. Maria and Alberto married in their early twenties, moved into their own home, and started a family almost immediately. Alberto's job was steady—not uncommon in his generation of Italian men—and although it did not make him rich, he rarely worried about unemployment. It was enough for Alberto to occupy the position he was born for: paterfamilias.

It's just as well that he wears this role so comfortably because it won't be ending any time soon. Alberto and Maria must now stretch their retiree pensions to cover the expenses of their adult children. Giovanni gives his mother about two hundred dollars a month, and Laura buys clothes for her daughter. Otherwise, responsibility for household costs is pretty much what it was when Giovanni and Laura were growing up. The tab falls to the Bank of Mom and Dad.

Does this "delayed departure" worry thirty-year-old Giovanni? Not really. Expectations are changing, and there is little pressure on him to be more independent. His family isn't urging him to marry, and he leans back in his chair and opines that "nobody asks you the reason [why you stay] at home with the parents at [my] age . . . nobody obliges me to move away."

Is this sustainable? Will Giovanni and Laura be able to take care of their parents when they can no longer care for themselves? Mother Maria isn't so sure. Her generation is taking care of both parents and adult children, but she sees young women like Laura, who have jobs and families, and wonders, *"How can they support also grandparents?"* Though that future may worry Maria, for now she is quite content that her grown children are under her protection. Why should they leave?

THE TOKYO SKYLINE looms neon across a vast region. A city of twelve million, Japan's capital city is a mélange of the old and the new: high-technology firms and skyscrapers mix in with small businesses, one-story houses, and neighborhood shrines. Kumi Sato has at least one foot in both worlds. A widow now, she has spent what feels like a lifetime caring for her children. Actually, Kumi worked as a young woman, taking a job as an "office lady" for a large electronics firm in Akiba, a central business district known for its bright lights and bustling trade in cameras, computers, and all things digital. Once she married, though, at age twenty-three, she quit—as did virtually all Japanese women of her generation—to raise a family.

When her husband passed away, Kumi re-engaged with the world of commerce by taking over the family printing business. Her job opened a new window on the world of younger workers since her firm employs several twentysomething workers. She does not particularly admire what she sees. The work ethic she defines as integral to the Japanese DNA seems to have been shut off in the next generation. "Young people now are impatient," she exclaims, "they don't work over time . . . they change jobs often."

Kumi's twenty-eight-year-old son and youngest child, Akiro, lives with her and shows no signs of leaving the nest. In fact, Akiro thinks he would like to "make some move by age thirty-five" but until then plans to take advantage of not having to pay for food or rent and being able to spend everything he earns "for myself"—on things like "CDs, DVDs, games, magazines, and books." Akiro is not responsible for cooking or any other household chores, though he tries to do things "when I notice." He graduated from a four-year university and since then has held a series of part-time jobs, working in a restaurant, at a gas station, and as a day laborer. He has no plans for further education, though he considers his current restaurant job no more than "a way to earn a living." Akiro regularly looks at the help-wanted ads in the paper, but does not seem terribly motivated to make a change. Kumi's friends, who also have children in their late twenties at home, urge her to instill a greater sense of responsibility in him. They ask, "What, you are not taking money from your children?"

She doesn't really need the money. What she needs is to know that her son is going to grow up and assume the life of an adult. That metamorphosis was unavoidable in Kumi's day. The post–World War II period in which she came of age was a time of widespread poverty and hardship in Japan. The boom years that followed were a blessed relief, but one that exacted an enormous commitment in work hours, particularly of Kumi's husband. Discipline, dedication, willingness to spend virtually every waking hour at the office—these are the qualities she associates with manhood.

What happened to all that? To hear Kumi tell the story, something untoward is germinating in the next generation. It is as if a bunch of aliens who look and sound Japanese landed from some distant planet and took up residence among the natives. This is a defective generation that does not have the drive and selflessness that is the essence of modern Japan. But who raised this alien crowd? Here Kumi falters. She doesn't think this state of affairs happened by accident. Society as a whole, in particular, parents like her, failed at their most fundamental task: grooming their successors. Her generation defaulted on a sacred responsibility to discipline its progeny. She is deeply troubled by her son's failure to live up to the ideal of masculinity and adulthood she sees as normative. At the same time, Kumi is convinced that this default is, well, her fault. She coddled him; she enabled this retreat from maturity. She berates herself for being too weak to demand more of him, to kick him out in order to pull him into line. When he explains that he plans to stay right where he is until the age of thirty-five, she merely shakes her head and wonders at her own indulgence. It is not the Japanese way.

But isn't Japan locked in the economic doldrums? Surely that is the reason Akiro cannot move on. The newspapers are full of stories of the "lost decade," or is it two by now? The bubble economy burst in the 1990s, and the following stagnation swallowed the job market whole. Giant Japanese firms put a stop to the time-honored system of lifetime employment. Companies like Toyota and Honda, Mitsui and Sony, were forced to do the unthinkable: lay off thousands of workers. An article in the June 9, 1995, *USA Today* noted "Japanese executives, labor experts and academics [saying] out loud what many have been thinking: that guaranteed lifetime employment for Japanese workers is becoming a thing of the past." A personnel manager at Dowa Mining said as much: "At our company, lifetime employment is gradually breaking apart."[3]

Eight years later, in the September 7, 2001, *Daily Yomiuri*, the president of Matsushita proclaimed that his firm "did not need middle-aged and senior workers, whose minds were too slow to adapt to new information technology." The article went on to posit that the then-current wave of layoffs of more than ten thousand employees at several major Japanese companies was an indication that the "thinking of Japanese management" had "undergone a radical change."[4] Starting in the early

1990s, the international press was filled with articles shouting the news: the Japanese system was cracking. Oki Electric Industry said it would cut two thousand jobs—7 percent of its workforce—by March 1995; electronics giant Hitachi planned to furlough two thousand two hundred workers, at 90-percent pay, for four days; Sanyo Electric would eliminate two thousand of its twenty-nine thousand jobs in three years; the Fuji Research Institute estimated Japanese companies employed eight hundred thousand people they didn't need, including "office girls" who served green tea to managers.[5] Nissan Motor announced plans to cut its workforce by four thousand over the next three years and said it expected to lose the equivalent of about 192 million Canadian dollars (in 1991).[6] Fujitsu, Japan's largest computer company, was reducing its workforce by six thousand over two years in an attempt to lower fixed costs and improve profits in the face of the continuing weak demand.[7] And the bad news continued—for years.

COMPARED TO WESTERN Europe, where unemployment rose to double digits during the same period, Japan remains an oasis of opportunity. A terrible labor market in Japan consists of 5 percent of the workforce out on the streets, which would be a welcome scenario in many other parts of the developed world, including the United States. In Japan, though, this level of unemployment is considered a catastrophe in the making.

Layoffs notwithstanding, the people taking it on the chin in this historic transformation in Japan weren't the old-timers, the workers with seniority who could rely on lifetime contracts. Younger workers in Akiro's generation were the people most likely to be out of luck and out of a job. *USA Today* chronicled the upheaval, explaining to readers that the long-vaunted Japanese system was headed for the junk heap of capitalism. What was to take its place? An army of part-time, expendable workers:

> Japan's economy has produced more than 17 million . . . "non-regular" workers toiling in part-time, contract or temporary-agency jobs. Easy to fire, these chronic part-timers are absorbing the shock of Japan's downturn: The government estimates that 158,000 have lost their jobs since October [2009].

When they first attracted attention in the late 1980s, irregular workers were viewed as social rebels, opting out of the dreary, 60-hour workweeks endured by corporate Japanese "salarymen" to enjoy flexible hours and undemanding jobs. The Japanese, who habitually absorb and transform foreign terms, started calling these outsiders "freeters"—combining the English word "free" with a German word for worker, *arbeiter.*

But what looked at first like a liberating social change proved to be the beginning of a wrenching economic transformation.[8]

The chances that Akiro will find a job like the one his father held one generation ago have all but collapsed. Layoffs that began in the early 1990s have left a moonscape full of craters for his generation. As a latter-day businesswoman, his mother is aware of the ups and (mainly) downs of the job market. But when she tries to explain to herself why her kid has turned out to be a disappointment, those structural forces recede into the background. What takes center stage are her own failings as a mother, the nagging worry that her marriage didn't quite measure up, and the sense that she and her friends made some serious mistakes in raising the next generation. It's a moral tale, and it isn't pretty.

NEWTON, MASSACHUSETTS, IS famous for its leafy streets, New England–style colonial houses, and well-educated, professional parents. The nearby universities—Harvard, MIT, Tufts, and dozens of liberal arts colleges—not to mention the concentration of health-care and computer-related industries, insures a steady influx of middle- and upper-middle-class families. Immigrants—especially high-tech professionals from Israel, India, and Russia—flock to this affluent community in pursuit of opportunities for the second generation. It boasts first-class schools from top to bottom; graduates of Newton high schools turn up regularly in the Ivy League. Poor black kids are bused in from inner-city Boston through the Metco integration program in order to partake of the town's exemplary educational facilities, but few actually live within its boundaries. All but the fairly well heeled are priced out.

William Rollo and his wife arrived in Newton in 1989 after having lived in Seattle, Philadelphia, and Summit, New Jersey. A Brooklyn native, William married Janet at the age of twenty-two and set about completing a residency in podiatry. Their eldest son, John, grew up in Newton and did well enough in high school to attend the liberal arts college Williams, one of the nation's most selective. Even so, he beat it home after graduating and has lived with his parents for several years while preparing to apply to graduate school. "A lot of my friends are living at home to save money," he explains.

Tight finances are not all that is driving John's living arrangements. The young man had choices and decided he could opt for more of the ones he wanted if he sheltered under his parents' roof. John is saving money from his job in an arts foundation for a three-week trip to Africa, where he hopes to work on a mobile health-care project in a rural region. It's a strategic choice designed to increase his chances to be accepted into Harvard University's competitive graduate program in public health.

John needs to build up his credentials if he wants to enter a school like that. To get from here to there, he needs more experience working with patients in clinics or out in the field. It takes big bucks to travel to exotic locations, and a master's degree will cost him dearly, too. In order to make good on his aspirations, John needs his parents to cover him for the short run. On his own, John could pay the rent on an apartment, especially if he had roommates. What he can't afford is to pay for both privacy *and* travel, to support himself *and* save for his hoped-for future. Autonomy turns out to be the lesser priority, so he has returned to the bedroom he had before he left for college, and there he stays.

John sees few drawbacks to this arrangement. His parents don't nag him or curtail his freedom. Janet wonders if they should ask him to pay rent, to bring him down to earth a bit and teach him some life skills, like budgeting. William is not so sure. He enjoys his son's company and was happy when he moved back into his old bedroom. Having a son around to talk to is a joy, particularly since John's younger brother is out of the house now, studying at the University of Vermont. That empty nest has refilled and thank goodness, says William, rather quietly.

If John had no goals, no sense of direction, William would not be at ease with this "boomerang arrangement." Hiding in the basement playing video games would not do. Happily, that is not on John's agenda.

William is glad to help his son realize his ambitions. He approves of John's career plans and doesn't really care if they don't involve making a handsome living. What really matters is that the work *means* something. It will help to remake the world, something William has not felt he could contribute to very directly in his work. Having a son who can reach a bit higher—if not financially, then morally—is an ambition worth paying for.

And it will cost this family, big time. William and Janet have invested nearly two hundred thousand dollars in John's education already. They will need to do more if John is going to become a public health specialist. They are easily looking at another fifty thousand dollars, even if John attends a local graduate program and continues to live with them. Fortunately, there are excellent options—some of the nation's finest—close by. Whatever it costs, they reason, the sacrifice is worth it.

Private Safety Nets

In Italy today, 37 percent of men age thirty have never lived away from home.[9] Their counterparts in Spain, Japan, and a host of other developed countries are following a similar path: millions are staying at the Inn of Mom and Dad for years, sometimes for several decades longer than was true in earlier generations. In the United States, we have seen a 50-percent increase since the 1970s in the proportion of people age thirty to thirty-four who live with their parents. As the recession of 2008–2009 continued to deepen, this trend became even more entrenched. Kids who cannot find jobs after finishing college, divorced mothers who can't afford to provide a home for their children, unemployed people at their wits' end, the ranks of the foreclosed—all of these people are beating a path back to their parents' homes to take shelter underneath the only reliable roof available.

To some degree, this has always been the way of the private safety net. Families double up when misfortune derails their members, and the generations that have been lucky enough to buy into an affordable housing market, that enjoyed stable jobs for decades, find they must open their arms (and houses) to receive these economic refugees back into the fold. Blue-collar working-class families and the poor have never known anything different: their kids have no choice but to stay home while they try to outrun a labor market that has become increasingly inhospitable. Their parents have had it hard as well, as layoffs have spread through the factories of the Midwest and the South; pooling income across the generations is often the only sensible survival strategy, even if the climate becomes testy. Those who remember the 1970s sitcom *All in the Family* will recall Archie and Edith Bunker's daughter, Gloria, and errant son-in-law, "Meathead," who lived with her parents because they could not make ends meet otherwise. This was the comic version of the accordion family, working-class style.

Until relatively recently, the middle class in most prosperous countries did not need to act as an economic shock absorber for such a prolonged period in the lives of their adult children. Their households might expand to take in a wayward divorcee or support a child who had taken a non-paying internship, but the norm for most white-collar parents was to send young people out into the world and look on in satisfaction as they took their places in the corporate world or the professions, found their life mates, and established their own nests.

What is newsworthy about current trends is less the return of the unfortunate to the parental fold but the growth in the numbers of young adults in their late twenties and thirties who have never been independent in the first place. Why, in the world's most affluent societies, are young (and not so young) adults unable to stand on their own two feet? And what kind of fallout is this "failure to launch" producing?

The media around the world picked up on these issues early in the 1990s, when a raft of headlines lamented the emergence of a generation of slackers. In Japan, the cover stories pointed at the young and called them out as "parasite singles," kids who mooched off their parents and refused to accept the strictures of adulthood. From the viewpoint of people like Kumi and her late husband, who stuck their noses to the workplace grindstone and the child-rearing treadmill, it appeared that Japanese youth were somehow defective. They seemed happy to accept part-time jobs and live at home, where their parents picked up the tab for daily expenses, freeing them to go out and party. In a country with famously rigid norms of appropriate behavior, the debut of this slacker generation was a social calamity capable of stopping the presses and flooding the TV talk shows. How could such a serious problem have festered beneath their notice? How had the orderly transition from youth to adulthood suddenly run off the rails?

Americans are generally more tolerant of social change, but here, too, the broadcast media and the daily newspapers began to fill with articles about boys in their mid-twenties sitting in darkened basements, whiling away their time on video games rather than buckling down to pursue adult goals. Psychiatrists diagnosed the problem as a kind of retreat from reality and hinted that indulgent parents were suffering from some kind of "'60s infection." Baby boomers, caricatured as being unable to say no, were accused of alternately cocooning their kids and indulging themselves. "Helicopter parents," who hovered over their progeny, following them off to college to help choose their courses, tending to their every need, were said to lack the backbone to let their children grow up by learning from their failures. If everything has to be perfect, boomers were admonished, your kids are going to be basket cases when they actually try to stand on their own two feet. No wonder Jack and Jill were coming home to live out their twenties: their parents were ready to wrap them in swaddling clothes all over again. Pathetic!

Structural Barriers to Independence

These complaints were largely off the mark. For the most part, young people the world over are still keen on establishing their independence. Twenty-six-year-olds who enjoy the comforts of home still look forward to the day they establish their own hearth. Yet, there are many reasons why that deadline is receding to more distant horizons. The contours of the household are stretching—creating accordion families—because there are few other choices, particularly in societies with weak welfare states (like Japan, Spain, or Italy) and because the advantages to delayed departure are significant compared to launching an independent life with insufficient resources in societies like our own.

Globalization has insured that the economic conditions that underwrote the earlier, more traditional, road to adulthood no longer hold. International competition is greater than it once was, and many countries, fearful of losing markets for their goods and services, are responding by restructuring the labor market to cut the wage bill. Countries that regulated jobs to insure they were full-time, well-paid, and protected from layoffs, now permit part-time, poorly-paid jobs and let employers fire without restriction. That may serve the interests of firms—a debatable low-road strategy—but it has destroyed the options for millions of new entrants to the labor market throughout the advanced post-industrial societies. Japanese workers who once looked forward to lifetime employment with a single firm have gone the way of the dinosaur. American workers have seen the emergence of contingent workers (part-time, part-year, and short-term contracts), downsizing, offshoring, and a host of other responses to globalization that have exposed the American workforce to wage stagnation and insecurity. European labor is arguably facing a very rocky future as the global consequences of the current financial crisis weaken the EU economies and threaten the social protections that made them the envy of the developed world.

Eventually, these conditions will envelop the entire workforce. For the time being, though, they are most evident in the lives of the least powerful: new entrants to the labor market, immigrants, and low-skilled workers. *The Accordion Family* dwells on the first of these groups, the generation trying to find a foothold in a rapidly changing economy, who must contend with the ill winds blowing through labor markets, which cannot absorb them as they once did, and housing prices that—foreclosure epidemics notwithstanding—are making it hard for this generation to stake a claim to residential independence. The new entrants fall back into the family home because—unless they are willing to take a significant cut in their standard of living, the last resort these days—they have no other way to manage the life to which they have become accustomed.

There is a cultural rub lurking here. In 1993, I published *Declining Fortunes*, which chronicled the emergence of downward mobility between the generations in the United States. I pointed out that the oldest baby boomers, the parents of the young people who are the subject of *The Accordion Family*, reveled in countercultural trappings in their youth and didn't mind living in dumps. The blue jeans brigade had no use for comfortable beds when they could bunk on the floor. New clothes were out of fashion because Goodwill hand-me-downs were just fine. Their younger siblings, however, were a different story. The trailing-edge boomers, those born in the mid-'60s, represented a different generational culture. Products of the Reagan years, they were more conventional and accordingly more desirous of the finer things in life.

With the advantage of hindsight, it seems clear that the older boomers, who rode the wave of social protest, were an aberration. The expectation of comfortable living standards was in place before them and returned to dominate the social imagination of their younger siblings when the leading-edge boomers moved into adulthood. The brief period in between—the heyday of the counterculture—has assumed an outsized importance in our cultural imagination, but it was an interlude in between far more conventional assumptions about what middle-class Americans should expect for their way of life. Today's thirtysomethings are not willing to "slum it" to protect their residential independence. Like Giovanni, they are happy enough to compromise on that freedom and privacy in order to eat well or ride their motorcycles into the sunset. Standard of living trumps taking on the trappings of real adulthood.

Meanwhile, their parents seem largely willing to accept—or in Japan, uneasily resigned to—the notion that a "boomerang child" in his thirties is the new normal. They aren't entirely at ease with the situation and downplay their mature children's presence in the home when speaking with peers. Giovanni's living arrangements aren't exactly celebrated. Yet, in truth, they aren't entirely hidden either. There are at least two reasons why. First, Giovanni is not an oddball. Most of his friends are in the same situation, and Italian parents are very aware of how the presence of adult children in their natal homes really is widespread. Second, Giovanni's lifestyle has some unacknowledged but nonetheless important, positive consequences for his parents. Maria and Alberto remain important, needed, because they are still parents. That was true when Alberto was twenty-three and a new father, and it is still true now that he is sixty-five. Nothing has changed. Given the alternative of being led out to pasture, as they see it at least, there is some merit in holding on to a valued identity.

Cultural norms—the expectations that people bring to the table when social change is in the air—matter for how parents around the world view these new family formations. Japanese parents expect discipline and order, and are horrified by what they see among their children instead. Italian families are happy to have their grown children live with them, however vexing it may be for Berlusconi. Spanish parents and their adult children are angry at the government for facilitating lousy labor contracts that have damaged the children's prospects, but they know that it can be a joy to be near the younger generation.

In America, we deploy a familiar cultural arsenal in crafting meaning: the work ethic and the hope of upward mobility. If Joe lives at home because it will help him get somewhere in the long run, that's fine. If he's hiding in the basement playing video games, it's not fine. The accordion family has to be in the service of larger goals or it smacks of deviance.

All of these adaptations are responses to central structural forces beyond the control of any of us. Global competition is taking us into uncharted waters, reshaping the life course in ways that would have been scarcely visible only thirty years ago. It's a brave new world, and the accordion family is absorbing the blows as best it can.

To understand how families are changing in the wake of globalization and what those changes mean, we focus first, in chapter 1, on how young people and their elders have uncoupled the subjective sense of adulthood from the signs we used to take as real markers of maturity and then, in chapter 2, on what forces are propelling this dramatic change. When adult children return to the family nest, they do not resume the roles they had when they were teenagers. In chapter 3, we see how they become "in-house adults," a new station in life that has to be carefully negotiated on both sides of the equation.

This is more than a practical problem; it has a moral face. The development of the accordion family is seen as completely normal and nonproblematic in some places and a sign of catastrophe and rampant deviance in others. In chapter 4, "I'm OK, You Are Not," we examine differences in the ways cultures are adjusting to accordion families (or refusing to do so).

Young (and not so young) people are the primary focus of our investigation, but they are not the only ones whose trajectories are changing. Their parents' life cycles are also diverging from the patterns of the past. How has the accordion family impacted the parents? That is the subject of chapter 5.

Suppose we didn't face the financial binds propelling the accordion family? What if higher education didn't cost us so much or rental housing was plentiful and inexpensive? Wouldn't everything be perfect then? Globalization has placed similar competitive pressures on the youth labor markets of the Nordic countries, but their response has been different: they protect young people from this onslaught by devoting tax dollars to insuring their independence. Is this the solution? The Nordic model obviates the need for families to serve as the main buffer, but as we will see in chapter 6, it has its own problems.

Political tensions are rising because of the way that fertility patterns are changing the composition of populations in countries with no history of immigration. Europeans are particularly aware that the accordion family is slowing the fertility of the native born compared to that of the immigrant newcomer, and this often feels like a threat to the national character (chapter 7).

Through these topical lenses, we will explore the social and cultural impact of the accordion family. It will emerge as an imperfect but nonetheless growing response to the pressures we face in a world of global competition.

CHAPTER 1

The Slippery State of Adulthood

ON THE SECOND MONDAY of every January, families all over Japan celebrate *Seijin no Hi,* the "Coming of Age" festival. Young people who turn twenty years old during that school year dress in formal clothes—kimonos with draped sleeves for women and business suits or kimonos for men—and are feted by their elders and public officials as they take their place in the adult world. The holiday marks the age at which a young person can legally drink, undertake important obligations, and generally claim the respect due a grown-up in a society where seniority matters. *Seijin no Hi* was first instituted in 1948, but the Japanese have held coming-of-age celebrations since at least the eighth century.

Few other cultures mark the onset of adulthood as formally as the Japanese do.[1] It is almost a curiosity in the country now since virtually no one actually achieves anything even close to adult status at the age of twenty these days. At twenty, most Japanese young people have no idea what it means to assume the weighty responsibility of marriage, child-bearing, full-time work, or putting a roof over their heads. They may be a decade or more away from the kind of maturity that was completely normative in the 1950s.

Take, for example, Katsu, who is thirty years old and lives with his parents and two younger sisters. Katsu's father is fifty-seven and works as an officer in a nonprofit organization; his mother is the same age, a housewife most of her adult life. Katsu has one younger sister (age twenty-eight) who works as a temp in a Tokyo high-rise office building and another (age twenty-six) who is a freeter. Katsu himself dropped out of a four-year university, hoping to pursue his dream of becoming a stand-up comedian. That didn't work out so well, though, so he joined his older sister as a temp. By the time we caught up with him, he had finally landed his first full-time job in a publishing company. The road from his *Seijin no Hi* to that job took nearly ten years to travel.

The older generation in Japan is perplexed by this path. Katsu's own parents were married for many years by the time they were his age. Nobu, Katsu's father, understood well that his role in life was to find a decent job right away and lay the foundation for a new family. Looking forward, Noriko, his mother, knew she would have to shoulder responsibility for the care of her in-laws as they aged. These were sober, serious people who knew they were destined for well-defined roles in Japanese society. Their children are caught up in a completely different migration to adulthood, and the shock of adjacent generations with such divergent routes to maturity is tearing holes in the social fabric of Japan.

Katsu moved out of his parents' home for a time but returned when he found himself unemployed; he hasn't left since. When he was loafing about without much money, it was hard to socialize with his working friends. He now expects to be living with his parents for at least the next five years.

Perhaps not surprising given his situation, Katsu does not see age, marriage, or parenthood as a significant marker of adulthood, though he does feel that having "social responsibility"—by which he says he means "responsibility for work"—is an important part of what it means to be an adult. More than anything, Katsu notes, maturity is not a station in life marked by what sociologists call "status transitions." It cannot be measured by jobs or a marriage license. Growing up is a state of mind. "When the person becomes self-possessed, I think that is an indication of true adulthood," Katsu says. And in this view, he is hardly alone. Katsu is part and parcel of a growing, international culture of delayed independence.

Men seem particularly ill-at-ease with adult transitions, but women often share their reservations (and patterns). Rin is a thirty-seven-year-old woman who lives next door to her parents in Tokyo. Although Rin has a college degree and has been working for nearly ten years, she doesn't particularly want to marry or have children. Those aspects of adulthood bother her, perhaps because of the confinement they imposed on her mother: subservience to a high-handed mother-in-law, many hours alone waiting for a commuter husband to finish a twelve-hour day. If that constitutes growing up, Rin suspects she might be better off ignoring the whole business:

I don't think it is necessarily a good thing to become an adult. So I don't mind if someone wants to remain a child. For those who want to be an adult, it's OK for them to be one. As for me, I don't want to be an adult. As far as I can see, adulthood means to cut up freedom into pieces or to throw away one's own freedom. To mutate oneself so one will be the same as others or the rest of so-called society seems to me the meaning of becoming an adult.

One of the reasons Rin is so determined to ignore society's demands is because she has absorbed conceptions of individuality that are decidedly un-Japanese. Her generation is breaking more than one mold; they are moving to the beat of their own drummer that is at odds with central values of solidarity and similarity, defining features of Japanese culture for centuries. Rin explains:

When you are on your own, when you exist just on your own, you do things you want to do based on the feelings from inside of you. But when I think of becoming an adult [and] social morals, shared illusions, or social conventions—there are many things like that, you know—it seems that becoming an adult means to fit yourself to them, regardless of how you really feel. In other words, fitting yourself to the mold that is demanded by society. There are many patterns for such molds—heart-shaped, bird-shaped, etc.— there are molds that are already prepared in society. And I think that becoming an adult means to bend and twist your body so your body will fit inside the mold.

In the United States, there is perhaps less to reject in the adult world. But the pathway to it is often strewn with obstacles and the imperative to push past them weaker than it once was. Lisa Caldwell majored in philosophy at Brown University but found herself unsure of the next step. With graduation over, she moved in with her folks and looked around for a job. A lawyer in her hometown of Newton, Massachusetts, needed assistance, which kept Lisa occupied for a few months. Because she had no living expenses, that stint gave her the wherewithal to move out on her own, first to San Francisco for two years and then to Brooklyn for another four.

It was a time of discovery for Lisa—as in discovering how much it costs to be an independent adult. Lisa piled up a mound of debt that, at age twenty-eight, drove her back into the arms of Mom and Dad. For many Americans, returning to the nest at that age would be pushing the boundaries of social acceptability. Twenty-one is OK; twenty-three is understandable. But once you're near thirty, which is coming up quickly for Lisa, the danger of being stigmatized lurks in the corner. Even so, Lisa found the opportunity to return to the place where she grew up comforting—and not just for financial reasons. Truth be told, she was drifting through her life, taking jobs that she found interesting, with little focus on building a career.

In Brooklyn, Lisa worked as an associate editor at *Media Week,* a job that she found "fun," mainly because she "loves English." During her San Francisco stint, she worked for an academic author who at the time was writing two books about women's issues, another area of interest for Lisa. Here and there, she tried her hand at acting, but that didn't quite satisfy. Back at home, with a bit more time and latitude to think it through, Lisa decided she had an interest in the "healing arts," meaning to her helping others with life's problems. To make a go of that, she knew, however, that she would need more education, probably a master's degree in social work. Given the mound of debt she still had from her years at Brown and thereafter, not to mention the high cost of graduate school, Lisa figured the best way forward would be to move backward temporarily: live with her parents so she could use the money she earned to pay off her debts and save whatever was left for professional education.

Given her "limbo life," Lisa finds it hard to bring the meaning of adulthood into focus. Her meandering path doesn't give her a clear trajectory of the kind that defined the experience of earlier generations. It has taken Lisa many years past college to find a focus in life, and it isn't clear even now that it will stick. It is ironic that this lack of direction is as much of an issue for a young woman like Lisa as it would be for any man her age. It was not long ago that women were not expected to develop career goals. If they worked, they were understood to be in a holding pattern before marrying, much as Japanese women are expected to be, even now.[2] If they worked after marrying, the accumulation of pin money was the goal, not the support of a family or the pursuit of upward mobility. Today, however, the genders have converged on the importance of careers as a source of identity. And, as a consequence, the experience of drift is just as problematic for women as it is for men. The genders have come together in their expectations[3] and, at least in the United States, in the barriers they face in moving toward independence.

"I guess [an adult] would be someone who takes responsibility and ownership of their life," Lisa says, "who's not kind of thinking life is going to happen or someone is going to help them out." For Lisa and many in her generation, adulthood is this kind of feeling or process much more than a rigid set of milestones. While she isn't there yet, she is edging up on the outer boundaries of adulthood. "So I'm still in this place, but I'm not an adult yet though I'm now becoming it," she explains. "For the past six years, I've just been living a life without any real responsibilities other than to myself and my dog."

For the living generations that preceded Lisa, this fuzzy orientation toward adulthood is baffling. Although Americans lack a *Seijin no Hi* of their own, back in the day, Lisa's parents would have had little trouble pointing out the landmarks.[4] Everyone understood where they were. When parents wanted to tell their friends what their kids were up to in life, they treated these markers as a roadmap: John has finished his education, found the love of his life, landed a decent job with potential for the future, tied the knot (finally!), and settled down to raise the next generation. Those days of status transitions—clear, publicly recognized steps toward autonomy, residential independence, and the birth of a new family—have given way to a more psychological perspective. You are an adult when you feel like one.

Feeling the Way to Adulthood

Giovanni Termina, the thirty-year-old we met in the introduction, has always lived with his parents in Bra, the third-most populous city in the province and home to the University of Gastronomic Sciences. A blue-collar man like his father before him, Giovanni works in a factory, except when riding his beloved motorcycle, and is a rather shy and understated person who dresses casually and enjoys walking in the mountains that flank his native city.

When we first made contact with Giovanni, he was surprised that a social scientist would seek him out for his personal reflections on the issue of adulthood. He doesn't think of himself as a source of the sociological imagination, and coming of age is not a topic he obsesses over. Giovanni doesn't see himself as aberrant for living with his parents or making so few moves toward independence. Many of his friends are in the same situation, and none of them thinks of it as a predicament requiring a lot of introspection. Though he is not responsible for the heftiest bills (housing or food), Giovanni doesn't exactly think of himself as a dependent. He is just a grown-up of a slightly different kind. "Being an adult is not about visible markers," he explains. Like Katsu and Lisa, Giovanni believes that adulthood

> [isn't] a matter of age or being married or not. Being adult means feeling this condition inside you, when you have reached your goals and you have satisfaction about your work and personal situation. You are adult when you don't need too much support from your parents, when you feel mature enough, and it is not even a matter of parenthood. It is mainly a matter of personal autonomy.

Giovanni has a ton of "personal autonomy." As a courtesy, he may tell his mother that he won't be home for dinner or that he's going away with his girlfriend for the weekend. But there is no rule that requires him to do so and certainly no sense that his parents' financial responsibility for his keep entitles them to veto power over his life. He is a friendly boarder, and that's fine with him—as it seems to be with them, at least for now. Their lack of control over him (something they don't aspire to anyway) leaves the psychological space for Giovanni to define himself as autonomous. It is an independence disconnected from the financial ties that bind: adulthood is a state of mind.

Carlo Morelli is thirty-two and lives with his parents in the Northern Italian city of Montà d'Alba in the Piedmont region. Renowned for its wineries, the area is a "mecca for gourmands," particularly well known for its truffles. In the fall, every town in the Piedmont region competes for tourists from throughout Europe and overseas (and other parts of Italy) with festivals celebrating wild mushrooms or wines aged to perfection.

Bald, tall, and stout, Carlo looks older than he is, possibly because he works so hard, holding down two jobs. The one that pays the bills is a responsible position as a building surveyor, a profession for which he trained as an apprentice. The other position, the one that makes him something of a big man around town, involves promoting local festivals and events. These are big boots for a man who completed his formal education at high school and comes from a modest family. Carlo's father is a farmer, and his mother owns a restaurant in the town. His sister, twenty-five, also lives at home but will soon be the only child left. At the ripe age of thirty-two, Carlo is ready to tie the knot and marry his girl in a big, traditional wedding in the church in the town square in Montà d'Alba.

Though he is now ready to settle down, Carlo has never felt that he was required to take this step in life. "In the past," he explains, "there was a social pressure that made people get married." No longer, though. "Now you are more free in . . . making choices," he says. That sequence—"the steps that you had to do"—defined adulthood; missing out on any part of it left the would-be adult in a kind of limbo, open to jibes and ridicule. Those days of lockstep development are over.[5] Yet men like Carlo are hardly ignorant of them; on the contrary, he knows how different the path is today from the one his parents embraced, the one that led to a sharp break with childhood and an almost instantaneous shift into the role of marital partner, worker, and parent. In his own era, Carlo can pilot his way toward this eventuality without much guidance—or opprobrium—from society. He doesn't worry about whether his neighbors will think he "failed to launch." One cannot be a failure if there is no social compact that requires a man to take these steps or suffer some kind of shame.

The more widespread a practice—be it racial or religious intermarriage, divorce, single-parent adoption, or any number of other familial practices once taboo—the less stigma it carries.[6] If nearly 40 percent of Italian men are still at home in the age group represented by Carlo and Giovanni, it becomes harder to point the finger and argue that those living at home are somehow odd, developmentally delayed, or worthy of disapproval. They are instead rapidly becoming if not *the* norm, then certainly *a* norm, one that gains legitimacy just by its ubiquity.[7]

Marco Fiorello, twenty-four, is a student living with his parents in Northern Italy. Unlike Giovanni and Carlo, Marco has never held down a job. Instead, he has been a student throughout his teens and into his twenties, living what one of his peers referred to as a "fairytale life" that has left him—in demeanor—younger than his years. Marco enjoys his studies and spends quiet evenings with his girlfriend at home rather than out on the town with his buddies. His relationship with his mother is formal and a bit strained; Marco doesn't feel comfortable speaking openly in her presence, which can make living in close proximity a strain at times.

Though his social class is distinct from that of Giovanni—who has worked consistently since leaving school at eighteen—Marco shares the view that growing up really isn't about assuming full responsibility for one's financial or residential autonomy. It is about identity, subjectivity, and forms of autonomy that don't depend on the ability to live on one's own. Since Marco enjoys a measure of control over his daily life, he certainly doesn't feel like a child anymore. Even so, he isn't quite at the stage where he would declare himself an adult, either—and not because he is financially reliant on his family. Marco is still at the self-indulgent stage of life, not having to sacrifice his desires to care for someone else. He muses:

> Personally, I think one of the first signs of being adult is being able to renounce something [you want]. Until you realize that renouncing something means obtaining something else [the respect accorded adults], you are not really an adult. It's a big step.

A step he isn't ready for just yet. Does this mean that the traditional path his parents followed, which involved getting married and having children, is no longer relevant to adulthood? Yes and no. The "yes" comes from the recognition that Marco shares with Giovanni: they both know that this is how the process used to work and that there are thousands of couples all over their region who exemplify it, even if most are sixty and over. The "no" comes from realizing there is nothing pushing at their backs to force Marco or Giovanni to learn that special skill of renunciation. Neither Marco's parents nor anyone else close to him is telling him that he is deviant or unworthy of respect because he isn't ready to sacrifice his whims for the sake of full autonomy. He looks around and sees other young men who resemble him, doing exactly what he is doing: stretching out their adolescent status for years more than anyone ever did before and enjoying every minute of this freedom.

And in this regard, Marco sounds a lot like an American counterpart, Kate Azarian, who is also twenty-four and lives with her mother (and another mother-daughter pair) in a house in Newton, Massachusetts. The summer after her graduation from Mount Holyoke College, Kate traveled for a few weeks and then came back home to help care for a dying uncle, who died that December. At that point, Kate was "ready to start working," but she "never had a really clear, defined career path" and ended up taking a job at Whole Foods supermarket, mainly because she felt that it was "important to have a job and . . . to be making money and have purpose." For Kate, the Whole Foods job was a "great opportunity. I met a lot of people I wouldn't have otherwise met."

In time, however, Kate moved on and, in the two years since her graduation, she has worked at an environmental nonprofit and held administrative assistant jobs. Most recently, she spent some time preparing grants for a man who runs a nonprofit that focuses on pediatric research and working on another project at the Harvard School of Public Health. She also does a lot of paid child-care work for families in her neighborhood. Kate says she will soon be working as an assistant teacher, her first "real nine-to-five . . . or seven-to-five" job since graduating from college.[8]

While Kate does acknowledge that financial self-sufficiency may be a marker of adulthood, to her mind being a grown-up is more about "having established your own social circle, your own networks, whether it's professional or personal or whatever." When pressed to characterize adulthood, Kate describes it as "this sense of self that I'm developing, that I hope to have . . . grounded in individuality and knowing a lot about yourself [and] also knowing about the world around you." For Kate, becoming an adult is a process of self-discovery, one she is not inclined to rush. She is also not hurrying toward—or down—a particular career path:

I am sort of looking for a career, but I'm also just looking for both what I think will make me happy and be contributing. So whether that is one narrowly defined career path or it's a bunch of different jobs, I'm not sure yet, because I am somebody who has sort of a wide range of interests but not a focused passion. Let me be clear, I really enjoy school, and over the last few years there have been moments, if you had caught me, I would have said, I'm going to law school or I'm going to public health school or looking to get a master's in social work, and that was all true.

But Kate has yet to make a firm decision about her future. And she knows she is privileged to be able to take her time. Living at home has been a huge benefit since it has made it possible for her to experiment with different possibilities but "not have to sign [her] soul away" for a job she didn't believe in.

Entitled?

Most middle-class twentysomethings living in upscale suburbs like Newton share elevated expectations for their destinies. Two generations ago, they might have had no choice but to stick their noses to the nearest grindstone and learn a trade or take a job that, in time, might lead to something better—but not before years of routine work or high-handed bosses.

The hit TV series *Mad Men* captures beautifully the period of the late 1950s and early 1960s, when young single women were venturing out into the work world (in this case, Madison Avenue advertising) and finding their options severely curtailed. They could become secretaries or, if they had attended college, teachers. But there wasn't a lot of opportunity in other fields, and the notion that work was there to help a young woman realize her personal ambitions was nothing more than a glimmer on the distant horizon. The popularity of *Mad Men* derives in part from the way it reminds baby-boom women of the narrow escape they had from the limited options that plagued their mothers. There could not be a sharper change than the one that separates the curvaceous secretary in Don Draper's ad agency, Joan Harris, from a modern young woman like Kate.[9]

Critics of American youth have come to see Kate's generation as suffering from a bad case of entitlement. A 2008 article in *Asia Times* noted the continuing reign of the American slacker and pondered whether America "might be the first country in recorded history whose culture celebrates not only indolence but also the sheer absence of ability . . . [where] slacking has become the entitlement of every young American."[10]But this assessment is wide of the mark. Kate doesn't feel the world owes her, and she doesn't perceive herself as goofing off. She hopes her education will provide her with the chance to see the world or help her land an interesting, meaningful job. A future of bureaucratic paper pushing is not her aim. Nor would her parents, who invested several hundred thousand dollars in her education, be happy if that was her fate.

There is a difference between high aspirations and entitlement. Along with her classmates and friends who grew up in this well-educated, professional suburb, Kate hopes she will lay her hands on the right kind of future. That said, it isn't a certainty, and she knows it.

Where, then, does the impression of entitlement come from? It hits the headlines when people like Kate respond honestly about two things: what they want and how much strain they are willing to put up with to get there. Kate's desire for a nice lifestyle and a job that is meaningful is clear enough, but she isn't exactly killing herself to get there. Taking time off to travel, moving to San Francisco as Kate did only to land in debt . . . these are not the pathways that "type A" youth indulge in. She is off on a meandering stroll rather than a sprint through a hundred-yard dash. Perhaps in time Kate will develop a greater sense of urgency about her future, but the elongation of the road to adulthood has dampened that fever, creating the perception that there is time enough for the strictures of adulthood. Kate's grandparents, who married and had their children young, were in a hurry to arrive at a station Kate doesn't expect—or at least feel pressured—to reach until she is at least a decade older than they were. Her parents waited a little longer, but they were settled by their mid-twenties. When pressed, Kate thinks maybe she will settle down at thirty-five.

Not a few older Americans would admit that, if they had it to do all over again, they would have preferred a more leisurely pace toward maturity; it simply wasn't the "done thing" in a generation for whom the road to domesticity was interrupted by a world war or the Vietnam draft. Few middle-class Americans are called upon to make that kind of sacrifice now; hence the experience of unhurried progress, reinforced by the long period of education needed to acquire a professional job and the wherewithal to be a homeowner, encourages young people like Kate to believe that there is no rush.[11]

That said, Kate hardly seeks a perpetual refuge from responsibility. She sees her time spent trying out different kinds of work—much of it not full-time or even long-term—as a way of figuring out just what kinds of responsibilities she ultimately wants to assume.

Her European counterparts, particularly in countries like Spain, are also trying to puzzle out their new life course. Roberto is a twenty-six-year-old living in his own apartment. He has studied acting and drama in a school of performing arts in Murcia (southeast Spain) and now lives in Madrid. Roberto comes from a reasonably affluent family—his father is a financial advisor, and his mother is a doctor. He received financial support from his parents throughout his formative years and even now, as they helped him buy his small apartment.[12] Like Kate, Roberto followed a meandering path that left him unsure of whether he merits the designation of adult. Sometimes he thinks he does, and sometimes he doesn't. He explains:

> The word *adult* for me is not associated with a concrete age. That would be false. When does a person become an adult? I don't know. I have left home. I've lived moments in which I have been economically independent, others in which I haven't been independent. I make decisions on my own. I live on my own. But I still do not consider myself an adult. Perhaps—this may sound obvious—when you have a child . . . all of the sudden you are not on your own. Because one of the most amusing things about young age is that you don't have to worry about anybody apart from yourself.

Osvaldo is twenty-five, an only child, and lives with his parents in Madrid. His father is in his sixties and retired early from his position at a bank. His mother still works. Osvaldo studied fine arts in school and worked briefly at an archeological site as a volunteer. He has been unemployed for some time now but wants to support himself as a painter. He has a lighthearted attitude that betrays a certain nervousness about the whole subject of maturity. Osvaldo says he isn't even close to being ready:

> Being an adult, I guess it means mostly a change of mentality, a way of thinking and acting. When you're an adolescent, you think about other things, don't you? When you're younger, you just think about having fun. Well, I personally consider myself to be an adult, and I think about having fun, too, right? The more the better. I don't know if I can explain [it] myself.

There are subtle differences between Americans and their European counterparts in the ways they characterize the psychology of emergent adulthood. Europeans mirror the Americans in their understanding of adulthood as not necessarily defined by a particular age or by residential or economic independence, but they focus more than the Americans on the social aspect. That is, Europeans see adulthood as a station defined by the way one relates to others: you are not the exclusive focus of your life; you have responsibilities to others that you cannot forego. Americans seem to focus less on this aspect and more on adulthood as a process of self-discovery.[13]

Parental Perspectives

While many parents in accordion families think about adulthood the old-fashioned way, as marked by settling into a career and starting a family, they have absorbed the new lesson that growing up today is a subjective, psychological experience, not a state of existence defined by concrete status transitions.

Take Stephanie Phillips, a divorced Newton mother who has had a long career as a nurse. When asked whether the old milestones—marriage and children—continue to define adulthood, she demurs, invoking instead the notion of "self-actualization":

> There are people who elect not to get married, some who are divorced, some are separated, people who live together without benefit of marriage, as they used to say, two women who live together,

two men who live together. No, marriage doesn't define adulthood. It's a sense of responsibility and accomplishment. When I went back to school to get my bachelors degree, the first college class I took was psychology. And I remember learning about self-actualization, and I thought, well, that ought to happen to me when I'm about sixty-eight or seventy.

Hers is a decidedly middle-class perspective. Self-actualization is a luxury for less affluent families. In low-income families, young people are expected to go out and get a job, often in their early teenage years.[14] There is little time to ponder and fiddle; if there's work to find, there are young people from Harlem to the South Side of Chicago who will snap up any opportunity, any chance to stand on their own two feet.

For an affluent parent like Stephanie, who can afford to give her children license to find themselves and take their time about it—but who would frown on perpetual childhood—a different set of markers emerges. It isn't about getting a job; it's about that sense of accomplishment that comes with growing maturity, whether or not the self-actualized have careers, cars, and mortgages. And this perspective is not just limited to Newton parents. Working-class parents in other countries seem to be expressing it as well.

Alanzo lives in the Northern Italian city of Legnaro, in the province of Padua. He is retired and lives with his wife and two daughters. The family is of modest means, but they were able to move out of their rented apartment and into their own house two years ago. Alanzo would not be able to manage the mortgage alone on his meager retirement income. His oldest daughter contributes almost her entire salary to the mortgage payments. Her economic future is being deferred in order to assist her parents in what is now a family resource: a home. Because his daughter helps out, she is defined—by her father, at least—as a kind of adult, the kind that can make a difference in the fate of the family. She is not goofing off, indulging herself, but a responsible earner, helping to take care of her kin. Alanzo observes:

Being adult means you are responsible for your house, for your parents, for your family, and if you don't have your own family,[15] your parents are in any case your family! You are adult when you think you have something to do for your family, when you take your responsibilities and when you understand you are mature . . . even if you are not married or if you don't have any children. You have to be responsible!

Adult children in Italy's working class are often called upon to commit their earnings to the household in which they grew up, much as Depression-era youth in the United States did as a matter of course.[16] Children in immigrant households often face similar demands in American cities today. "Failure to launch" may come about on account of the economic stresses with which their families are struggling, rather than the limited options for youth independence. Under these conditions, parents and children redefine adulthood into a more specific form of obligation that actually leads away from autonomy.

Joan McBride, a Newton mother, recounts her own transition to adulthood and the attitudes and values that supported it. She knows it was a clear pathway, with milestones that everyone understood, and that her parents were not going to support her while she "found herself." Unlike the millennial generation, Joan says she would have been horrified at the thought of being dependent on them anytime after the end of her formal education:

I think in my own generation, part of being an adult was to be independent of your family, to establish your own residence separate of your family. It seems more common [today] that young people are more often living with their family. That was taboo: you didn't do that, or you would have felt like such a failure if you had to go back home when I was growing up. It didn't cross our minds that we would after college go back home for a period of time. Even if you struggled financially, it was an expectation that you would be doing that. You start off in a struggle, then earn a little more money and get on your feet.

The thought of going back home to live and save money to then go out and establish yourself at a little higher level financially with a better apartment was not at all in the cards. In fact, when I graduated from college, I spent a year as a volunteer in a domestic Peace Corps type of program. It wasn't Vista, but it was similar, and when my father knew I was just being a volunteer—they gave you a place to live, and they gave you a stipend of fifty dollars a month—my father took me aside, and he said, "Joan, I hope you know that you are on your own now, having put you through college."

Coming of age in Spain in the same (baby-boom) generation was often, it seems, an even more abrupt encounter with responsibility. Veronica is married and mother of three adult children—two daughters and a son. Both of her daughters live independently, but her son lives at home with her in Madrid. That would have been completely impossible, she recalls, in her youth:

When I was a child, 80 percent of my generation didn't receive any attention, because [our parents] had very serious economic problems I'm telling you about the postwar years—and so they didn't care much about our studies or anything. And so you became an adult the moment that your parents, either because they had no money or because they were really selfish, said, "Now you start working." And so you passed from childhood to young age from one day to the other, in a jump, and you had no teenage [years].

In Italy, the same stark transition was the norm. There was no slow transition to maturity. One day you were an adolescent, and the next day the weight of the world was on your shoulders. Vittoria, an Italian mother of five living in Calabria, remembers how she and her new husband were on their own from the minute they exchanged their vows:

[When] we got married [at twenty-three], we didn't stay living together with my parents or with my parents-in-law. We decided to live on our own. We rented a house, and we took the responsibility of our problems. No one gave us anything for free. Neither now that we are sixty: no one is giving us anything for free!

But times have changed, and all of the living generations have had to come to terms with the elongation of adolescence, its fracturing into stages that now include a kind of trial period of greater liberty and responsibility short of the ultimate state of adult independence. What the economic slowdown is really doing is making it harder to bring that trial stage to a conclusion. What started out being a few years to get on your feet has turned into a decade or more in countries like Japan, Italy, Spain, and, for growing numbers, the United States as well. The adjacent generations can see the difference in one another's pathways, whether or not they understand why it has transpired.

Is Money the Issue?

In many respects, the fuzzy, "feeling-driven" process of coming of age reflects the economic difficulties of being truly autonomous. It costs more and hence takes longer to achieve. But more than money is at work here. We know this is the case when we cast an eye toward countries that have bent over backward to make the transition to residential independence a high priority. The Nordic countries are a case in point. Nowhere else has the national investment in youth independence been greater than in rich social democracies like Sweden and Denmark. Young people are extended extraordinary opportunity to live on their own, given the large amount of inexpensive public housing, generous allowances for higher education, and direct unemployment benefits provided to those who have never worked. Young Scandinavians are not shy about accessing this largesse: the second most common form of support after a paid job in the Nordic countries is a student stipend.[17]

Given that Scandinavians are largely free to live on their own, surely they must feel more independent than their counterparts in Southern Europe tethered to the home front. Well, not exactly.

Robert Jensen is twenty-four and lives with a roommate in the center of Aarhus, the second-largest city in Denmark, home to the nation's leading university. Bicyclists are everywhere in Aarhus, threading their way around its lovely parks and tree-lined streets. It is a hip city, full of young people in cafes and clubs. Robert grew up outside Aarhus, in a small town called Hinnerup, but he left home at about age twenty

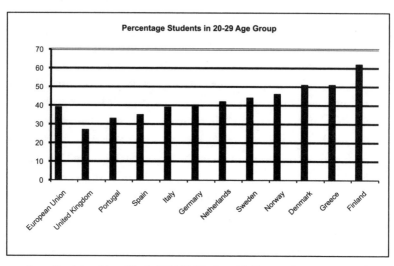

Source: Eurostat 2008 data, Office for Official Publications of the European Communities, Luxembourg.

to take the job he still holds in an insurance company. A high-school dropout, he went no further in school, electing instead to find his way in the work world. He was no older than his parents were when they moved out of the family home. Little has changed between the generations in this respect. But he says a lot has changed in the way he thinks about his development, even though he has been self-supporting since he was only twenty:

> It is hard to say when people really are adults, but at some point you start feeling that everything should make sense. A sort of unity. Then I think you might get to the point [where you are adult], when you start to get the meaning of things. You can look upon your family and the society and the problems there might be there. . . . Once you start looking beyond the end of one's nose, then you are an adult.

When asked whether growing up had anything to do with having a job, Robert replied: "No, I don't think so. These days everything goes so fast, you might be a business hotshot in two, three years' time, but inside you might still be just a little boy."

Barba is a twenty-six-year-old woman who lives on her own in an apartment in Copenhagen. She grew up in Aarhus and moved to Copenhagen when she was twenty, after spending several months traveling and after her father, who works in journalism, offered her a job in the city. Given this economic stability, which makes it possible for her to live autonomously, one might expect Barba to stake a claim to adulthood. Not so. She, too, embraces a psychological model:

> [To] be an adult, I don't really know. That is a funny question because I don't personally feel that adult, so it depends, sometimes I feel like a child. I guess you make your own decisions, and you are responsible for yourself and your own actions and the impact it has on other people.

When asked what it means to be responsible for herself, she waffles. It means "all kinds of things," she says. "All kinds of decisions here in life: education, work, housing, whether you want to move abroad, the little things, too." As for whether age matters, Barba equivocates: "I don't think so. Of course there are certain things legally speaking that you can't do until you have reached a certain age. But other than that, it depends on how responsible or mature people are." When queried if it has anything to do with one's financial situation or having a job, she explains: "It depends. I have been working since I was thirteen or something like that, in my younger years. But well, others might get by until they finish their educations at the age of thirty with support from their parents, not having had a job." And when asked if people dependent on their parents can still be called adults, she is sure they are entitled because getting help "simply has something to do with how privileged you are."

Abigail is a twenty-five-year-old fitness instructor who has lived independently for the last three years in Copenhagen with a roommate in an apartment owned by her mother. She is studying to be an occupational therapist and hopes to finish her training in a year or so. She muses:

> When are you an adult? That's a hard one. Well, I am twenty-five, and the age might tell you somehow that you should be an adult, but you don't have to feel like an adult just because of that. Being an adult has something to do with being responsible for yourself,

yes. I think it is hard to say what it means to be an adult, but definitely being responsible for yourself and to others, too, and look a bit further than your own nose. Well that was what comes to mind when you say adult.

Well, there is also something about family and work, but there are also people that never grow up, so I think it is hard to say. But the thing that comes to mind is being responsible for your own life and your own actions. I know a lot of people at the age of forty-five that might not be.

I have an uncle that hasn't grown up. But then I also have a cousin who is eighteen who is very grown-up, but I think it depends on what kind of upbringing you have had. She became a mother at a very early age and was responsible for some things that she just couldn't say [and] had to stand on her own feet.

Maja is twenty-two years old, tall and slim with shoulder-length dark hair and a bit shy. She grew up in the small town of Horby in the south of Sweden but now lives in a typical student apartment overlooking a park in the southern part of Lund. She has a big living room, a small kitchen area, and a bathroom and bedroom—all reflecting the prevailing styles of the 1970s, when the apartment was built. Still, the apartment is comfortable and cosy. Maja is very interested in music; she plays the guitar and is a member of a classical music group. She reflects:

[To be an adult means to have responsibility] for your own person. And also perhaps if you have children. [And] to sort of understand different contexts sort of in life and to be able to sort of handle consequences, and when something goes wrong, to be able to sort it out or admit well OK, I need some help now. And you go ask for help, or you solve it. . . . [It is] to be able to solve it basically.

Does Maja think that age, marriage, or a full-time job is integral to being a fully grown person? Not really, she explains. It is entirely possible to be a mature adult without any of these status markers.

What we have here is development by introspection, by how you feel, by the extent to which you can care about the world beyond your narrow preoccupations. Adulthood is about situating the self in a larger context; a supremely psychological process that has little to do with obligations or duty.[18]

For Scandinavians, it seems, you have truly come of age when you feel that way, when you define yourself as responsible, even if the aspects of life over which you hold ultimate responsibility are significantly more than your American or Italian counterparts. That this has transpired in a society that has poured billions into supporting many aspects of youth independence, from their educational stipends to their housing options, from direct unemployment benefits to those who have never worked as well as those who have, suggests that the financial barriers to independence at work in the United States or Spain are not the whole story.

A secular trend that reflects extensive investment in education, delayed entry into the labor market, the receding importance of (and incidence of) marriage, and declining fertility is creeping around the globe and ensnaring the weak welfare states (which do little to facilitate youth independence) and the rich social democracies (which do a great deal). This doesn't mean money is irrelevant, but it does suggest it isn't the whole story. Global competition, increasing rewards to human capital, the relentless process of rural to urban migration (where children are costly), and the positive pleasures associated with women's movement into the work world are reshaping the pathway to adulthood across the developed world, whatever the domestic policies.

Destigmatizing Delayed Adulthood

From one perspective, adulthood is still defined by a clear set of responsibilities; it simply takes longer to get to the point where a young person can reasonably assume them. When that goal becomes so distant, when it stretches into the thirties, parents may look for ways to destigmatize the condition. This seems not to have been the reaction in Japan, but elsewhere we see the invention of new kinds of benchmarks that shift the emphasis to a psychological concept of maturity, unhinged from traditional manifestations of adulthood. Jane Azarian, a Newton mother who has long been an activist in feminist circles, sees her daughter's world in these terms. She doesn't completely discount financial independence as a marker of adulthood, but other qualities are more important in her mind:

I think that being able to support yourself is important. [But it is also important] that you are an attendant to the world, you're not just an adult that is buried in the movies and parties and isn't paying attention to the world. You have to be plugged into the world beyond your family and your next-door neighbors, and that to me is a sign of an adult. And not just aware but figuring out some little thing you can do to be part of making the world a better place.

I also think that being in respectful, caring relationships, not necessarily being married and not necessarily having children but caring about the people in your community and doing something that is one-on-one. If personal meets the political in the things that you do that help an individual, and there are things that you do that help lots of individuals, not necessarily the ones that you see. And I believe that it's important that you do both kinds of things. And do I see it as a sign of being an adult? Yes, I do. That's my definition.

Larry Keegan grew up working class in Brooklyn. He jumped these developmental hurdles "on time" because no one was going to catch him and provide the support that would enable him to slow down and discover himself at a more leisurely pace. He might be the kind of person inclined to be judgmental about the differences between generations, but he is instead fairly even tempered about them. Fate—in the form of the economy—has intervened, he says, to create a different set of conditions for his kids:

The milestones are still the same. It is just a lot harder to achieve. Which is probably what is causing young adults today to figure new solutions to how to do it. A young adult is someone who is willing to take full responsibility for their actions. Someone who is financially independent. Somebody who has a plan of where they are trying to go. And in trying to achieve where they are trying to go, I would say the obstacles are much greater.

In a recent article, Robin Henig, a writer for the *New York Times Magazine*, helped to destigmatize delayed adulthood in ways that underline the psychological theory emerging in the minds of people like Jane. Henig recounts research that claims the brain is still plastic, still growing, still forming new connections well into the twenties. In "What Is It About 20-Somethings?" she reviewed research promoted by Jeffrey Jensen Arnett, a psychology professor at Clark University, that suggested a physiological reason for the spread of delayed departure: the brain just isn't ready yet. Arnett suggests that "emerging adulthood" is no "social construction" but rather a stage of development through which everyone must pass before their bodies are ready for full independence. If the brain is the culprit, it cannot be a source of embarrassment to be living with Mom and Dad. It's just natural.

It is difficult to square this account with the variations we have seen in the space of less than forty years in patterns of adulthood. The gene pool doesn't mutate that fast. If leading-edge boomers were dying to be out on their own, ready to put up with cheap digs, fraying blue jeans, and a diet of pasta in order to maintain their independence, while their younger siblings stuck close to home to preserve a higher standard of living, it is hard to imagine that brain development could explain this divergence. Instead, social conditions are promoting a new way of thinking about developmental pathways. This shift in perspective is not apparent only in the United States but in other countries where social and economic changes have promoted a similarly elastic definition of adulthood.

Laura Fuentes is rare among our respondents in Spain. She moved out of her parents' home two years ago, at age twenty-five, to live with her longtime boyfriend, a computing consultant. She seems almost surprised at herself, remarking that she never expected to do that. She has a degree in economics and a further certification in business studies. She is also currently taking an English-language course while she works with her father at the family business in Madrid. She says:

> [If a person lives with his parents] he can be an adult, of course. But well, if he is the *sopa boba*[19] and he does nothing, then I do think that person has not grown up yet. But if you live with your parents because you are saving or because you have been studying a lot and you have started to work late or if you are preparing for a public ex-

amination [then you might be an adult]. Because in many cases you can't get independence before thirty. I don't consider that they aren't adults. The main thing is that you assume your responsibilities and that you don't depend on your parents for everything.

Spanish parents living in Madrid today have seen a dramatic change in the country's social atmosphere. Their children have far more freedom; gender roles are more elastic; the authoritarian atmosphere of their youth has collapsed and a kinder, more congenial relationship between parents and their children has emerged.[20] Spanish society is nonchalant about premarital romance, in keeping with the relaxed sentiments of the rest of the developed world.[21] On occasion, one hears laments about broken values or the consternation that extremely short skirts provoke in villages where widows wear black forever, but on the whole Spanish parents seem relieved that they no longer have to contend with the rigidity that dominated their early years.

For accordion families in Spain, this means that it is not a stigma to have children living at home for many years more than was typical in the past but a necessary adaptation to an unkind market. And it is an adaptation with a silver lining: continued closeness of the children to parents who in earlier generations would have constituted a reason to run.

Maria Moreno is a middle-aged woman living in El Pilar, a neighborhood in the north of Madrid, constructed mainly in the 1970s, with very tall buildings. El Pilar used to be populated by the lower middle class and some sectors of the working class. During the years of the political *Transición*[22] from the authoritarian rule of Francisco Franco to the modern democracy that is Spain, El Pilar was a beehive of political activism. Maria was not there for those exciting times. She arrived later, having grown up in a rural village in the north of the country. Maria and her husband raised four children without much help from anyone else, and their youngest child, Juan, still lives with them. She spent her working years in a bank, even though she wanted to be a teacher. She is concerned about many issues facing young people in Spain today but saves her greatest passion for the topic of gender equity and what she sees as the real progress between her generation and her daughter's.

In the village where Maria grew up, young men ended their school-
ing and began their work lives at a very young age. She remembers:

> There were people who started working at fourteen. Those people
> were not [thought of as grown-up]. But if you were eighteen or
> twenty and you had a stable job, you were considered an adult. Of
> course, if you were that age and employed, it was also expected that
> the time had come to start a family.
>
> At the time, people stayed with the parents until they married.
> I remember that one of my sisters-in-law left her parents' house,
> and that was regarded as something very bad. At the time, there
> were very few people who left. Her parents were very upset, and
> people would criticize her. [It was] something that today is seen as
> perfectly normal. Well, not the most normal thing, because it's not
> that they leave so often, because they can't [for financial reasons],
> but at the time it was not accepted. [At the time] in fact, there [was]
> almost nobody. I'm referring to the people from Madrid, because
> those like me who came from outside, of course. But you went to
> halls or private houses.[23]
>
> You would never rent a flat . . . that kind of independence, never.
> [Buying or renting a house was only something you did] if you were
> going to marry. Or well, perhaps there were people who bought a
> house but actually got it five years later. And if you had not mar-
> ried, you wouldn't move to the house. It was very strange to do that.
> If you were eighteen or twenty and you had a stable job, you were
> considered an adult.

Agata Calatrava is married with three children and lives in a humble
suburb of Madrid. Her eldest son and daughter have moved out, but her
youngest son still lives with her and her husband. Like many women in
the parental generation, Agata remembers her childhood as restrictive
and troubled. She was under the parental thumb with a vengeance: "I've
been directed for all my life. . . . They had us very . . . like tied down, I
can't explain. They didn't let you be yourself. You couldn't say, 'I'm going
out now because I feel like it.' You had to ask for permission; if they let
you, fine, if not, you stayed at home." Marriage was Agata's only route

to freedom. It was the only way she would ever be able to decide what to do without the heavy-handed interference of her traditional father. She recalls:

> I was very normal [for my age]. Between eighteen and twenty-two, it was the age to marry, more or less. I got married at nineteen, and then I really started to live, strange though it may seem [laughs]. Because, well, I had freedom to do whatever I wanted: going out, going in, to do as I please—what I have never had.

That taste of freedom was almost intoxicating. It was also a shock. The distant relations between parents and children in her youth meant that no one talked to Agata about what she should expect, how she should behave. She was essentially on her own, and though she wanted to get over the hurdle, she didn't really know what lay on the other side. The contrast between the way this metamorphosis took place then and the way it unfolds now could not be more striking.[24] Not only is the change slow and unformed these days, each step along the way is discussed and debated by parents in the company of their children.

Laura is about the same age as Agata, and she reflects the same intergenerational transition:

> I had never been out from my parents' house until the day I married. My daughters, they have become independent earlier. They come in, go out. To be truthful, I have envied that freedom. And it is not licentiousness, it is freedom. And I don't think it is bad, eh? You must have the opportunity to choose. I think that young people now, you can choose much better than we could because you have other means that we didn't have.

Laura had to contend with the traditional confinement of young women in Franco's Spain; it was not entirely unlike the traditional Muslim world, in which the movements of girls are constrained by male authority.[25] Whatever the limitations of the accordion family for Laura—as for Agata—the freedom modernity has bequeathed their daughters is almost miraculous.

Though older women see the modern world as a relief for the liberty it affords their daughters, this is not as much of a gender story as we might imagine. Men, too, felt the heel of authority at their backs in Franco's Spain. They were freer to move around outside the house than women were, but they, too, were compelled to follow traditional conventions, including in marriage and fatherhood.

Juan Porta is a working-class father and husband in his mid-fifties. His life followed the predictable Spanish pattern of rural to urban migration. Growing up in a village, he worked as a sheepherder as a child before coming to Madrid at fifteen to begin working as a pastry maker. The job occupied Juan for decades and provided the wherewithal for him to marry at the age of twenty-two. Eventually, he brought his wife, Lidia, to Madrid, where they raised two daughters who still live at home. The parents do not try to push the girls into the mold that shaped Lidia's life: no sex outside of marriage, early courtship and wedding, and motherhood soon after the marriage banns were signed. They are free to make their own choices, including the one that led them to stay at home.

Nonetheless, Juan worries that his daughters will never be able to afford an autonomous life. The cost of housing skyrocketed when Spain (like the United States) experienced a multiyear housing bubble. While the bubble has burst, housing is still prohibitively expensive. That burden, coupled with the difficulties the next generation is having finding work in a country with unemployment running at more than 20 percent, leaves Juan pessimistic about their futures. He understands why they can't grow up like he did; the conditions simply are not the same:

The young these days, since they don't have the means, they stay with their family, and so some are still there at thirty. They aren't in any hurry, even if they have a boyfriend. [Back] in the seventies, if you had any problem with the company or with your boss, you just left and you could then work [somewhere else]. Right now, you can't. If you work here, you work here, and if you don't have a good relationship, the company sacks you and [it will be a long time] until you find a new job.

The lack of security his children face troubles Juan. At the same time, relative to the culture of his youth, where liberation from home was an almost desperate desire, he feels that mandate has diminished now. Without the sense of confinement that Spain's young people felt in the 1970s, today's youth experience less pressure to break away. They have less to free themselves from. "[Young people] have more freedom than in the past," Juan explained. "So in certain respects things have advanced," personal liberty is less constrained, hence continued dependence is not as limiting.

Spanish parents like Juan fear for the economic future of their children, as do American parents watching the unemployment numbers rise to heights not seen since the early 1980s. Yet on both sides of the Atlantic, they see virtue in the social changes that have brought boomer parents closer to their Gen-X kids. They can talk to one another in a fashion that was unknown in the past. This is particularly true in Spain, where a harsh kind of traditionalism prevailed long after it was swept away in other cultures.

Is Freedom Always Good?

Japanese parents don't necessarily share this conviction. They are far more ambivalent about the consequences of this loosening of authority and diminishing distance. Is increased familiarity between parents and children necessarily a good thing? Or is there a good reason for generational distance? Instead of looking at the next generation as liberated and free, the Japanese worry instead that they are aimless and unworthy.[26] This kind of adulthood is a symptom of dysfunction, a problem in search of a blameworthy party.

Kumi Sato, the sixty-one-year-old widow we met in chapter 1, has followed an unusual trajectory, taking over the family business after the death of her husband. Japanese women do not routinely reenter the workforce after they become mothers, much less widows. And when they do, it is rare to find them in an executive role. Kumi's pathway was somewhat unorthodox from the beginning, for unlike most other Japanese girls, she left home in her teenage years to attend a sewing school, relying on her parents to send her money for her keep. However, when she was twenty years old, Kumi became an "office lady" for a large firm and became financially independent. As was the custom in her country, after she married, she quit her job. Because Yosimichi, Kumi's husband, was the eldest son in his family, the new couple moved in with her in-laws, as was the custom. Kumi assumed the role of the dutiful daughter-in-law and mother (eventually) to three children.

It might be argued that Kumi herself knew little of real adulthood and lacks the legitimacy to criticize her son who is living at home since, with his part-time earnings, he can hardly do anything else. Yet Kumi sees herself as quite knowledgeable indeed, not only about the appropriate behavior for a real adult but for right conduct in general. She has always understood what society demands of people if they want respect from their families and community. This is what her son lacks, and this, she thinks, is her own fault:

> When you are living with your parents, the rent is free [laughs], the food is free [laughs]. I take care of everything: laundry, cloth-ing, food, and residence. In that way, my child has been indulged. Friends of my son [have come] to Tokyo from the provinces for work. They are independent. But not doing so and still staying at home means that my child is not fully independent. But the fact that I am allowing it to happen suggests laxness on the part of a parent [laughs].

All that laughter betrays nervousness about the decisions Kumi has made as a mother. Living in an agentic culture means that mistakes are, if not intentional errors, at least moral faults—the only real question is whose. Kumi seems to think the answer is clear: hers.

Natsuki Endo is a fifty-seven-year-old married woman who lives with her husband and three adult children in Hachioji City, a com-muter town twenty-five miles west of Tokyo. Natsuki's three children all live at home. Her son, age thirty, works at a publishing company. Her oldest daughter, twenty-eight, is a temp worker who has not been able to do better, even though she holds a bachelor's degree. Her youngest daughter, twenty-six, is a freeter who graduated from vocational school, a stigmatized alternative in Japan.[27] Natsuki does not think any of her children are truly admirable; instead they are stuck and growing older.

"None of my children is adult yet," she laughs. "They are not entirely independent financially, even if they contribute money a little. It's not like they live on their own renting their apartment somewhere. So they are still children."

Her critical attitude is widely shared in Japan, not just among parents in accordion families. Atsushi Etsuko, is the fifty-seven-year-old president of a subsidiary of a major Japanese trading company. He and his stay-at-home wife raised two sons. The oldest, now twenty-six, finished a master's degree, while his younger brother, twenty-four, only went as far as earning a high school diploma. Both young men have landed "company jobs," and neither of them lives at home. The Etsuko brothers have bucked the tide. Atsushi hopes they will start thinking about the next step in the march to adulthood, settling down to a life as family men, but for now he recognizes that their jobs and residential independence put them ahead of the pack. He isn't impressed with the rest of that pack, wallowing in freeter jobs, spinning their wheels:

> Marriage is perhaps the second biggest event in life; the biggest event for them is to give birth to children. I think women become full-fledged by this. On the other hand, for men having a job is very important as it leads to establishing the basis for life, even though it may seem important for them to enjoy their lives. Young men who are freeters now do not realize that. In that sense, both young men and women do not realize what is important for them yet. I feel that the ability to think through is becoming weaker among youth.

The current generation—his own children notwithstanding—comes up short compared to Atsushi's generation. He was one of four children who worked hard to complete a university degree. He worked part time to pay for his tuition and commuted from home to save money. But by the time he graduated at the age of twenty-two, he was completely independent financially and landed a job that made that a permanent condition. His sons have followed fairly closely in his footsteps, and hence Atsushi has little to complain about from a personal standpoint. But he joins parents like Kumi, whose freeter children are such a worry to her, in critiquing the next generation. There is blame to spread around, even when it doesn't apply to the person dishing it out.

The Japanese appear to be an exception to the growing cultural adjustment to delayed adulthood. They retain a strong normative sense of what is appropriate and what is deviant in the evolution from youth to adult. They simply do not like what they see.

American parents are more forgiving and more malleable in their expectations, particularly if they believe their own choices in life were more constrained than they would have liked. If their own affluence can buy their children more discretion, more time to reach the right landing spot, so much the better. William Rollo from Newton thinks it's just fine for his son, John, to travel and become a cosmopolitan. He wants John to have advantages he didn't have, including the freedom to sample alternative futures so that he is truly content with the choices he makes. That, after all, is what William says he has worked for, to give John options:

> A lot of what he is doing is [trying] to understand what he would like to do for a living. I spent a lot of time doing what I have been doing for the last twenty-five years, and I probably would have liked to have done what I originally went to school for, and it didn't work out, so I would like for him to find out for himself what he would like to do now and go ahead and do it.
>
> That's kind of why I am willing to let him go by not being as strict about paying his share. I continue to do what [I do for a living] in a large part because we wanted to live in a nice place for them to go to school and to help pay for their college education for both of [our sons]. I did that willingly; no one forced me to do it. When it comes down to the end, I think my biggest accomplishment was the kids I produced. I'm feeling that if they turned out OK, and I think they have, and I say that honestly.

Though William is a successful podiatrist, he came up from less elevated circumstances. He wasn't poor, but he didn't grow up in the kind of privilege he has conveyed to his kids. Giving them a boost, making sure that they will benefit from his hard work, is half the reason for being a parent in the first place. If that means protecting them from the pressures of the market through their twenties, then so be it. "My generation, whose parents grew up in the Depression and World War II,"

William explains, "didn't want to see their children having to live like [they did]." He adds:

> I grew up in a little apartment, and I shared a room with my sister until I was like sixteen, and my sister was six years younger than me and we didn't really have a bedroom. It's nice that I give my kids more than what I had as a kid. At least in this society, every generation that comes after doesn't want to work as hard as the generation before. Just like the generation before didn't want to work as hard as the parents before them had to work.

Of course, not all middle-class parents can ensure their children want to follow in their footsteps. Some have to redefine what constitutes a respectable career to incorporate different pathways. Gary Mack went to law school and works as a computer network consultant. His son dropped out of the University of Massachusetts and wants to be a blacksmith. Gary explains:

> I suppose there could be [a stigma] if people thought that a child living at home was living at home because they are just good-for-nothing leeches. Then there would be that, but there are plenty of other reasons why kids would live at home. If I knew of somebody whose kid was living with them at home, I would not at all think of it as stigmatizing. If I knew more about the family situation and I knew that the kid was a lazy, good-for-nothing leech then, yeah, but I wouldn't have concluded that simply because they were living at home.

Gary's son wants to live a solid life as a skilled blue-collar worker. And that's just fine with Gary, even if it's hard to explain to his neighbors. But a hard-working, gainfully employed man who can take care of his family—that's a success story in his book. He is willing to support his son to underwrite that future.[28]

To be sure, not all Newton families find these arrangements easy to swallow. Teddy Yoo lives with his parents because he cannot afford the alternatives, but he is not happy about it. Teddy worked in a financial

services firm as a customer service representative but lost that job. Perhaps because his living situation is forced by financial limitations, he
casts his situation as a form of humiliation:

> [Living at home] is a good thing monetarily but a bad thing spiritu-
> ally. Because you are living in your parents' household, and it's their
> rules, and they have those silent and unspoken expectations of you.

Teddy's distress is amplified by his complex relations with his immigrant parents. Tension between immigrants and their more assimilated children is common no matter what the national origin, but Teddy
sees it as a rift specific to Asian parents, with their high expectations
and strong sense of self-sacrifice on behalf of the next generation.[29] He
explains:

> Living here is very spiritually deadening because my parents are
> your typical Asian parents. They support you financially but not
> emotionally. They say the right things, but they always had this ex-
> pectation of me when I was a kid that I would be a doctor or a law-
> yer and you're going to go to Harvard. And Asian parents are like
> that. Some Asian males say it's the white mom. The white mom is
> someone that says: "Oh so what if you stole your boss's car from
> work and totaled it? I still love you, and you are a great boy." This
> is an exaggeration, [but it means that] the white mom will always
> be supportive no matter what and give you money no matter what.

Second-generation immigrants—those born in the United States of
foreign-born parents—do not always experience the kind of conflict
brewing in the Yoo household.[30] Some are nostalgic for the close-knit,
multigenerational household that was common in their parents' lives
in the old country, wherever it was to be found. When their own children boomerang back into the natal home, it feels like a throwback
to an earlier era in their family history. Take Esther Goodman, a divorced mother living in Newton whose parents emigrated from Yugoslavia. With a son, daughter, and the daughter's child living at home,
she says:

I grew up in an extended family myself, so I am repeating that pattern in a way. It was my grandparents, parents, myself, and my sister living in a single-family home together. Despite the fact that after college I never considered returning home, the fact that my daughter and granddaughter are here is quite natural given the home that I grew up in. I was very close with my grandfather as a child, and I am having that sense with my granddaughter. There is that same availability of grandparents. That is part of the experience.

My granddaughter even said one day when she came home from kindergarten, "I really like living with you" or something like that. It had to do with other children in her class going on some long trip to visit a grandparent and how they didn't get to see them that much and regretting that. She said, "I am really lucky that you live right here." It's a nice experience to watch her grow. I get a lot of pleasure watching my daughter and granddaughter together. I enjoy seeing them together and seeing that sweet interaction.

Elaine Mark is a Newton mother who grew up in Zimbabwe, where her Jewish family settled after World War II. Like Esther, she has fond feelings about accordion households. It feels to Elaine like part of the natural order of things:

I always went home when I was at a certain point and needing to make a decision for my next point in my own family. So I would go home, so I assumed that this was what everybody does. In Europe, for example, a lot of people never left home to go to college or university and assumed that is where you go and maybe get married and you go somewhere else. Here I think it is very strange that everybody goes away to live in a dorm at the university in the same city. That's strange.

Conclusion

If adulthood was once a station in life, marked by cultural conventions of marriage, parenthood, and a "real job," it has become something else in the globalized world we inhabit now. Adult children are migrating home or refraining from leaving in the first place, and there they stay for many years longer than was the case in most countries for decades. It is disruptive to our sense of social order to think of these stay-at-home thirty-year-olds as perpetual adolescents. And indeed, that is not how they describe their state of mind. They see themselves jumping over psychological barriers, feeling that they are taking greater responsibility for their actions than they did in those dreaded teen years. When a twentysomething claims to "feel like an adult," we credit this as a meaningful assertion because they have captured something real: a sense of responsibility and increased mastery, a capacity to imagine a more defined future and plan for it, at least to a greater degree than was common in earlier stages of life.

Adults who came of age in an earlier era are not likely to think this is an adequate substitute for the real thing. But they are coconspirators in the effort to develop this psychological side. All too aware of how much harder it is to afford education and residential autonomy than it was back in the day, American parents join their Spanish counterparts in recognizing that life is simply more costly today, the job market is problematic, and all that combines to limit the capacity of their kids to do what they did in the distant past. Yet even in countries where cost isn't the question—as is largely the case in Scandinavia—the spread of a "psychological theory" of adulthood is unmistakable. A secular trend is underway that removes the imperatives to leap status hurdles to get to the holy grail of adult respect. Instead, thinking more like a grown-up makes everyone feel like one, and that seems to be the consequence of the spread of accordion families.

The economic conditions that have made it so difficult for today's young people to find a footing in the labor market, coupled with the emergence (and then collapse) of housing bubbles throughout the developed world, have conspired to make it financially difficult to be independent and all the more important for families to band together to pool their resources. Accordion families are, then, a natural response to economic insecurity, particularly in countries where the welfare state is weak and hence owner-occupied housing constitutes a critical private safety net. If multiple generations can pile into one house, the costs of housing per person decline at precisely the moment where earnings are stagnating or falling. It is an eminently sensible adaptation to growing inequality, the force of globalization, and the absence—in countries like

Italy, Spain, Japan, and, to a degree, the United States—of supports like those routine in the Nordic countries. In Sweden and Denmark, where the residential independence of youth is practically a plank in the welfare state, we see virtually no evidence of accordion families. They exist only in the rural areas where the continuity of land ownership and management between generations is important.

Yet we must be cautious in assigning economic forces too much causal power in the emergence of the more subjective, psychological model of adulthood. For it appears to be robust in Scandinavia as well as Japan. Why? Residential independence in the Nordic world does not signal the kind of autonomy that full adulthood implies. Scandinavian youth are living on their own but are often in school for a longer period of time than any other part of the developed world.[31] The average age of educational completions hovers around twenty-seven. Entry into the labor market in Finland averages about the same age. Marriage is increasingly unfashionable in the Nordic countries and when it happens tends to be very late indeed. The companion markers that once went together (residential independence, marriage, and parenthood) have come apart in the social democracies. The pattern produces independence without full adulthood.

Hence the feeling that you are a grown-up when you can convince yourself that, subjectively, you have "arrived" has permeated these societies as well. Money matters—but it is not the only constraint that encourages a psychological orientation toward maturity as opposed to the status transition model.

Where money really does matter, unassailably, is in the growth of the accordion family itself. The transition to adulthood—whether accompanied by residential independence or not—may be marked by a subjective orientation. But the formation of multigenerational households of the kind we have identified here is the consequence of market pitfalls.

CHAPTER 2

Why Are Accordion
Families Spreading?

"THERE'S SOMETHING HAPPENING HERE," as the old Buffalo Spring-field song suggests, but "what it is ain't exactly clear." We need to understand the growth of multigenerational households, though, because virtually every aspect of our lives is affected by the emergence of accordion families. And emerging they are: 3.4 million American parents shared a home with their adult children in the United States in 2009, up from 2.1 million in 2000.[1] This is an astounding increase in the space of less than ten years.

Accordion families are hardly new. Before social-security systems created opportunities for retirement, elderly relatives who could no longer provide for themselves moved in with their children and lived out their days in rocking chairs by the hearth. Daughters and daughters-in-law provided countless hours of unpaid nursing care and companionship to aging parents.[2] Their support was feasible, though personally taxing, because so many women were not in the paid labor force, and their working-age husbands could provide for the family. In East Asia—especially in Japan—this form of the multigenerational household was emblematic, enforced by powerful customs that required the wife of the eldest son to commit to the care of her husband's parents, often many years before they were disabled by age. Though expected and reinforced by social norms, the practice took a toll on the mental health of generations of daughters-in-law.[3]

Declining wages for men coupled with rising expectations among women for a life in the workforce began to chip away at this form of the accordion family. In the United States and in much of Western Europe, men's wages began to stagnate in the late 1960s,[4] and families responded by sending women out to work. It is hard to know whether the feminist movement was the chicken or the egg in this transformation, but either way, it played an important role in legitimizing and then celebrating the cause of women in the labor force. Today, more than half of women with children under the age of one work at least part time.[5] While many choose this path willingly and would not give it up for the pleasures of the domestic life, most have no other option if they want their families to be anchored in the middle class. The pressures are even greater on less-affluent households, which often must deploy husbands, wives, and teenagers into the world of work and hold those wages in a central pot.

With everyone carrying a lunch pail and no adults at home, the custom of caring for the in-house elderly began to fade. Nursing homes emerged as the organizational solution. Costly and isolating, what emerged out of the poorhouse or the convalescent system turned into warehouses for the elderly who were living longer and longer but were too much of a burden for working women to handle.[6] Japan, the country best known for the daughter-in-law model of elder care, now faces a surging demand for nursing homes.[7] European countries have tried to limit this surge by increasing in-home care. The United States has led the way in developing institutions from assisted living to nursing homes, which is not surprising, since American women have led the way in labor-force participation.

In the 1970s and early 1980s, the combination of elders moving out and young people leaving home—which was the norm in the American middle class—actually increased the percentage of single-generation households.[8] "Empty nests" piqued the interests of the media and the vacation industry, both of which could see a new phenomenon across the landscape: parents who had sent their children off to college, whose elders were either healthy or living independently from them. Ours was the first society to imagine such a configuration, and it became a psychic worry for parents, unsure what to do with themselves in the absence of their little darlings, and a boon to the travel industry, which could create new package tours for the affluent, newly freed from the constraints of looking after dependents at either end of the age spectrum.

It didn't last. Starting with the sharp economic downturn of the 1980s, a steadily increasing proportion of young people in their twenties in the United States—and in many other economically advanced countries—either returned home or never left at all. Economic opportunity melted away, unemployment rose to double digits, the cost of higher education started to grow steeply, and the combination of these trends was so damaging to young people's fortunes that they reversed course and headed home. Instead of reaching out to incorporate the elderly, whom the accordion family had stretched to incorporate in the past, households started expanding to retain the young.[9]

The United States is not the only country to see this trend emerge. Other parts of the developed world are way ahead of us—if we could describe this as a race—because they have even larger proportions of adult children sticking close to home. As noted before, in Italy today, more than 37 percent of Italian men ages thirty to thirty-four still live with their mothers.[10] Japan looks very similar.

Not everyone is so happy with this state of affairs. Spain is one place where the difficulties of creating an autonomous household are causing extraordinary rifts between citizens and their government. Less than a third of Spaniards ages twenty-five to thirty had left home in 2001, compared with more than half in 1977—and the change has registered in public debate.[11] The forces that have made it necessary to stick to the natal household are neither invisible nor amorphous to the Spaniards; they are obvious, awash in class politics, and require political response. "Why did the government give business owners the right to offer lousy part-time work contracts?" they want to know. "What special interests are profiting from the skyrocketing cost of housing in Madrid?" they continue. Low wages and high housing costs are preventing young adults in Spain from moving on, frustration is growing, and fingers are pointing at the elites. In recent years, the anger has spilled over into the streets, where sit-down strikes and street demonstrations protesting the high cost of housing have erupted with increasing frequency.[12] In response to public outcry, the Spanish government in 2007 unveiled a plan to help struggling young people move out of their parents' homes by offering a monthly cash subsidy to people ages twenty-two to thirty whose salary was less than twenty-two thousand euros. The government also planned to allow renters whose annual incomes were less than twenty-four thousand euros to benefit from tax cuts as property buyers.[13]

Citizens of Norway, Denmark, Finland, and Sweden could be forgiven for wondering what the ruckus is about in those warm Southern European countries. Young people typically leave home at age eighteen in Stockholm or Oslo. Living with one's parents in Copenhagen or Helsinki past the age of eighteen will set tongues wagging; it's a social curiosity. Then again, it isn't a very challenging assignment for young people to leave home in Scandinavia. A Danish teenager who finds a high school in another city that is more to her liking than the one she attends in her hometown can rely on the municipal authorities to help her find affordable rental housing and can live on a government stipend provided to students. The state is a partner, a willing one at that, in enabling young people to strike out on their own.

The forces that create the accordion family are both universal and particular. Global competition has spread throughout the developed world; labor is on the run, fighting to hold onto jobs, wages, and benefits. These are common problems that seem to know no national boundaries, even in the people's paradise of Sweden. But the response to these pressures is not universal. Some governments step in to create a durable buffer between citizens and the market; others are far more laissez faire and leave their people to sink or swim largely on their own. Where the family is the principal "haven in a heartless world," it is also the main shock absorber that pulls its youth (and in some places its elders) inward. "All for one and one for all—because no one else is looking out for any of us" might as well be the motto in the laissez faire countries of the developed world.

To understand how these features pattern against the international landscape—and why some cultures are almost hysterically upset about the changes that have taken place, while others are shrugging their shoulders—we must look carefully at where, exactly, the accordion family has emerged and where it is absent. We need to understand how job markets have changed and who has been most profoundly affected by these trends. Globalization has increased the rewards flowing to the well-educated, but it takes time to join those ranks; the cost of further education (college and professional school) has meanwhile been rising steadily around the world. Saving money by staying at home is the only way many young people can afford to pursue that advanced degree.

The confluence of these trends places the move toward independence on the back burner in societies where the government has not intervened to smooth the transition. In the Nordic countries, we see virtually no signs of "failure to launch"; in the United States, we see more evidence of the accordion family than we have known since the coming of age of the baby boomers, but less than we had before World War II; and in the weak welfare states of Western Europe and Japan, it is epidemic.

Locating the Accordion Family
Europe may be one continent, but it is composed of many different social worlds, especially where the accordion family is concerned. In Southern European countries like Italy, 73 percent of young men (age eighteen to thirty-four) were living in their parents' home in 2007. Neighboring Portugal looks similar: 66 percent of the men in this age group are bunking with their parents. At the other end of the spectrum, we find the Nordic countries, where in Finland, for example, only 21 percent of this age group is still living at home. It is the rare adult child who is living at home.

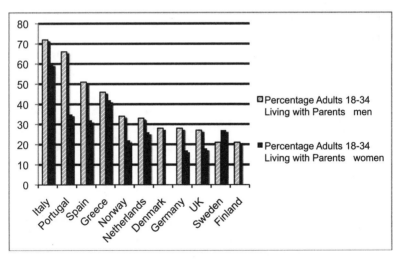

*Sample of women in Finland and Denmark too small to assess.

Source: *Family Life and Work: Second European Quality of Life Survey,* European Foundation for the Improvement of Living and Working Conditions, Dublin, 2007.

The United States sits somewhere in the middle of this continuum, though accordion families become more prevalent in hard times. According to the Census Bureau, nearly 60 percent of young Americans between the ages of eighteen and twenty-four were living with their parents in 2005.[14] The Pew Charitable Trust found that 13 percent of parents with grown children say that one of their adult sons or daughters moved back into the home in 2009.[15] The American Association of Retired Persons, the largest organization that works on the issues that matter to people fifty-five years and older, commissioned a survey to find out about housing trends in the United States and how the economy is affecting the living situation of adults. Their findings were eye-opening: as of 2009, about one-third of the AARP respondents between the ages of eighteen and forty-nine were living with their parents or their in-laws.

The inclusion of eighteen-year-olds is likely to give us a false impression of the frequency of accordion families since many of these households include high-school students who have always lived at home. So let's look instead at the group we would normally expect to be entirely independent, those thirty-five to forty-four years old. For the most part, these are men and women ordinarily too old to be dependent on their natal families and, for the most part, too young to have parents so aged that they need custodial care. They are most likely "boomerang" adults who have had long periods of independence but have come back into the fold because they are in trouble. Eleven percent of adults in that age group are back home with their parents.[16]

Why have they returned home? Recessions put families under pressure to reduce expenses and corral their members into households where they can pool income and share expenses. When AARP asked people how likely it is that they would need to move in with family members or friends (or receive them in their home), about 15 percent indicated that "doubling up" was a distinct possibility. Loss of income, changing jobs, and foreclosure were the main reasons they gave for possibly having to take this step. The eighteen-to-thirty-four-year-old group was more likely than the older people in the AARP study to have actually made a move: 20 percent of them had already moved back to their parents' homes. Parents know this tidal wave is headed in their direction.

Parents are the ultimate safety net, at least for the fortunate families that can afford to stretch the income of its stable members to cover the cost of caring for the least fortunate. But recessions are not the only reason families are stretching the fold to include their adult children. The Great Recession merely intensified trends that have been gathering force for some time. A higher proportion of adult children are living with their parents in the United States now than at any time since the 1950s. Their number has been growing as a percentage of their cohort or generation for decades now, and this has been the case in good times (the late 1990s and the early part of the 2000s) and bad.[17]

Young Men Living at Home (Single, No Children), by Race and Age, 1900-2000

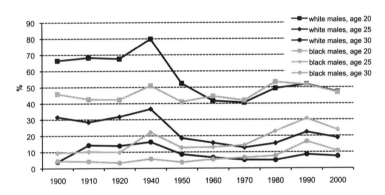

Young Women Living at Home (Single, No Children), by Race and Age, 1900-2000

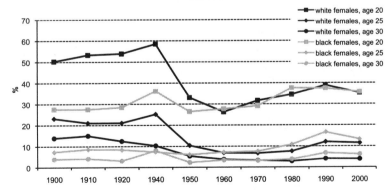

Source: R. Settersten and B. Ray, "What's Going on with Young People Today? The Long and Twisting Path to Adulthood," *Future of Children* 20 (2010): 19–41.

There are many reasons for the growth of accordion families. Some are structural, meaning that they are connected to macro-level changes in the international economy, the ways in which governments have responded to global competition, or something as mundane as who is eligible to borrow money to finance a home. Others are cultural, having to do with changing expectations and beliefs about what should be the appropriate configuration of a household. Naturally, these two dimensions of social experience are related.

Baby boomers that came of age in the United States in the early 1970s were fortunate to ride a wave of economic growth that created the structural conditions favoring youth independence. A mere ten years later, their younger siblings were stuck with unemployment rates in the double digits. The early years of the Reagan administration were extremely hard on young people entering the labor market, and that pushed them back into the arms of their families.

Those hard facts that dictate what people can earn (and, hence, where they can afford to live) have a softer side as well. How much do people value independence or privacy? Do young men feel like adults when they are eighteen—as they typically did before World War II—or do they still feel like kids who need to develop more ballast before they can really handle the world on their own? Do women want creature comforts like a nice car or elegant shoes, or are they perfectly happy to slum it in blue jeans from Target, which don't cost very much? These cultural values play an important role in determining what young people spend their earnings on. In a generation where expectations for consumption are high and the options for high earnings are dubious, it seems sensible to stay in the natal home, sacrificing autonomy in favor of cool clothes or the money it takes to pay for a master's degree. When personal autonomy is valued above all else, and there are jobs out there that will underwrite it, sleek cars recede into the background and independence comes to the fore. What the labor market provides is one thing; what individuals floating around inside it want is quite another. Living arrangements reflect structure and culture at the same time.

Of course, neither cultural expectations nor economic opportunity stand still. By the early 1980s, the last time we were mired in a recession with 10 percent unemployment, no one took economic security for granted. The same is true in the midst of the recession of 2010. There is nothing like a brush with an impossibly crowded job market and college graduates selling home-baked goods on street corners to make an entire generation more concerned about their standard of living than their blue-jeaned ancestors.[18]

Even though the connection between structure and culture is there, it is helpful to divide them for the purposes of clarity. What, then, are the structural forces making it harder for young people to strike out on their own? And how, exactly, are cultural expectations changing here and abroad?

Globalization

Global competition is the most profound structural force affecting the residential location of young adults in the developed world (or the underdeveloped world, for that matter). At first blush, this would seem too remote a pressure to matter. Yet globalization is a prime mover in determining the economic stability (or volatility) of young adults and their parents. New entrants to the labor market are often the first to feel the brunt of increasing competition in the labor market and the downward drift of wages that results. Young people are less powerful and may be largely unable to protect themselves from changes in labor-market regulations that increase the flexibility employers have to meet the competition they face or the desires of their shareholders to maximize returns by holding the payroll down. The availability of white-collar workers in low-wage countries and the development of Internet communications technologies, such as Skype, force Americans to compete against their English-speaking counterparts in India and Jamaica.

Though competition is affecting workers all over the world, the consequences for the youngest among them are dramatically different depending on nationality. What governments do to cushion the blows of globalization matters a great deal in shaping the opportunity landscape and therefore the pressures on families to buffer the least favored: young workers.

If we look back to the 1970s, it becomes clear that the prospects of new entrants to the labor market have deteriorated fairly steadily across many countries in the developed world.[19] At the beginning of that de-

cade, the unemployment rate for twenty- to twenty-four-year olds in
Japan was 2 percent; by the end, it was up to 7.1 percent. Italian youth
lived with 9 percent unemployment in 1970; by 2008, that proportion
had doubled to 18.7 percent. France saw a six-fold increase in youth
unemployment, and Germany went from virtually zero unemployment
in this age group to more than 10 percent. Even more disturbing is the
length of time that young workers are going jobless: between 1980 and
2007, it has more than doubled in Japan. In Germany in 2007, 32.3 percent of unemployed youth were out of work for more than a year, which
is a significantly larger group than it was only a few years before.[20] Long-
term joblessness is more than a financial problem. Skills grow rusty,
references are harder to tap, and the prospects of getting back into the
workforce dim the longer a worker goes without a position.

The impact of unemployment has been concentrated disproportionately among young workers, particularly in Southern Europe. In
2011, the overall unemployment rate in Italy was 8.7 percent; but young
people, ages fifteen to twenty-four, were in a much worse condition in
the job market: nearly 29 percent were unemployed, an all-time high.[21]
The United States saw a more modest increase (from 8.2 to 10.2 percent) in unemployment among young adults, but the picture looks truly
dismal when we focus on teenage workers: 27 percent of the sixteen-
to nineteen-year-olds in the active labor force—meaning looking for
work—are out of luck.[22] Racial differences are pronounced, with black
youth the most disadvantaged: in the most recent recession, their unemployment rates are twice that of whites.[23] It would appear that youth
unemployment is getting worse as each successive recession slams into
the American economy. The problem has become much more acute
in the Great Recession compared to periods of economic contraction
over the previous thirty years. Moreover, where the unemployed in the
United States once had to contend with short-term layoffs, the European pattern of long-term joblessness is spreading here, too; in 2010, it
is at its highest level since the 1930s.[24]

MEANWHILE, EUROPE HAS seen the emergence of the NEETS, which
stands for "not in education, employment, or training"; a fancy way of
saying "just plain idle." These are people not working, not in school, and
not in the military. They are disconnected from all the major institu-

tions of society and their numbers are growing at an alarming rate in the United Kingdom, Spain, and Poland, with slightly less but notable growth in Greece, Italy, and Finland.[25] We are not immune to the problem in the United States, and we might be said to have a larger problem than Europe.[26] We know very little about what these young people are doing all day; we just know there are many more of them than there used to be.

Young people in Japan also face increasing problems in the labor market. Historically low unemployment rates have given way to what are—by Japanese standards—skyrocketing levels of joblessness. In 1999, 10 percent of Japanese males under twenty-five were unemployed.[27] In 2002, 22 percent of university graduates and 11 percent of high-school graduates did not have a job, a record high.[28] By 2002, there was only one opening for every two graduating high-school students searching for work.[29]

While the Japanese have had to face a sharply deteriorating labor market, the change has not affected its workers uniformly. In the 1990s, the proportion of the labor force consisting of regular employees (those with long-term contracts) actually *increased* overall in Japan. Yet Japan's teenagers and workers in their twenties went the other direction: fewer of them had regular employment. Large companies are hiring new graduates at far lower rates than in prior generations—one-eighth of the peak rate for high-school graduates and two-thirds of the peak for university graduates.[30] Young adults who graduated from poorly regarded high schools were left with even fewer options, and it's from their ranks, among others, that we see the emergence of a new kind of Japanese worker: the freeters, employees on temporary or short-term contracts. Freeters are assumed to be unwilling (rather than unable) to land real jobs, the kinds that came easily to their fathers' generation.[31] In 2006, 48 percent of those between fifteen and twenty-four and 26 percent of those between twenty-five and thirty-four were described as freeters.[32] Those levels represent a stunning increase: in 1988, only 17 percent of young workers were freeters. The rate of increase among the youth is twice what it is among workers in older age groups. As Manubu Shimasawa, a professor of social policy at Akita University, has explained, "Japan has the worst generational inequality in the world . . . the older generations don't step aside."[33]

These new conditions are reshaping pathways through the Japanese labor market for new generations of entrants. In a country where lifelong employment has been taken for granted for decades,[34] young people now have extremely high rates of job turnover: half of high-school graduates and 30 percent of university graduates left their first job within three years in the late 1990s.[35] Only a decade earlier, Japanese ages eighteen to twenty-four were the least likely to have changed jobs among all the countries covered by the Fifth World Youth Survey.[36]

The disproportionate impact of globalization on young people is not a given. It is powerfully influenced by the deliberate actions of governments responding to the demands of employers to lift constraints to fire people. These rigidities are being dismantled in many countries as employers flex their muscles, threatening to unleash runaway shops in friendlier countries. Accordingly, national governments—even in the social democracies—are loosening the strictures in ways that have disproportionately negative effects on young people.

When the Japanese government lifted some restrictions, including limitations on part-time employment, the consequences varied across the age groups. As Japan's economic recovery began to gather force, part-time and temporary employment expanded at a rapid rate. In 2004, a quarter of the workforce was employed part time, up from 15 percent in 1997. Two million workers signed up with temp agencies. Few of them were mature workers, protected by laws such as the Doctrine of Abusive Dismissal and the seniority wage system.[37] It was young workers who fell into the part-time trap and became freeters.

The same generational split developed in Spain. Starting in 1984, Spanish firms were allowed to arrange short-term contracts with any employee, a sharp departure from past practices. Today, a third of all Spanish employees have short-term jobs, the highest level in Western Europe. Older workers, who had permanent jobs before the reforms, had more bargaining power to protect their insider status. We see the emergence of a bifurcated labor market with young people pushed into less-secure positions. The percentage of twenty-five- to twenty-nine-year-old Spanish men in temporary employment rose from 20 percent in 1987 to more than 50 percent less than ten years later.[38] The most insecure jobs—temporary employment—also skyrocketed among young workers.[39]

This age-based dichotomy did not unfold in countries that created buffers, in the form of government policies, between young workers and the pressures of globalization. Seventy percent of French men have a permanent long-term job by age twenty-nine.[40]

Trouble in the labor market spells holes in the pocketbook. This is a universal sore spot. However, whether or not money trouble translates into a prolonged stay under a free parental roof depends a lot on nationality. Generous welfare states—the social democracies of Northern Europe, for instance—cushion the blow with higher-education grants, affordable rental housing, and even unemployment benefits for those who have never or barely worked. Conversely, the weak welfare states of Spain, Italy, Japan, and post-Thatcher Britain are apt to leave the unemployed and underemployed to their own devices, pushing them into the private safety net: the family.

Housing Markets
The single biggest cost young people face in establishing their independence is housing. Rent or mortgage expenditures take more out of their pocketbooks than any other expense. All over the developed world, housing costs have been rising as a proportion of overall consumer expenditures.[41] That has not escaped the notice of European citizens. We know a lot about how they are responding to the economic pressures of globalization because an annual opinion poll—the Eurobarometer—provides us with lots of information about the attitudes of residents in every European Union country. In 2007, a special poll surveyed young people, asking why they thought accordion households were forming. Twenty-eight percent cited the lack of affordable housing as a reason for the delayed departure from the parental nest, while 44 percent said they "could not afford to move out."[42]

Plentiful, subsidized rental housing, a pattern typical of Nordic countries, tends to lower the age of home-leaving because rents can be kept within reach of young workers or students in need of transitional housing. A dearth of rental housing and little government support for homeowners—generally the case in Southern Europe and Britain[43]—often fosters later departure from the nest. In Spain, average monthly rent is half of the average monthly wage and the interest rates for mortgages are 5 percent higher than the European average.[44] When housing costs are high and job prospects are low, the family home looms as the only realistic solution.

In countries where privately owned homes are the main form of housing, young adults face the hurdle of saving up to buy a house in order to move out of the home where they grew up. Ironically, it is the poorest part of Europe where homeownership predominates and governments are the least likely to lend a hand in making it more affordable. In Spain and Italy, more than 70 percent of the population owns its own dwelling.[45] This is much higher than, for example, France, where only 54 percent of primary residences are owner-occupied. Most Spaniards buy a house *before* leaving the parental home,[46] with only a quarter moving out to a rented dwelling as compared to three-quarters of the French.[47] At the same time, it can be very difficult for young Southern Europeans to finance residential independence: in Italy, as in most countries, a regular paycheck is necessary to obtain access to credit, leaving most young people dependent on parental housing because they cannot buy homes.[48]

In many ways the United States has been more generous to young people looking for housing. The GI Bill (officially titled the Servicemen's Readjustment Act of 1944) provided, among other things, a variety of loans for returning veterans to buy homes.[49] At zero interest and no down payment, the GI Bill provided a huge shot in the arm for the American housing market and helped to usher in the postwar expansion of the suburbs. More than 4 million homes were purchased with Veterans Administration loans.[50] Baby boomers by the millions were raised in those owner-occupied houses by parents who were relatively young homeowners from modest backgrounds. Since the boomers were such an outsized generation, their historical experience defined new norms and expectations that have remained. Owning a house is an essential part of the American Dream. Yet the economy has conspired to make it far more difficult to achieve. Nearly 80 percent of Americans age seventy-five and older are homeowners. Young people have no such luck: only 23 percent of Americans under the age of twenty-five own their homes.[51]

When housing becomes more expensive and lending policies more conservative—as they tended to become in the wake of the Great Recession and the foreclosure crisis it provoked—young people either fall into the rental market, which is more robust in the United States than in many Southern European countries, or they retreat to their parents' home in order to save money for a down payment. There are clearly more options available to them than to their counterparts in the weaker welfare states of Spain, Italy, or Japan, which is why accordion families have blossomed in the United States but not to the degree we see in those countries.

Education

We typically think of education and living arrangements as independent spheres of life. Yet they are closely connected. Depending on how college students are housed, the pathway to residential independence can look very different. Accordingly, enrollment patterns and the age of completion of education make a difference in the distribution of accordion families.[52] In Germany, Austria, the United Kingdom, and Ireland, less than 20 percent of eighteen- to twenty-four-year-olds are enrolled in school. By contrast, about half of this age group is in school in the Nordic countries and in the Netherlands. The Southern European countries, as well as continental countries such as Belgium and France lie in between these extremes.

The explanations for these variations lie in different patterns of labor-market entry and regulations governing compulsory education. Italians can leave school at fourteen, while Germans must remain to the age of eighteen. The other European countries are somewhere in between.[53] The age at which students complete their education is only partially related to home-leaving because students may or may not live away from home while they *are* enrolled. There is almost no student housing at Southern European colleges.[54] Only 2 percent of Spaniards take student housing as their first independent dwelling, while it accounts for 33 percent of first independent homes for the French.[55] In Sweden, most students live in residential halls or on their own since they are supported by study grants and loans from the government.[56]

The preference for student residence at home or on campus is not simply a matter of availability. In some countries, such as the Netherlands, Sweden, and France, young people expect to live away from home while studying, and moving out to study is seen in a positive light.[57] In others, like Spain and Italy, moving out to attend a university is regarded as a burden. It may also be unnecessary since the long history of regional independence in countries like Italy means that one rarely needs to migrate in order to study a particular field.[58] Italian universities tend to duplicate one another on the theory that every region needs its own full-service university. In highly centralized systems with elite and specialized study centers—like those found in France—those who cannot move may not be able to study in their fields of interest.[59]

Financial support for students is another element in the puzzle. Spain provides no housing allowances and little social housing for students, while France has both and extends them to low-income nonstudents as well.[60] Swedish students are supported by government grants and loans.[61]

For American college students, class powerfully affects education-related patterns of residence. Only 25 percent of the student population is what we might call "traditional students": they live on campus in dormitories or rent off-campus apartments, go to school full time, and are supported by their parents. The vast majority lives at home, works at least part time and struggles to complete degrees. No doubt the ranks of the nontraditional student are growing because the cost of higher education is galloping ahead of inflation. One of the few ways to protect themselves against the sticker shock is to live at home while studying. That said, for the privileged students who do move out, the availability of transitional housing means that they can break free of the home front while in college.[62]

Thereafter, however, residential freedom depends on earnings—and an increasing proportion of America's newly minted BAs are headed back to their high-school bedrooms. By some counts, 85 percent take up residence with their parents, a record proportion and a sign of the abysmal prospects for employment in the midst of the Great Recession.[63]

Family Income and Wealth

To this point, we have been thinking mainly about structural conditions young people have to contend with as they migrate toward independence. But we know the economic condition of their families makes a huge difference in their options. Wealthy parents can decide to buy an apartment for their children and facilitate their physical separation from the family, even if they are tethered financially. Middle-class parents may be unable to subsidize that first apartment, but at least they don't need their children's income to survive. If their kids are willing to find roommates and live a little rough in order to be independent, they do not have to stand in the way. Poor families may need to restrain their children from moving out because they cannot manage if they don't hold the collective income of all workers in the family inside a common pot. Of course, adult children in those low-income households may not be able to afford to live on their own anyway, but even when they can strike out on their own, their families may try to dissuade them. All in all, the socioeconomic status of parents is likely to influence the age at which the younger members can make a go of it on their own.[64]

Though there is clearly a correlation between family wealth or income and the residential patterns of the next generation, the connection is complex; it doesn't necessarily tell us whether resources are changing hands. They could, but do they? The Eurobarometer sheds some light on the extent to which young people are financially supported by their families. Respondents are asked, "Where does your income come from?" and the survey permits multiple responses. In 2001, about 45 percent of Italians and 42 percent of Spaniards ages eighteen to twenty-four were supported solely by their parents. In France that same year, the number was close to 12 percent, while in Britain it was about 6 percent.[65] With the exception of Finland and Denmark,[66] European youth have become increasingly dependent on parental resources, with a particularly sharp upswing in the countries of Southern Europe.[67]

The American case is inconclusive and even a bit contradictory. Some scholars argue that children in affluent families are less likely to become independent until they are eighteen or nineteen, but thereafter, families with money produce children who can become autonomous (at least in terms of residence) sooner than those who are broke.[68]

Cultural Change: What We Value

Labor markets, housing, and education—all of these institutional arrangements matter in patterns of home-leaving. But it might be argued that the way these structural elements of national economies are organized is itself a reflection of their history, of patterns that have built up over centuries to which these institutions have responded. The European Union notwithstanding, there are long-standing differences in family structure and relationships that demarcate Europe's regions. These differences predate the development of modern welfare-state structures and may indeed have helped to shape the contours of social policy.

In the eighteenth and nineteenth centuries, Northern Europeans left home to work as servants at much higher rates than their counterparts in the Mediterranean, where young people left largely to get married. In the strong family of Southern Europe, economic hardship has historically been shared by the family group rather than falling onto the shoulders of young adults.[69] In the "weaker" family of the Nordic societies, families put their young people on the road, particularly when they couldn't provide for them.

This historical trend has bequeathed to modern European societies expectations for either autonomy or dependency expressed in the development (or underdevelopment) of the welfare state. In countries like Italy, Greece, and Portugal, families are expected to absorb the financial burdens of caring for unemployed, young adults and students, while the state compensates for the weak family in the North, making it easy for young people to rely on government to support their independence from the natal home.[70] Long-established cultural differences have created a paradox: Southern Europeans, with their strong families, are least able to ensure the continuity of those families as their fertility rates plummet to lowest-low levels.[71]

Delayed departure from the family home may also be a by-product of what demographers term the Second Demographic Transition, in which fertility drops sharply—at present, to the lowest levels in recorded history.[72] Debate continues over the causes of the "birth dearth," but among the principal culprits is the disappearance of an economic rationale for childbearing, now superseded by a change in values in which children come to be defined not as economic assets but as precious for the way they fulfill their parents' hopes and dreams.[73] This cultural shift may be responsible for delayed and reduced fertility and may have, at the same time, led to greater variation in the way the life course unfolds. If children are "priceless," it may be more acceptable for them to deviate from old-fashioned and rigid norms that used to govern the march to adulthood.

Japan is well-known for its familistic culture with strong bonds of respect and deference between parents and children. The premodern conception of "stem families"—in which the oldest son brings his bride into his parents' home, and they remain a three-generation household—strengthens intergenerational ties, even at the expense of bonds between spouses.[74] The stem family is no longer the expected form, but its historical legacy has been to create in the Japanese a stronger disapproval for cohabitation outside of marriage than is evident in, for example, the Nordic countries or the United States.

Much has been made—especially in the popular press—about the development of the freeter labor force in Japan. The idea that young people are not giving themselves over, body and soul, to the firm, has excited concern that Japanese youth are made of less sterner stuff than their forebears. The question is whether the development of the freeter reflects lack of opportunity for full-time work (a change in structure) or a taste for freedom and a rejection of the "nose to the grindstone" life of the salaryman (a change in cultural values). Clearly, some of each is at work in Japan today. A survey of high-school students by the Japan Institute of Labour found that while half of all freeters tried to find a regular job and gave up when they were not successful, the other half *chose* to become freeters from the start. Many freeters are focused on self-realization and responded that they chose to be freeters because they were not sure what type of job was best for them or they wanted to do things other than work. While the young Japanese are undoubtedly constrained by the difficult labor-market situation, it does seem that there is a cultural shift with emphasis on enjoying a flexible lifestyle and earning some money without too much effort or commitment.[75] Japanese youth simply don't seem to aspire to the kind of life that was expected and respected in the older generations.

Consumption Norms

In places and periods in which high value is placed on autonomy, young people might be willing to take a significant drop in their standard of living or the quality of the jobs they can expect to land in order to pur-

sue or preserve their independence. Only 12 to 14 percent of eighteen-
to twenty-four-year-olds in Europe would be willing to "accept any job"
if they were unemployed.[76] Higher percentages insist on jobs that are
stable, well-paid, and appropriate to their qualifications or that meet all
three of these conditions. This does not suggest a group that feels it has
its collective back against the wall but instead a population with choices
and fall-back positions. One of the most likely is to remain dependent
on the family purse.

Employment is not the only domain where expectations have risen
while the means to realize them have fallen. Standard of living is another. Young people seem to have concluded that it is better to stay
at home than experience a loss of creature comforts. The Eurobarometer asks respondents about the role of "home comforts without the
responsibilities" as a factor in delayed departure and more than 30 percent of respondents in all countries (more than 40 percent in Greece
and Italy) agreed that this was one reason to "stick around."[77] "Parasite
singles" in Japan are believed to be living with their parents—rather
than taking up their social obligations—in order to maintain their living standards.[78] This shift has come as something of a shock in Japan,
and popular books pointing to the evolution of this new youth culture
have generated considerable public discussion. With fewer children
per family and greater prosperity, parents may be better able to support their children financially and may no longer think of their children as potential income earners for the family. Few coresiding, young
Japanese contribute income or pitch in to help with domestic chores
in the parental household. Surveys suggest that youth believe their
standard of living would decline with marriage and departure from
the natal home. There is a close association perceived between the two
events.[79]

The question of whether this evolution is voluntary or provoked by
economic barriers to which families are adapting is difficult to settle.
Japanese economist Yuji Genda discounts the notion that the change is
elective and cultural, pointing instead to the many structural obstacles
that young Japanese face in the labor market. Nevertheless, he concedes that a result of these structural factors is young people staying at
home to maximize their living standards.[80]

Tying the Knot or Not?

If the emergence of the accordion family was a neutral fact, a benign adaptation to the ebb and flow of social change, there would hardly be a need for a book like this one. There is nothing neutral about this evolution. Accordion families are symptomatic of, and causally connected to, basic demographic features of society that have profound consequences for the economic health of the United States and other advanced countries. Some of the most serious social tensions erupting across the developed world—immigration, public spending, and deficits, for example—are simmering in some places and boiling over in others. They are emerging at the same time and for some of the same reasons that we see accordion families sprouting, including lack of economic opportunity for young people.

When adult children cleave to their parents, they will come to marry much later in life, if they marry at all. In the early part of the twentieth century, men and women wed when they were in their mid-twenties. It took that long for them to amass the economic wherewithal to establish new households. The prosperous years following World War II saw men's wages skyrocket and, accordingly, the age of marriage fell to its lowest level in a hundred years. Those days are gone now. Between 1960 and the present, the average age at first marriage has increased throughout Europe, the United States, and Japan by as much as seven years, with those in many countries delaying marriage until their early thirties.[81]

Moreover, a growing proportion of men and women are not bothering to marry at all. Demographers estimate that one in seven Japanese women will remain unmarried for their entire lives. Italian marriage rates have plummeted to among the lowest in the European Union, a remarkable change in one of its most Catholic countries.

Late marriage—and no marriage at all—depresses fertility. Japanese women typically had their first child around the age of twenty-five in 1970. By 2008, the mean age at which they had that first baby had climbed to nearly thirty. Parents who wait that long to get started have many fewer kids overall than their counterparts who have their first child at age twenty. The countries we focus on in this book have all experienced declining fertility.

Completed Fertility Rates for Selected Countries

Denmark	2.0 (1970)	1.8 (2004)
Italy	2.4 (1970)	1.3 (2003)
Japan	2.1 (1970)	1.3 (2004)
Spain	2.1 (1970)	1.2 (2003)
Sweden	1.9 (1970)	1.6 (2002)
US	2.5 (1970)	2.0 (2002)

Source: World Fertility Patterns, UN Department of Economic and Social Affairs, Population Division, 2007, http://www.un.org/esa/population/publications/world fertility2007/Fertility_2007_table.pdf.

Demographers consider a fertility rate of 2.0 to be "replacement level." Anything less and the population is shrinking. Italy, a country famous for its love of the *bambini,* plummeted to 1.19 in 1995. Although it has been improving in recent years, Italy is still one of the countries with the lowest fertility rates, exceeded only by Germany. Just about the only country in the developed world that is not actually shrinking is the United States, and we owe that good fortune mainly to the presence of immigrants from Mexico, who tend to have larger families than the native born. If we take immigrants out of the equation, the United States does not look very different than, say, Sweden. The gap between immigrant and native-born fertility rates in the United States is nearly 30 percentage points.

We cannot claim that the accordion family causes delayed marriage or low fertility per se since many other factors enter the equation, and it is quite likely that many of the same forces that push young people back into the parental nest are contributing simultaneously to changing patterns of family formation. What seems clear, though, is that these phenomena go together and collectively have problematic implications for society.

Graying
The most serious of those problems is the aging of these societies. When few babies are born, the composition of the population tips in favor of the old. That may be a blessing as long as the elderly are productive and

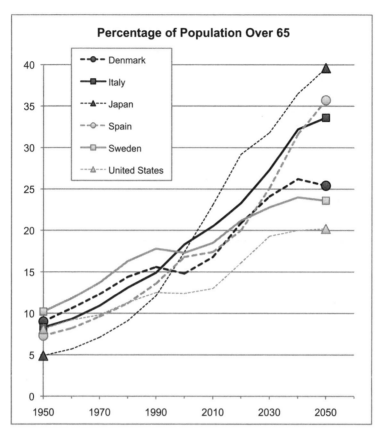

Source: Organisation for Economic Co-operation and Development, Paris, France.

healthy, and indeed they are increasingly long-lived today. But at the end of the road, an aging society is likely to see a downturn in productivity, higher costs for health care, and a shrinking base of workers who must support a growing proportion of retirees through a social security system. A recent series of articles in the *Economist,* titled "Into the Unknown,"[82] dwells on the consequences of population aging in Japan, painting a dire picture of the country's fate:

> Japan is heading into a demographic vortex. It is the fastest-aging society on Earth and the first big country in history to have started shrinking rapidly from natural causes. Its median age (44) and life expectancy (83) are among the highest and its birth rate (1.4 per woman) is among the lowest anywhere. In the next forty years its

population, currently 127 million, is expected to fall by 38 million. By 2050, four out of ten Japanese will be over 65.

The *Economist* foresees an economic calamity in these trends. As its working-age population contracts to a level below what it was in 1950, Japan will see its economy shrink at a stunning pace—unless it can find a way to boost productivity to compensate. "From then on," the magazine warns, "demography will seriously aggravate Japan's other D-words—debt, deficits, and deflation." Pension costs will eat up an ever-increasing proportion of the country's resources. The problem is so acute that even now younger Japanese workers are refusing to pay into the state pension system. Half the workers under the age of thirty-five now fail to make their payments, which are legally required.[83]

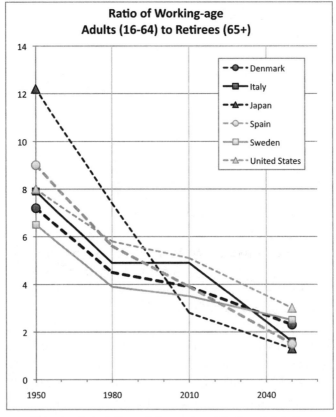

Source: Organisation for Economic Co-operation and Development, Paris, France.

If this was just a problem in Japan, we could look at it as an interesting test case of the consequences of a graying society. But all around the developed world, particularly in countries loathe to turn to immigrants to cure the population problem, we see something similar.

The costs associated with the support of a large elderly generation by a small, working-age population are enormous and set the stage for tense domestic squabbling about which group is more important: young people or old people. Who deserves the lion's share of public spending? How much of the burden can families shoulder, and what can we expect from government (read, the rest of us)? And can we afford *any* of this under punishing, recessionary conditions? All over the developed world, conflicting pressures are building: boost public spending to revive employment or cut it drastically to trim ballooning deficits? There is no consensus; just a heap of trouble.

These problems are acute in the United States as well, but they would be far worse if we did not have such a large immigrant population buoying the tax receipts and providing the workforce, particularly in service-sector jobs that support elder-related needs like home health-care workers. Draconian policies designed to placate anti-immigrant anger are waging a losing battle, for we need the newcomers to pay for our baby-boom retirees.

At least we have a tradition, fraught as it may be, of building a nation out of the immigrant fabric. This is far less the norm in Europe and basically unheard of in Japan. The birth dearth in those regions is, in fact, leading to in-migration, but it is largely illegal and almost universally unwanted. There is no "melting pot" tradition in Italy, Spain, or Japan, and they are not ready to invent one now. Yet without some means of replenishing the population, these low-fertility countries are in serious trouble. If opportunities for their young workers continue to build elsewhere, they could witness brain drains that will push their productivity down even further.

Conclusion

What has emerged out of this maelstrom is a "new" or in some cases a recycled "old" form of multigenerational household. In the weak welfare states, where the family is on its own in a sea of demographic and economic trouble, middle-class parents are opening the accordion and accepting their children back in the fold. In many countries, they never let them go in the first place. The pressures are even stronger on working-class and poor families who actually need to hold the earnings of their younger members inside the family fold just to stay afloat.

In the strong welfare states of the European North, the opposite is the case. They pay dearly for the privilege, through high taxes, but those resources underwrite youth independence and obviate the need for the expansive private-safety net that is the accordion family. In the social democracies, we still see a very young age of departure from the family home.

These demographic facts are hardly the whole story. The accordion family is greeted with equanimity in some places, alarm in others. The reasons for this variation have everything to do with how different societies diagnose the problem of delayed departure or whether they think it's a problem at all. And even where they do define this evolution as problematic, there are often silver linings to these family clouds. This cultural back channel has been little studied and is our prime focus in this book.

CHAPTER 3

In-House Adulthood

LIVING AT HOME AT THE AGE of thirty *is* different from being a teenager or a college student at home. When things work well, a kind of "in-
house adulthood" develops, in which the younger generation has more
autonomy and the parents have less responsibility. Not-so-young adults
become like beloved boarders or roommates rather than children to be
supervised. Mom may still be doing the laundry, putting dinner on the
table, and covering most of the bills, but she is not demanding to know
whether Sally will be home at eleven every night.

It makes a world of difference when in-house adulthood unfolds in
the comfort of a middle-class home. Accordion families in the working class or among the poor face an entirely different landscape. Tight
quarters, money worries, the coercive attempts of parents to confiscate
the adult children's income—none of this improves the parent-child
bond. In *All Our Kin,* her classic book on the African American poor
of the Flats, a community in southern Illinois, Carol Stack wrote about
the ways parents stir up trouble among their married children to un-
dermine relationships and pull their children back into the natal fold.
Stack showed that parents and siblings undermined marriages in order
to recapture the income lost to a separate household.

These pressures are far less evident for the American middle class.
There, the accommodation of the accordion family is made much easier
because affluence and space make almost any relationship simpler to
maintain. Yet there are also cultural reasons why the gap between parent and child in a community like Newton is so small. The distance between millennials and their folks, in terms of tastes in popular culture,
closed some time ago. Clashes over music, movies, the length of men's
hair, politics, and social mores are less common than they were between
the millennials' baby-boom parents and the World War II generation.
Boomers did almost anything they could to avoid living with their par-

ents after the age of eighteen. Few of them lived at home during their college years or even thought about returning to the family nest when they finished college. All of that has changed.

Take Jennifer Warren. Jennifer is trying to make a go of it as an opera singer, a singularly complex career choice. Her parents agreed to let her use their home as a base while she takes her best shot. In fact, her mother was thrilled that Jennifer was on her way home, as much for her company as for the ways in which her presence would rekindle Jennifer's relations with her younger siblings. But moving in does not signal the resumption of her former life as a dependent teenager. It is a new Jennifer with a different set of ground rules. Her parents give Jennifer a wide berth and a lot of privacy. They do not get annoyed when she uses "their things and the car."

As a courtesy, she mentions her schedule, but she is clear that she is not asking permission. And while she is not required to do so, Jennifer says she tries to help around the house:

> There are no concrete responsibilities. You have to do dishes every night. I make sure to clean up my own mess, [and] sometimes if they have just left stuff out or stuff in the sink, I will do that. For laundry, I take care of my own laundry. If they ask me to clean for a special occasion, I will do that.

Jennifer's bedroom is on the top floor—which also consists of an empty bedroom and a bathroom—and, while her boyfriend currently lives in Paris, her parents are comfortable with him staying in Jennifer's room for a week or so when he is back in the country.[1]

This would have been completely unacceptable back in the 1950s when Jennifer's grandparents' generation was raising the baby-boom generation. World War II–era parents were raised on conservative expectations.[2] The beat generation and the common experience of premarital sex in the prudish Cold War era notwithstanding, the social rules called for the avoidance of overt intimacy until marriage.[3] The sexual mores of the succeeding generation were, of course, a sharp departure from these conventions. The introduction of the birth-control pill in the 1960s divorced sex from pregnancy. Jennifer's mother could lead a liberated life without compromising her future and so, of course, can her daughter.[4]

The relaxed attitude toward intimate relations between the sexes, the freedom of young women to go out on their own, the liberty that young men have to postpone adopting the role of family provider—these all actually preceded the emergence of the accordion family. What is different now is that the intimate lives of the coresident generations, the boomers and their kids, are carrying on under the same roof. That is a new configuration.

The new arrangement is born from a desire to support and admire the new person this adult child has become. In some households, it is easier for the young person to garner that respect from parents than it might be from roommates. Where one might have to tiptoe around housemates, parents will bend the rules and understand the fragilities that come with the territory of in-house adulthood more easily. Jennifer's mother makes the point herself:

> Last year [before Jennifer moved back] was very intense because she was performing in *La Bohème*. She had her singer recital, and she had all of her papers together and all this sort of stuff. She would just come home at night after the rehearsals and want to go to bed. There was her roommate, who had been her really good friend in undergraduate school, who had been watching a movie or something, and when Jennifer came in, [her roommate] was ready to talk. Jennifer was just exhausted. Like with your parents, you can say, "I'm so tired, I'm going to bed." Everybody's used to that. But to do it to your roommate, your roommate feels a little insulted.

The practical benefits for Jennifer are considerable as well. When she is performing on the road, her parents will step in and take care of chores and obligations that her housemates would not have been willing to do for her. Her mother continues:

> Look at this week: some important mail has arrived just when she's just in Paris for a couple weeks. We can open the mail. We're per-

forming [the role of] a social secretary. These are important contracts for things she's doing this year. And we can tell her this mail has come, and these are the things you need to know about. Your next gig. We do that for her. She has her stuff here; she realizes she needs some gown for a performance. I can go up to her closet and get it and send it to her.

I think we're a bit of a life-support system here, even though she may not sleep that many nights in the house. This is [a] kind of organized, safe storage, with people you can trust and [ask to] go get [things] for you. She'll probably call home and say I need . . . [t]here's just a whole bookshelf in [her room] of scores. We're [a] whole lending library, too. We can get access to her materials. I think she needs that. Plus for her, home will probably be the place she comes to decompress. Probably she's had intense auditions, intense whatever, she can just come back here. Certain things get handled for her. If she gets sick, it's good to get sick here.

In many respects, Jennifer is an adult functioning in the outside world. She is a professional who travels, signs contracts, and is respected as a performer. But she is not on her own. She takes refuge with her parents, who provide her with a support structure, understanding, and a willingness to overlook her faults in ways that no one else would.[5] They enable her to live a fairly autonomous existence. In this, her life is very different from what it was when she was a kid. She is an in-house adult with all the privileges that seems to confer.

Jane Conlon adopted the same laissez faire rules with her daughter, Caroline, since they were the rules she grew up with. She explains:

I'm not telling Caroline she can only go out one night a weekend with her boyfriend. I say go sleep [at his place since] it's easier, and I don't have to clean up your room. But they are very simple rules. Simple house rules. It's just a common respect. You know, pick up after yourself and wash your dishes and that.

Jane doesn't quiz Caroline about where she will be at night because her daughter volunteers those details. Caroline knows her mother will worry if she doesn't. Both parties have adjusted to the needs of the other. Jane is less comfortable extending that liberty to her adult son, Max, who also lives in the family home. His progress toward in-house adulthood is a bit more halting. She shares:

> There was a little more trust with Caroline. So [I didn't check on her whereabouts] so much. And I pretty much know where she is. She checks in all the time. The second one, Max, well, every night he goes out, I say, "Where are you going?" and I'll say, "What time will you be in?" Just out of the common decency, so that we can go to sleep. Because I can't sleep 'til I know he is safe. And yet, when they were in college, I could care less what time they got in. What I didn't see didn't bother me. But when they're living here, if they're not in by three, four o'clock in the morning, I start to get a little nervous.

How does this balancing act strike Caroline? It is a little harder for her to adjust to the loss of autonomy she experienced during her college years, when she answered to no one except herself. She doesn't want to feel that she has regressed, and these expressions of interpersonal trust are important indications that she hasn't. Caroline remains very embarrassed that "my mom still does my laundry." While the arrangement seems to work for her, Caroline does note that initially it was hard to find the balance between closeness and autonomy:

> I love my mother, but when there are like two women there, like mother and child, it's really hard to have two strong personalities sharing one space. It's also complicated because my boyfriend lives in Brighton, and so I spend the majority of my weekend nights there. It's kind of like I only store things at my parents' house, and I come home to shower and eat on occasion and to get ready for things. And that is so funny because my mother is overwhelmed when I am in the house and then is upset when I am not in the house for too long. So at first, we just could not figure out the balance.

Ultimately, though, the arrangement has worked because the trade-offs helped Caroline feel her way toward a career that she wants badly.

This is a palatable way to reach that goal, and since her parents grant her a new status that differs from her old high-school position, she has not compromised more than she can tolerate.

TEENAGE LIFE IS notorious for the conflict it engenders between the generations. Though it passes in time, the stress can leave a gulf between parents and children that is hard to close. In the best of all circumstances, the accordion family creates the circumstances in which more egalitarian relations emerge between the generations. That lays the groundwork for a positive adult-to-adult relationship that will last decades after the children establish their independence.[6]

Deepak Patel, a second-generation immigrant whose family settled in Newton, is currently a graduate student in political science. He graduated from Cornell and lived in Latin America for several months before spending two years working as a teacher in the slums of India. Thereafter, he came back to the United States and lived with undocumented immigrants in Astoria before moving back to Boston to work. He took up residence with his parents and has not regretted the move, especially because he is not paying a price in the form of surveillance. He says he has his freedom, the roof over his head, and the uncomplicated affection of his parents:

> It was really good because I was old enough that I could do what I wanted. I could go out and come back when I wanted. I had a car. I was pretty much living like an adult, and my parents were pretty much hands-off. They were happy to have me there, but they were really very different from what they were in high school. It was a good experience. I mean they were always sort of—they never really constrained me compared to people that I've talked to. I really could say that I'm going out with friends and I'll be back, and it wouldn't be a problem.

For many adult children at home, living with parents creates an instant "consulting firm" at their fingertips: people who know them very well to whom they can turn for advice and network connections.[7] Tom Donnelly, a young man who returned to his Newton home after he graduated from Brown, wants to find work in sports public relations. He isn't entirely sure how to reach that goal, and he says he often turns to his parents for guidance:

> And a lot of the times I really appreciate the advice, and then there are other times when I just sort of want them to leave me to my own devices. I do know that when they try to provide me with advice that they mean well. Well, my dad has always been a pretty good mentor to me. My mom has always been there to provide emotional support, but when it comes to recounting experiences and parting advice it has always been from my dad—from the time that we started looking at colleges and he gave me advice about that to now, when he's sharing with me what exactly the job market is like and which areas I'd probably be happy in.

One of Tom's neighbors, Steve Norton, has been working as a teacher's aide at an elementary school for a year and a half and then shifted to tutoring to make a living. He has been thinking hard about what he really wants to do for a career and says he is grateful that he can turn to his parents for advice:

> I've become closer with my parents and have learned a lot from them. I've had the opportunity to really think about different jobs that are out there. So the experiences of having an apartment and paying rent and living independently [are] what I've had to give up. Those are experiences that are definitely important, I think, but I think I've gotten to learn a lot from my parents and have [had] a lot of experiences like traveling and have had time to think about the job market in ways that I wouldn't have had. So it's great.

Similar accounts of the pleasures and benefits of coresidence can be found in other cultures as well. Carla Giudice lives with her sister and mother in Montà d'Alba, a small town in Northern Italy. She has a degree in Chinese language and now works for a big company in Alba. A tiny woman with brown eyes and hair, a big smile and a vigorous voice, Carla finds that living with her mother—on new terms—is far more pleasurable than she expected. Beyond the convenience, she says, there is an emotional grounding that is a source of comfort:

> [Living at home] depends [on] the way in which you do it. I mean, even if I live with my mother, I'm totally autonomous and responsible for my living, and if I had to live alone tomorrow I will be totally able to do it. I know that there are people that stay at home because it is simpler and because their mothers do everything for them, and so in that case it isn't a good thing. I live at home not because I'm too strictly linked to my mother but because I work near here, and so I enjoy my family's company, and I don't waste money in renting an apartment since I can live with them and we enjoy each other. I feel completely independent, but it's a pleasure for everybody. I don't consider my [current] job [to be my real goal], and so when I will find the final [job], I will be able to live alone or with my boyfriend in the right place.

Carla's mother, Giovanna, also likes the arrangement. While she pays all the bills, Giovanna notes that Carla "helps me a lot . . . she washes clothes, she cooks." Giovanna enjoys having her daughters at home and makes an effort to respect their privacy and treat them as autonomous adults.

The advantages of in-house adulthood are understood in Spain as well. Isabela has two daughters, one of whom—a business graduate working for six years in the private sector—lives with her parents. They live in a comfortable apartment in a tall building in Barrio del Pilar, a typical middle-class neighborhood of Madrid. Isabela delights in her ability to give her daughters a measure of freedom while offering them the security and support that living at home provide. She encourages them to call if they need a lift home from a party so as to avoid danger, but she says she doesn't insist that they follow restrictive rules:

> My daughters have sometimes phoned me around two in the morning and said, "Mama, we have no way to go back." And I haven't had any problem to go and pick them up wherever they were. And my husband is the same. And I have never made them be afraid in a way that they had to conceal anything from me.

It is not just the parents who enjoy the emotional benefits of the accordion family in Spain; their millennials also appreciate the latitude of in-house adulthood. Twenty-five-year-old Osvaldo sees living at home as normal: "I mean, it hasn't [anything] to do with autonomy. I come and go whenever I want. I have complete freedom to move."

Boundary Conditions

There is an art to being a parent in a household with adult children in the next bedroom. Authority hangs in the background and could be invoked at any moment, but when the occasion arises, a heavy-handed parent can destroy the delicate fiction that their adult children are, well, adult. To manage this tightrope walk, parents must learn new boundaries and recast the parental role as lateral rather than hierarchical. Respecting the privacy of the protoadult is essential. Bedrooms and topics that might have been fair game in the past move into "off limits" or "by invitation only."

Asmita Patel lives in Newton but grew up in India. Her immigrant background makes all of these adjustments as a mother that much more complicated since she is balancing her native concepts of age-appropriate behavior and those of her host country, which are in flux. When her son, Deepak, finished college, he had ambitions to travel. She had other ideas for him but had to learn to stifle them. "We love having our kids around home," Asmita explains. "Just as soon as he finished college, four or five days later, he was gone to South America. We hoped that he would stay home a little longer, but he had made up his mind that he was going." Had she expressed her desires, she risked undermining her relationship with her soon-to-become in-house adult. "We knew that it was not a battle that we were going to win," she concedes, "so we never waged one." Asmita avoids talking to Deepak about things that might invoke the vertical authority of a parent over a dependent child. She has learned how to back off and back down, pulling back sharply, in ways she never would have contemplated when her kids were young, from expressing her opinions about her kids' plans or behavior.

Stephanie Phillips, the divorced Newton mother who is a nurse and whose son served in Afghanistan, describes just how tough it can be for a parent to come to terms with the fact that boundary rules must be observed:

It's incredibly difficult. You realize there are locks on doors. You knock on doors. Even though you've changed literally thousands of diapers, you must not go in if they're anywhere near the bathroom. [But if] they want to talk to you, they can march into the bathroom. You dare not when it's them.

Of course, the adjustment process can become a very delicate negotiation, in which the feelings of parents are the sticking point, rather than the sensitivities of the child. Parents may come to feel that they are being taken advantage of, and their adult children have to guard against that. Dan Morton works in TV production and was planning to move out of his parents' house soon. But for the time being, he says he tries to be sure that he contributes to the household[8] or at least is not adding to the burdens of running it:

I call them when I leave work to see if they need anything from the store almost every day. If they are home and I am driving, I am happy to pick it up. Sometimes, it is not often, I always ask, but they hardly ever need anything. Usually three to four days a week, I am home for dinner. They seem to have adjusted their dinner to when I get home, around 7:15 p.m. I work eleven to seven. If I work late, which is often in [a] news-based organization—news doesn't wait for you—it could happen at 8:00, 9:00, 10:00, or 2:00 a.m.

Dan looks for opportunities to participate in the daily rituals of his parents' household, in part because he enjoys it but also to underline his genuine appreciation for their hospitality. He doesn't want to be seen as someone who is just "crashing" for a time. Dan shares how he has carved out a place for himself in this new configuration that means something to his parents:

They wait for me to cook. Sometimes, mostly they wait for me to get home before they cook. But I definitely cook; I was a chef for two and a half years. I know a lot of tricks; I teach [my mother] how to do certain things that she never knew how to do. I inspired her to grow an herb garden in the backyard.

Parents know there is a danger lurking in the shadows of the accordion family. It is all too easy for the adult child to lapse into the "take care of me" mode that would not only represent a burden but a compromise of the implicit American bargain: you can stay here as long as you are taking steps to become independent. Larry Keegan says he asks certain things of his son—things he might not have asked of him when he was younger—that represent a contribution, however modest, to the functioning of the household:

> Just yesterday, the TV in our bedroom broke, and so I was talking with one of my sons in the morning, and I just said to him it would be really good if when you got home you switched the TV, so that the TV in our room would work for my wife, [so that] when she got home she could watch TV as she decompressed from a day of work. So I got home at night, and it was done.

Learning how to avoid battles is an art form that takes on great significance in the accordion family. When the kids are young, battles are markers of authority appropriate for parents to wage. Once they are older, that hierarchy is muddled, and the assertion of authority is a challenge to the emerging adult. If he or she can be backed into a corner, then more than a test of wills has happened. An assault on a fragile status has occurred and can puncture the working agreement: we ignore the deviation between what should have happened—a young person becoming a grown-up—and what actually happened—the transition to adulthood stalling out.

Teddy Yoo and his parents seem unable to strike this balance. Instead of recognizing that the post-college Teddy is a different person than the high-school model, the family is locked in conflict over just how autonomous he should be. Teddy admits he is at the boiling point over the surveillance:

> I really resent [being questioned]. I really don't like being asked all the time. Because I feel it's not that I'm doing bad things, [and] I never even have had a girlfriend, it's just that they say, "We want you home for dinner, so you should tell us where you are going and

if you will be home for dinner." When you have a bad relationship with your parents, even them asking you where you are going is bad. Because you relay it to them badly. Even the littlest thing brings up the bad relation, so you can't cope. So I tell them, but sometimes I don't tell them. I say that I'm going here, but I go somewhere else because I think that they don't understand. They say, "Oh you just want to spend money again."

These kinds of battles are not easily calmed. The evolution of a more egalitarian relationship depends in many respects on the quality of the parent-child bond before the great return. Rarely do we find explosive tensions developing between the generations if the relations they shared in earlier years were positive, open, and supportive. The Yoo family experienced generational conflict throughout Teddy's adolescence; his escape to college helped the relationship by putting some distance between them. Necessity forced Teddy back into close proximity, and this rekindled tensions latent—and sometimes out in the open—for many years.

When relations are supportive, terms can be negotiated in ways that suit both the moment and the budding independence of the adult child. Tom Donnelly was fortunate to enjoy this kind of support for many years, both before leaving for college and after his return. While not without the occasional wrinkle, on the whole he says he enjoys the opportunity to be near, without feeling cramped:

I think the fact that I have such a good relationship with my parents [means] that I can come home. While my dad still loved and respected his own mother, it wasn't really warm and fuzzy, and my mom was even worse [with her parents]. She grew up in a household that just wasn't filled with a lot of love and a lot of compassion, and the two of them have told me a couple of times to feel lucky that you can come home to an environment like this, whereas your dad and I never really had that option.

So I guess that is just a blessing that I can count that they're there. And another factor is my little brother. He is actually going off to college in the fall to be a freshman at Brown. While I haven't even seen him that much in the last three years, I feel like the time that I am going to see him is going to diminish even more. But this summer, since I'm not doing anything, and he is not really doing anything other than looking for a job, we will get to spend a lot of quality time together.

The strength of their emotional bonds enhances this family's capacity to step in and advise Tom on the more mundane matters of pro-toadult life: finding jobs, buying a car, and the like. Tom does not feel undermined or infantilized when he needs his parents' advice. By and large, he says he's glad it's there for the taking.

Less Than Perfect

In 2006, Paramount Pictures released the hit comedy *Failure to Launch*. The ever-handsome Matthew McConaughey plays Tripp, a thirty-five-year-old bachelor with "an interesting job, a hip car, a passion for sailing, and a great house," which happens to be the one he grew up in. His parents are desperate to get rid of Tripp and hire Paula (Sarah Jessica Parker), an attractive interventionist who has made a career of seducing men like this out into the world. Tripp starts out looking like a jerk and magically undergoes a metamorphosis into a desirable hunk, whereupon Paula falls for him. Following the predictable Hollywood plot twists, Paula eventually lands her man, and they sail off into the sunset. But Tripp had to overcome the stigma associated with living at home, a visible manifestation of subordination that is hardly compatible with the sexy character he becomes.

Independence is not simply a personal aspiration; it is part of the cultural capital that young people use to evaluate one another against some imagined ideal. A young woman who has a nascent romantic interest in a young man may find it difficult to think of him as her dream-boat if he is tethered to his parents' home. The accordion family can be socially problematic for young people, even if it is financially helpful.[9]

John Rollo lives with his parents and grandmother in Newton. One of the reasons he claims not to be embarrassed about the arrangement is that his girlfriend is indifferent to his living arrangements. "My girlfriend does not care that I live with my parents and my grandma," he explains, "so if she doesn't care, I mean [why worry]?" Conversely, of course, if she did care, he might have second thoughts. Most young men do.

Dan Morton is also perfectly comfortable living with his parents while he plots his career in TV production. But it does put a crimp in his social life; not because his parents mind if he has a girlfriend over, but because the rest of the world is not as enlightened as his parents. Dan explains:

> My dad actually mentioned to me before I moved home, as part of the agreements of keeping the home respectful, that he has no problem with me bringing a girl home. That's not to say that the fact that I have permission makes it any easier. We go back to that stigma, I live at home: "Oh, that's OK, that's such a good idea, saving money," "Oh, he lives at home." It is a stigma. It's not because I am not allowed to but because I don't want to bring girls home, girls don't want to come home to Newton. It is like, "Oh, we are all out in Somerville; I am going to stay in Somerville." I can't blame them. I'd rather stay in Somerville, too.

Dealing with adult children's romantic relationships can be difficult for both children and parents. Amy Manzo is twenty-five and works in a child-care center. Until very recently, she lived with her parents in the same hometown of Newton. To hear Amy tell the tale, she got out just in time. Had she stayed any longer in her parents' home, she says, her love life would have been in trouble:[10]

> Toward the end, [living with my parents was hard] because that started making a lot of issues for my boyfriend and I. We would get into a fight [in the house]; we would kind of sugarcoat it and [pretend we] are OK. When we got outside, it would be a different story; we would fight, so he said we've got to move. Or we would be watching a movie, and my mom would come down and say it's time to go upstairs or keep the door open.
>
> Living together in an Italian household . . . horrid! No boys are allowed upstairs, unless it was my brother; that was the only way

that they could go upstairs. [My boyfriend] slept [in the TV room], and I slept all the way upstairs. My room was next to their room. If we were [in the TV room], the door was open. If we were upstairs, the door was open. They would walk by. Mom would pretend like she had to go [to] the basement or go get food, and she would just sneak in and ask, "What are you guys doing?"

Being an accordion parent means learning to be more accommodating about sexual behavior. This is an irony for many boomers, the first generation to break with convention and insist on the freedom to sleep with whomever they pleased. For some, becoming a parent is an exercise in relapse, back to the culture that was common in the traditional 1950s. But in the twenty-first century, the accordion parent has to learn to stifle that urge if she wants to respect the boundaries required for her child to be an in-house adult. Lily Heller explains how she has learned to put her moral qualms about her son's private life on hold:

He has his privacy. I mean he has his room, and he can go in there. You know, if I want him, I will knock on the door. I don't open the door. I will knock. [His girlfriend] even stays over sometimes. The modern mother here.

At first, it felt a little awkward. I happen to like her a lot. And it's not about what I like. It just feels a little awkward for me. I am used to it now. I am from a generation with my family, my mother and my parents, [who] would never have been able to tolerate that. And you know, so I was brought up in that, even if I didn't believe in it. So it took me an adjustment to accept that: this is what people do these days. I mean he lived at college, so I know they were together, and her parents know I have a two-bedroom condo. They know she doesn't have her own room.

ZARZA DE GRANADILLA is a small village in the province of Cáceres, a part of Extremadura, a region in the western part of Spain. Together with Andalucía, Extremadura was once one of the poorest parts of Spain. No longer. The investment injected by the European Union into the south and west of Spain have made a significant difference:

new highways, new development schemes, a flood of expatriates leaving the cold, dreary parts of Europe to sunny Spain—all of this has brought greater prosperity to this part of the world. Veronica Flores, a forty-two-year-old woman with long hair and dark brown eyes runs the village's only flower shop, Zarza. Her house is a narrow building of two floors. The flower shop is on the ground floor; the home, which is modest but comfortable, occupies the second floor.

Her two children, a daughter age twenty-three and a son age nineteen, live at home. Esperanza works in Veronica's shop, and they spend most of their time working side by side. They have a reasonably good relationship, but Veronica is not happy about Esperanza's boyfriend. She says she is especially upset about his overnight visits:

> My daughter had a boyfriend, and four days after she's brought him home. Four days after, she gets into the room with him. [I tell her,] "Listen, dear, I don't think this is very normal." But she doesn't care. Four days afterward, she opens that door for him.[11]

Veronica hasn't adapted to the idea of in-house adulthood but rather expects persistent deference to her authority. Since that is not forthcoming, she just laments the difference between her life and her children's pathways:

> You have to accept it. No matter how much you tell her off, they don't care about what you tell them. And so that's the situation. The young are not in a hurry to marry, to make a new life, to have children as we did. In the past, we wanted to leave.

Conclusion

In the most successful accordion households, the experience of being at home is not a rerun of the past. Adult children do not relapse into a second episode of teen life. Instead, an in-house adulthood emerges, following delicate—and ongoing—negotiations over personal privacy, autonomy, and the extent to which the returnee should contribute earnings to the household. Parents no longer demand the kind of information they would have asked for as a matter of routine when their adult children were sixteen. They bite their tongues when they are tempted to ask, "Where are you going, and when will you be home at night?"

More relaxed attitudes toward intimate relations between the sexes, the freedom of young women to go out on their own, the liberty young men have from the obligations of the provider role: these are major changes that have paved the way for the emergence of the accordion family. The sexual revolution of the 1960s long predates the trends we are describing here. Baby-boom parents authored those social changes, and their children have taken them in stride. It would be the height of hypocrisy for parents who cohabitated before they married to object to their daughters bringing a boyfriend home for the night or the year. And generally, they don't.

At least in the United States, then, the economic conditions that created the impetus for accordion families came about at a culturally propitious moment and left less friction in their wake than might have been the case in earlier times. This is less so in more conservative countries, where financial pressures push generations together even as their social expectations may pull them apart. This is a very stressful balancing act, and in some cultures, there is nothing balanced about the outcome.

CHAPTER 4

I'm OK, You Are Not

IN THE LATE 1990S, a spate of articles appeared in the Japanese press exposing a truly bizarre social malady for which there seemed no easy explanation: young men were taking to their bedrooms and refusing to come out—for ten years. The *hikkimori* (shut-ins) captured the dark side of the country's imagination. Who were these boys? What pathologies lurked behind the closed doors of their family homes? One by one, what appeared to be perfectly normal parents—hardworking salarymen and their stay-at-home wives—confessed that they had not been able to lure their sons as far as the kitchen for years on end.

Hikkimori stories were followed by gruesome accounts of patricide and other unspeakable crimes in the midst of a society that was, and still remains, legendary for its orderly culture, rigid social structure, and commitment to obedience. Kumi, whom we met in the introduction, is convinced that distance is growing between parents and children, despite their coresidence. It can turn deadly, she explains:

> You know, there are incidents where parents are killed by their son, often. That may be because parents cannot help complaining when they live together, perhaps. They say things that are unnecessary. That may be the cause of the trouble. I don't know. But in our case, we hardly have any conversations, even when both [my son and I] are at home. Well, my son and I follow different schedules. So we don't have much conversation.

Others see the same scary possibilities out there in the social vortex. Atsushi Etsuko, the trading company executive whose two sons have landed on their feet in company jobs, looks upon her sons' generation with fright:

[Young adults] treat human life lightly. There are news reports that they buried someone while she or he was alive or they murdered someone—there are so many incidents like that. That is because they see other human beings only as things.

To read the country's press—and, indeed, to interview ordinary Japanese—is to encounter a country whose citizens often seem fearful of the future. Apocalyptic incidents are recalled constantly in casual conversation because they represent the tip of an unsettling iceberg: it's a nightmare out there.

Kotone has been supporting herself since she was twenty-five. Now twenty-eight, she has a master's degree, and her work involves submitting reports and applications to the government for registering agricultural chemicals. Kotone's younger sister continues to live with their parents, a situation that concerns the family. The problems within the household are understood against a backdrop of worry about the whole culture; the tabloid side of life is a constant refrain when Kotone talks about Japanese society:

There was an incident in Japan recently. A girl was making her mother drink poison, and she was keeping a diary of her observations of her mother. Young people are confused about the real world and the world of fantasy they create. The number of children or youth who cannot tell the difference between the virtual and the real seems to be increasing.

At first blush, the accordion family would seem to have little to do with these visions of mass deviance. Yet in a society that prides itself on social order, the prolonged presence of thirty-year-old children who seem unwilling to grow up and take their place in the natural progression of the generations elicits a similar reaction: the whole society is somehow falling apart.

In the American context, as long as a young man or woman appears to be making headway toward a profession or a meaningful career, the family can take heart and understand its role as facilitating an honorable future that is just harder to come by than it once was. In a country that prides itself on self-made men and women, this momentary departure from the norm becomes acceptable when seen in this light. It wouldn't be the same if Junior were holed up in his room practicing air guitar. There are limits, but they are flexible.

In other societies, like Japan, the transformation is a social problem of almost hysterical proportions. The deviant behavior of the nation's adult children is lumped together with *hikkimori* to indicate that the whole social system is in danger. The new abnormal takes on the quality of a crisis. The newspapers, magazines, and airwaves in Japan are periodically saturated with stories of wayward youth and extreme behavior, where the moral of the story is that Japan itself is in serious trouble, unable to contain its people inside a shared understanding of appropriate behavior.

Reactions to the accordion family are not random anywhere. The explanations that ordinary people offer for this change are connected to what we might call moral cultures. In using the word *moral* here, I mean to invoke Emile Durkheim, the nineteenth-century founder of sociology in France. Durkheim was concerned with the ways in which religious institutions, educational systems, and the very division of labor in society express underlying social structures. The beliefs ordinary people are taught inside these institutional contexts, he posited, are not unrelated to the social order in which they must function daily. Accordingly, he argued that what appeared on the surface to be a very personal decision—like committing suicide—expressed fundamental aspects of the surrounding society: how tightly it integrates individuals together, whether it provides for rules of conduct or leaves people to sink or swim on their own.

Societies that create powerful commitments toward the ruler—for example, Japan in the World War II—will more easily see the emergence of suicide bombers than will societies that cannot compel that kind of allegiance. Protestant nations that let their people determine their own patterns of worship see greater levels of suicide than Catholic nations or orthodox Jewish communities that surround their people in a cocoon of rules and institutions that enforce them. What seems individual on the surface turns out to be a property of the collectivity.

Relying on Durkheim's approach, we might say that the beliefs people have about the emergence of the accordion family derive from a more general experience of social change engulfing each of the societies we are concerned with here. That experience is at once *universal*, in the sense that we are all affected by globalization (by the increase in competition restructuring labor markets in advanced economies), and *particular*, in that we bring to this experience divergent histories and local variations in everything from the structure of the welfare state to the state of housing markets.

The similarities are visible in the common demographics of the accordion family. Throughout the developed world, we are seeing young people falter in their entry into the labor market as they confront weaker job prospects, less security in employment, greater demands for advanced educational credentials, and creeping underemployment, with fewer jobs available to meet the expectations of well-educated workers than are needed to absorb job seekers pouring out of universities in Italy, France, and the United States. Everywhere, this is producing a rocky road for not-so-young workers, making it harder for them to leave home. Yet what these trends mean, whether they are defined as a social problem, a welcome change, or an unremarkable mutation, depends on the surrounding historical and cultural context. And here the variation is everywhere and ripe for the kind of comparative understanding that Durkheim tried to develop.

Unnatural States

Many Americans embrace the idea that social change is natural, that society progresses toward ideals not yet realized. Without minimizing the conflict over what direction the country should pursue, the notion that change is necessary comes with the territory. Among older Japanese, the opposite sentiment prevails: there are, or should be, invariant customs. Changes that "no Japanese had imagined before" cannot be for the better.

Kana, a sixty-six-year-old widow, lost her husband the year before her interview. Her thirty-one-year-old daughter lives with her, while her eldest daughter and her family live next door. The eldest daughter did not marry until she was almost thirty-five-years-old, a marked contrast to Kana, who became a mother at the age of twenty-five. They are an upper-middle-class family with a nice home in the middle of a comfortable but not lavish Tokyo neighborhood. Kana is not struggling financially, and she has her family all around her; a protection against the loneliness of widowhood. But she is worried about the shape of Japanese society.

Kana isn't really sure why the natural progression toward adulthood, family life, and retirement has broken down. She *is* convinced that the very social structure of Japan is at risk, that it is already listing in the direction of the West, where, she believes, it's every man for himself and, instead of rules that guide behavior, a free-for-all chaos reigns. Kana explains:

> In the past, both adults and children followed a certain model according to their age. You graduate from a university somewhere and join a company somewhere. And if you worked consistently, you received a lump-sum retirement allowance when you retired and bought a house with that money and spent the rest of your life [there] until [you were] seventy or eighty. There was a model like that in society. There was a societal model for those high-school graduates as well.
>
> But now, such models do not exist. If a woman remains single forever and lives on her own, then she would need to live with a low salary and a low standard of living for the rest for her life. It was the same for a man who was a high-school graduate. So in reality, now, each individual lives on their own, without being protected by their family.
>
> Japanese people are estranged in a country without any asset or legacies. Each individual lives with pain, each individual feels loneliness in life. It is a situation no Japanese had imagined before.

Yui is a fifty-year-old married woman who lives with her two sons, ages twenty-three and twenty. Her husband lives separately in Tokyo to be close to his work. Her eldest son is a company employee. Yui joins Kana in thinking that the continued dependency of children on their parents bodes ill for Japan:

Unless children live outside the parental home, they can never learn the difficulty of living on one's own or what it means to live on one's own. They would not have a chance to learn that sort of difficulty or concern for others as they grow up. I think children are dependent on their parents, but that dependency has come to be taken for granted. So living together is not a good thing for the child's independence.

Society itself is seen as crumbling around the edges because the younger generation refuses to take its place in the social order. And that is an unnatural state.

It's Our Fault

The shadow of World War II hangs heavily over Natsuki's generation, even though they were born a decade after it ended. Economic devastation cut a broad swath through Japan and shaped the early childhood of the oldest generation of Japanese alive today. While the United States embarked on a postwar expansion, an almost unparalleled period of growth and prosperity, Japan had to contend with the destruction of its basic industries, food shortages, high inflation, and severe unemployment. Cities and factories were heaps of rubble, twisted metal, and burnt wood; the economy was almost totally paralyzed from wartime destruction, rampant black marketeering, and runaway inflation; people drew water from communal faucets and used holes in the ground instead of toilets. Few Japanese had any money, but there really wasn't anything to buy anyway. People were so desperate for something to eat that they hitched rides on freight trains to the countryside, where they traded old clothes for sweet potatoes. Some scavenged for grass and bark to survive. On the streets, former soldiers and amputees begged for food. Many people's growth was stunted by malnutrition.

Relatively little money flowed into Asia to rebuild the war-torn nations. Most of the aid money the United States invested was earmarked for Europe and the Marshall Plan. However, the American government, under the auspices of the Supreme Commander of Allied Powers, did play a significant role in Japan's initial economic recovery, as did the Japanese government. Military hostilities in the Korean Peninsula further helped the Japanese economy as the U.S. government paid the Japanese government a lot of money for special procurement.

Ten years after the end of the war, the Japanese economy finally took off. A period of rapid economic growth followed between 1955 and 1961, which created the foundation for what has been dubbed the Golden Sixties, or the "Japanese economic miracle." The parents of the millennial generation caught this wave in mid-childhood, but the memories of deprivation stayed with them and formed a backdrop for the crushing blows that fell when, in 1991, an asset bubble burst and a decade of stagnation gripped the country. Natsuki Endo, a fifty-seven-year-old woman who lives with her husband and three adult children, remembers how hard the postwar period was for her family and draws a direct link between that experience of hardship and the desire to protect succeeding generations from it. "We did any jobs in order to eat," she remembers. "Our time was like that. So, those [parents] who had dreams and could not fulfill them want their children to achieve their dreams."

According to Natsuki, these aspirations backfired as the millennial generation crested into its late twenties. "They do not take their lives seriously," she complains. Natsuki manages a full house. Her son, thirty, is a company employee. Her oldest daughter, twenty-eight, is a temp worker and has a bachelor's degree. Her youngest daughter, twenty-six, is a freeter who graduated from vocational school. But this is not the way things are supposed to be. By now, these adult children should be married, have their own kids, and live in a separate space (even if it is one that is connected to the parents' home). The culprits? Natsuki and her husband, she believes.

Just as Depression-era Americans wanted their baby-boomer children to have it better, postwar Japanese parents who saw hardship in early childhood and graduated into the boom years of the 1960s also wanted to give their kids an advantage. But the self-critical qualities that permeate Japanese culture lead many to fear that, with the best intentions, they coddled the next generation too much. They worry that they may have created a monster they cannot tame: kids who do not know how to be independent and lack the desire to mature into full adulthood.

The Absent Father

In the rush to capture the affluence that followed from the high-growth period of the 1960s, when Toyota, Honda, and Mitsubishi were becoming household names around the globe, Japanese fathers seemed to disappear from the life of the family. Salarymen, those infamous workaholics, stayed at work for ten hours and then went out to drink with their friends from the firm, finally rolling home when the family dinner was long since over, the children were in bed, and the lonely wife was waiting for the husband she rarely saw. Who questioned the wisdom of this devotion to the modern Satanic Mill? Virtually no one at the time. But the long-term consequences of father absence seems to be haunting Japanese families now. They—in particular the mothers—look upon problems cropping up among the millennials as evidence that monomaniacal devotion to the company might have had a dark underbelly.

Natsuki and her family live in Hachioji City, about forty kilometers west of Central Tokyo. Hachioji is a commuter town for people who work in Tokyo and is also home to many colleges and universities. Natsuki looks out from her modest home upon a society that she thinks is spiritually troubled. The society is hollow, she says. Why? The family lacks its central pillar: the father. With her husband gone all day and long into the night, Natsuki believes something fundamental is missing in the moral education of her children. There is no real communication of values from her generation to the next, and this is leaving a vacuum. Marching headlong into that empty zone are antisocial attitudes undermining the unique qualities of Japanese culture and values. The media and the young promote empty aspects of the West, and there is no effective counterbalance. The only person capable of setting a different tone—her husband—is unavailable emotionally and physically.

The complaint has an oddly familiar ring for Americans, for we also recognize the fallout from fathers not around, particularly for sons, who need masculine role models. We dwell on the absent dad as a key explanation for the problems of fragile families in the inner city, where harried single mothers are on their own with the burdens of raising kids. The absent father in poor households represents a refracted version of the Japanese diagnosis of the ills of their society.[1]

The first feminists, especially Betty Friedan, sounded a parallel lament about the isolated middle-class wife. In her hands, the complaint became a clarion call for the women's movement that urged mothers into the workforce and onto the public stage as authors of their own ideas, no longer derivative of the men around them. But for ordinary, middle-class women, the problem was less about being a major player on the public stage and more about being abandoned to their suburban isolation by husbands who commuted into the cities to work.

Don Draper's beautiful wife on *Mad Men* captures this kind of madness with eerie perfection. Betty Draper, once the belle of Bryn Mawr, an educated woman with cosmopolitan tastes, finds herself marooned in a domestic scene that is, above all, a crushing bore. Betty is also lonely. While Don circulates through the city, enjoying (or suffering through) the distractions of the business world, consorting with women who represent the rebellious ideal of the coming feminist revolution—glamorous and dangerous working women—the elegant Betty develops a nervous condition that makes her hands shake uncontrollably, landing her on a psychiatric couch.

This fictional portrait had millions of real-life parallels, and the roaring success of Friedan's *Feminine Mystique* was no surprise. It spoke to the souls of millions of women stranded in the American suburbs. As in the bedroom communities of Tokyo, women and children inhabited an isolated landscape while men folk were out in the world. Oddly, though, when psychiatrists of the time turned their attention to psychopathologies like schizophrenia, they rarely pointed to the absent father. Instead, they looked (accusingly) at the neurotic mother.[2]

So, too, in Japan, where suspicion landed on the archetypal Japanese mother later than it did in the United States. In the absence of her husband, she was criticized for an unnatural level of devotion to her children, especially her sons. With competition for entrance into prestigious colleges rising to a fever pitch, mothers were said to have dropped everything in favor of grooming hyper students, in school all weekend, staying up late at night, all in the name of that elusive golden ring: entrance to a name-brand university. Even if the urge to promote upward mobility was not a primary goal, for many Japanese mothers, so the theory goes, the absence of the father promoted a suffocating attachment to her children.[3] After all, who else did she have in her life?

These are not simply the pet theories of psychoanalysts or cultural critics. They are explanations compelling to ordinary people puzzling through what has gone wrong with the Japanese family. Fifty-three-year-old Chicko certainly sees this point. She lives with her husband and both their sons, ages twenty-four and twenty-one. The eldest son is a graduate student, and the youngest is a college student. Chicko's husband, who is fifty-five, took early retirement to care for his parents. "In Japan still, for [a] mother, particularly those who have children above twenty," she explains, "mothering has played a big role in their life." Chicko continues:

> They got married and began to take care of their family. Since balancing the family and work was difficult in reality, [they had to give up their job, and] they necessarily have devoted themselves to child rearing solely. Now it is difficult for them to let their children leave, after they have lived with their children for so many years.
>
> Unless parents understand that it is inevitable that their children will leave them sooner or later, they will spoil their children and delay their independence, telling them, "You do not have to rush to marry." This is absolutely the case. And even if the child got married, [the mothers] tell their children, "If your marriage does not work out, you can come back anytime."

During the 1990s, psychiatrists in Japan coined the term *mazakon*, or "mother complex," to describe the more innocuous versions of a sociopathology revolving around emotional incest between mothers and their sons. Psychiatrists at the University of Tokyo argued that the "entire culture has [the] undertone" of *mazakon*. According to this theory, Japanese sons grow up with overindulgent mothers who "smother them in affection, preventing them from developing emotional independence" and leaving them unable to assume the responsibilities of spouse and father. Researchers argued that sons are not the only ones subjected to this treatment: the Japanese state treats its citizens like children.[4] The extent to which this is a real phenomenon is, of course, difficult to assess. There is surely greater variation within the Japanese population than this uniform description implies.[5]

Nonetheless, mothers of stay-at-home children in their thirties came of age at a time when it was normative for a Japanese woman to view her children as her reason for being. (The Japanese term is *kodomo ga ikigai*). The ideology has contributed to the perception that delayed departure—particularly among men—is the mother's fault. It has induced a kind of blindness to the powerful impact of the prolonged recession that began in the late 1990s and continued for more than a decade. As we have noted, that lost decade has taken a severe toll on the Japanese labor market and has clearly had a negative impact on the opportunities available to workers in their twenties and thirties today. But when asked why families are stretching like accordions to shelter their children, it is notable that economic hardships of the moment play virtually no role in the explanations that come back.

While many Japanese accounts of the problems with accordion families focus on one gender or the other, some lump them together in a critique of the postwar generation, whose early life experiences of hardship created problems down the line. Miki, now sixty, was her parents' twelfth child; her mother was forty-five and her father forty-eight when she was born. Accordingly, Miki was "raised and educated in a very old-fashioned manner." Her life, by her own admission, "was not as free as others in [her] generation." Miki was married two weeks after she graduated from university and never worked. In the Japanese tradition, because she married an eldest son, she and her husband moved in with his parents and depended on them financially. Miki's adulthood was primarily defined as being a housewife; the family was her workplace, and she feels she performed her job perfectly.

Miki does think economics has something to do with why Japanese youth are not growing up properly. Rising affluence has made parents soft and unable to impose discipline on their children. When families *had* to be careful with their money because they had little, parents could steel themselves to be tough. As the pressure lifted, their appetite for strict child rearing diminished. They indulged the next generation because they had the wherewithal to cope with the consequences. These days, parents can afford to keep their kids at home for years on end, so they do, whether it is good for them or not. Miki explains:

In Japan, there is a tendency not to make children independent when they are young. I have heard, by contrast, that overseas parents make their children independent when they are young. But in Japan, living together is taken for granted, so it is common for parents not to make children live on their own.

Young people do not do things under their own responsibility. This is [an] indulgence, I think, for both parents and children. Parents cannot be strict with their children. It is as though they have become a little cowardly compared to the past. Between parents and children, there is [an] indulgence based on familiarity. Thus parents do not force their children to leave home.

Life has become affluent as well—not the enrichment of the mind but economic affluence. Since parents are not in financial trouble, they allow their children to stay home. In that way, parents are not making their children independent. We hear a lot about NEET recently. That means that parents are allowing their children not to work. Even though they may think this is a source of trouble, they cannot say anything to their children. If parents say anything, it may lead to domestic violence [from children against their parents]. Parents may be afraid of that. Neither parents nor children can talk to each other.

Daiki agrees with Miki that affluence is the source of the problem. Now fifty-seven, he married at twenty-five and took care of his wife and three children entirely on his own. His twenty-eight-year-old son now lives with him, as does his ninety-one-year-old mother. Daiki's is the most sociological of the explanations for why his children took so long to find their footing. "In the past, before our generation, it was normal for young adults to be independent," he explains. "In order to reduce the number of people in the family who need [to be supported] because the family could not afford it, they married their children off or sent their children to Tokyo for work from the provinces." He continues:

Now parents receive pensions, own a house, and are affluent economically. That is the fundamental reason [for the increase of youth living with parents]. There are also many children coming back to the parents' home after having a divorce. In addition, there are cases where married children live with their parents. That is because their parents are affluent and have large premises, allowing the child and the spouse to live there. There is two-generational housing—that is what corporations advertise as a style of housing for profit. But that is all because our life is affluent. [This arrangement would] be impossible in a place where there is an ongoing war or with a much wider economic disparity. In a place where whether or not they can eat is the issue, they cannot do such things. We can do such things because we are affluent.

The Rearview Mirror

Wealth may have made parents soft; the desire to protect their children may have discouraged them from insisting that their children learn the hard way to stand on their own two feet. But one hears a more depressing folk theory from parents who believe their children may not want to marry and set up a separate household because they have seen what marriage meant to their parents and are not keen to repeat the experience. Miki muses:

I wonder if our married life did not look so happy to [our daughter]. That may be the reason why she could not decide on getting married. The traditional life of a Japanese mother, wife, and daughter-in-law involves selfless devotion, silence, and subordination. I worked hard at mothering and was playing the role of a daughter-in-law and a wife. I was thinking I was very happy. But perhaps [my daughter] was really looking at the inside [laughs]. She was seeing through the reality. So now I think maybe we weren't that happy. That is the reason why she [did] not have hopes or dreams for marriage. There are many situations where parents deceive each other about their marital life. I think children are watching that, and that may be the reason why there are many young people who do not get married.

Growing disillusionment with the experience of married life may be inducing younger Japanese to put the whole experience off or forego it altogether—a bittersweet pill for women of Miki's age to swallow.[6] To reject a mother's pathway is to quietly criticize her choices, which didn't feel like choices at all back in the day.[7] Even mothers who applaud the relative freedom their daughters enjoy today feel a bit aggrieved when the next generation's pathway stands as an implied critique of the traditional past.

Sonoko is a sixty-six-year-old recent widow who lives with her thirty-one-year-old daughter. Her oldest daughter and her family live next door. Sonoko, too, sees the value of marriage diminishing as the Japanese baby boomers come to relish freedoms denied to her generation.[8] She thinks that women of her age may try to catch up to modern times by seeking to liberate themselves from unhappy marriages:[9]

> We see a lot of middle-aged couples getting divorced. Several years from now, there will be a system where the divorced wife can receive half the pension [of their husbands] if they were married for twenty years or so. So there are many middle-aged women who are considering divorce, waiting for that system to be established. Japanese society was not previously like that. Young people today are brought up by such a baby-boomer generation. In that sense, the relationship between husband and wife has been shallow.

Saki is a fifty-seven-year-old woman who lives with her husband, twenty-four-year-old son, twenty-one year-old daughter, and ninety-year-old mother-in-law. She does not generally need to take care of her mother-in-law, who is in good health, and she runs her own nonprofit organization that helps Japanese youth to train for soccer in Latin America. Her son works with her and plans to take over the business in the near future. Although Saki's own career is far from the traditional norm, she, too, thinks her children are rejecting the idea of marriage because of the model they have seen close up:[10]

> Young people are looking at their parents [laughs]. So far, including my generation, it has been the main task for women to take care of their husband in Japan. But now, because of increasing information and work, women can see different worlds, and they are challenging such things, and that is why marriage is delayed. For example,

when I speak with my daughter, she often says she does not want her marriage to be like mine and my husband's.

The rejection of marriage has grown to the point where the stigma of being unmarried—particularly an unmarried woman—has all but disappeared. Estimates are that more than 25 percent of today's young women in Japan will remain unmarried all their lives, a trend that is a stunning departure from hundreds of years of history.[11] Yet there is little hand-wringing among the youth. As *Los Angeles Times* reporter Sonni Efron reported in 2001, times have changed:

> Only a decade ago, Japanese women who failed to marry by age 25 were warned not to become "Christmas cakes" left unsold on the shelf past their expiration date. But millions of them are now flouting their elders' advice—and getting away with it. Japan today is a paradise for singles.[12]

Parasite Singles and Lazy Freeters

One might imagine that young people in Japan would defend their generation and reject the idea that they are troubled. Instead, most young people in Japan seem to accept the characterization of their cohorts as damaged. Where they differ is in their diagnosis of the problem. Jun is a twenty-three-year-old young man who lives with his parents. He will be graduating from university soon and hopes at that point to find a full-time job and become financially independent. He also thinks that young adults are in trouble and agrees that it is mainly the fault of the older generation. His is a psychological frame with a development twist: parents can shape children, but society doesn't shape anything. Society merely receives the end product, which in this case is defective. Jun explains:

> I think it is more the problems of parents of young adults than young adults themselves. Parental influences on children are great. Parents rarely take responsibility for the crimes committed by their children. Society does not accuse them for their children's crime. So

whatever was committed by children only comes back to [the children]. That is the reason why parents think there is nothing wrong with them and they do not feel responsible, I think. I don't think society is responsible [for children's delinquency] particularly.

Postwar parents receive the lion's share of the blame for this state of affairs, from themselves and from their children.[13] But there is no shortage of blame to go around, and a significant amount of it boomerangs back onto the millennials themselves. A strident tone has spread throughout the Japanese media that excoriates them for mooching off their parents, failing to strive, and being willing to accept, and even embrace, their deviant pathway. In 1999, Japanese sociologist Masahiro Yamada published an instant best seller, *The Age of Parasite Singles,* which first described what he called "parasite singles," a term for a single person who lives with his parents into his late twenties or early thirties in order—and this seems key—to avoid taking responsibility for his life (financial and otherwise). Yamada pointed to the rising number of adult children living with their parents into their thirties, leaching off their largesse, without regard to the burdens they create or the social imperative to move on.

Many of them were also freeters who stand as an aberration, though an increasingly common one, in a country where lifetime employment for a single firm was both the goal and, for a certain part of the male workforce, the norm. Conveniently overlooked in this equation is the fact that the lifer pattern was never universal. It existed only in the larger firms.[14] Japan's giant manufacturing firms, banks, and insurance companies could afford to provide these guarantees, select their workforce from among Japan's leading universities, and start them at modest wages and let them rise slowly all in exchange for security. Surrounding these core firms was, and still is, an ocean of small businesses—from parts suppliers to ancillary services—which look more like the contingent workforce that has become so familiar throughout the developed world. Increasingly, new entrants to the labor force, apart from those at the very top of their game in terms of educational credentials (and personal contacts), are relegated to this tertiary sector.

But these facts on the ground rarely enter into Japanese explanations for delayed departure. Instead, personal character takes center stage, and this is as true for the younger generation's opinions as it is for their parents'. Youth are also inclined to minimize the changing economic landscape as a force behind the accordion family. Instead, the willful behavior or misguided motives of individuals and generations is the culprit.

Hina is twenty-three years old and lives with her parents and younger brother. Her father is a forty-nine-year-old company employee, and her mother is a fifty-year-old English teacher. Her younger brother is nineteen and in college. Hina is currently in the second year of a master's program in piano, and she teaches piano. When asked why young people are living at home for so long, Hina launches into a soliloquy about her badly behaved generation. "Young adults snap easily and become violent," she says, recoiling into her seat. "Or they become involved in odd religions or cultures. They don't have much hope for the future. There is probably an increased number of people [my age] who do not care about their life."

Absent entirely from Hina's account is any mention of the structural pressures on the Japanese workforce. There are freeters but no forces producing them. No mention of changing contract regimes, of the reduction of lifetime employment opportunities, of the lost decade of Japanese economic stagnation. Instead, magically, slackers have emerged who seem content with their lot in life, even if it makes an independent existence as an adult a near impossibility. If Kenji ends up a freeter, it must be because he wasn't really trying to do any better. He is the master of his own destiny and, in a convenient tautology, he must not deserve a destiny that is any better than the one he has.

Shigeyuki Jo, the author of *The Truth of Generational Inequalities*, complains, "Every avenue seems to be blocked, like we're butting our heads against the wall."[15] The wall is made up of more senior workers who have the jobs sewn up and are not moving aside to let in younger workers. But these structural problems are often invisible to the generation whose life has been constrained by them.

What, Me Worry? Italian Attitudes toward the Accordion Family

In 2006, Italian economists Marco Manacorda and Enrico Moretti tried to explain why eight out of ten Italian men between the ages of eighteen and thirty lived with their parents.[16] They argued that the high rates of delayed departure in Italy (for both men and women), while no doubt related to limited employment opportunities for young people, declining fertility, and decreasing migration rates, are also strongly influenced by the attitudes of Italian parents. It is not, however, parental altruism—which the authors note has long been invoked to explain this phenomenon—but instead the desire to keep their children at home.

Italian parents like having their children at home so much that they actually "bribe" them to remain there in exchange for money transfers. Of course, these bribes would be much less effective if the state offered greater support to young people (in various forms). Manacorda and Moretti argue that if Italian parents were less eager to keep their kids at home and less indulgent of them, Italian young people would have more incentive to find jobs and become independent.

"Italian parents benefit from the companionship and other services their children provide," they explained in an interview in the *Guardian* in 2006, and most "importantly, from the opportunity they have to get their children to 'conform' to their precepts when they live together."[17] What is the evidence that these bribes are proffered to satisfy the needs of parents, rather than the financial straits of adult children? Italian parents report that they are happier when their adult children live with them, which is the opposite of what the authors find for parents whose kids have failed to launch in Britain or the United States. Manacorda and Moretti suggest that intergenerational cohabitation produces higher youth unemployment rather than the other way around. Young Italians are succumbing to their parents' entreaties to stay put and hence exchanging "higher consumption today [for] lower independence and possibly lower lifetime satisfaction."

There is another potential explanation for the higher satisfaction Italian parents have with life when their kids are home. As Durkheim would have noted long ago, the odd man out in a social system—the person who is deviant by the norms of her society—is apt to feel at best awkward and, where a moral reading of their conduct is available, stigmatized. The first few (thousand?) Italian families with adult children in residence may well have been unhappy because they were defined as deviant. But the pattern is now so common that the reverse may be the case: the Italian family whose children leave home at the age of eighteen may experience a sense of uneasiness, a sense that they have done something wrong to chase their kids away.[18]

Moreover, the shift to delayed departure was sufficiently gradual that for many families it did not constitute the kind of radical break with tradition that we perceive from our contemporary vantage point. We are less apt to notice gradual changes of this kind until we turn around and realize that the elongation of life on the parental payroll has stretched to remarkable lengths.

Living at home until marriage has been the normative pattern in Italy for centuries and remains so. What has really changed is not so much the duration of residence but the age at which marriage takes place. That has been creeping steadily up, but for most people marriage is still a likely destination.

Whether it makes sense to characterize the monies that pass between parents and children as bribery or a necessary support in the face of catastrophic youth unemployment and meager state support for job creation and social protection seems at least debatable. Indeed, it is debated—at the highest reaches of Italian government. According to Minister of Social Affairs Giovanna Melandri, the issue of *mammoni* (mama's boys) is a complex one.

> "There are certainly lots of young adults who would like to move out from their parent's shadow," she said, "but the opportunities are not readily apparent. It's a matter of the [Italian] government investing in opportunities for the new generation . . . creating avenues for employment and creating opportunities that make it not only attractive to find an apartment but fiscally possible."[19]

Though jokes abound over Italian men and their mothers, the problem—if that's what we should call it—extends to young women as well. It is a pattern Minister Melandri worries about because it can shut down options for them in later life. "Consider that many times a sibling continues living at home well into their thirties," she reflects, "and eventually evolves into becoming a house-nurse for his or her aging parents. What's the trade-off? The parents die, the house goes to the child, they finally marry, have children, and the entire cycle continues anew."

They may or may not finally marry. Many an Irish spinster in the nineteenth and early twentieth centuries could testify that the house and the options that come with it may arrive too late in life.[20] In any case, Melandri has been hard at work with the new Romano Prodi government—trying to generate interest in new business proposals that cater to the young, including rental options and home-purchase plans that focus on short- and long-term employment contracts.[21]

IN HIS WIDELY read 1997 book, *Less to Fathers, More to Children (Meno ai Padri, Piu ai Figli)*, Nicola Rossi, a professor at the University of Rome and an MP from the Democratic Party of the Left, criticized the Italian public for the way it favors older generations. Too much money is spent on pensions, he argues, while young people get short shrift. It follows, Rossi argues, that this imbalance gives parents remarkable bargaining power over their children. And many use it to keep their kids at the home. Perhaps. One person's bargaining power is another's expression of love and parental obligation. Based on Rossi's theory, one could just as easily speak of parental bargaining power in feeding children in the first place, but no one would credit such a perspective. Nonetheless, it is clear that the structure of social spending leaves young Italians without the kind of backstop that the Scandinavians find in the welfare state.

One thing is certain: the increasing trend toward prolonged residence in the family home is part and parcel of a society in which job prospects for young people are dismal[22] and family formation has slowed to a crawl, leading to very low fertility rates in a society once known for its *bambini*.[23]

But do these structural developments worry Italian parents? Yes and no. They are aware that opportunities are more limited than they should be. But this is not the focus of their attention. They simply don't believe the persistent presence of their children is a problem. Limited job opportunities—sure, that's a problem. But if it could be solved in ways that leave the *bambini* in the nest, this would not unduly disturb most parents.

Alina Legato grew up in Sicily. At sixty-six, she lives with her husband and thirty-four-year-old son, Angelo, a PhD student in Siena. Alina loves having her son around and would like him to remain with her for as long as possible. To underscore the point, she has made life for him very easy at home. But she also acknowledges it is best for children to move out of the parental nest, as hard as it is for her to imagine the day: "The more he stays, the more I am happy. But he has to leave, it is a natural evolution."

Alina says it has been hard to come to terms with the need to "cut the umbilical cord" with her son:

> I really loved him a lot! When the other mothers grumbled about their crying children, I woke up at night and stayed, astonished, looking at him over the cradle. I also gave him my marriage veil, and he broke it down with his little feet. I cried with joy! My motherhood has been an incredible experience to me, so I loved him so much. It was a strong pain when he changed and kept me far away from his life, even if I wanted him to be independent and adult.

Despite the strength of these parent-child attachments, somewhere deep down in their bones, Italian parents also know that separation is inevitable at some point and that their children have to learn to be productive adults, so that they can take care of themselves. Angelo's evolution toward independence, which is still not complete, has occupied Alina's dreams in a troubling way. She explains:

> I felt he was an adult quite late, let's say when he was around twenty-three to twenty-five. In that period, I had the decisive impression he was detaching from me, and he was creating his own identity. He did not want me to [watch over] him any more. He started keeping me far away, and I felt it, so I painted a picture. I was in Favignana [Sicily] at my parents' place. I felt Angelo's change, and I painted a pregnant woman and a sky full of birds. It was like a spark. The umbilical cord was cut.

There are some regional differences in attitudes toward intergenerational cohabitation, as there are on other issues in Italy. Northern Italy is a far more prosperous region and, in terms of political economy, resembles European states like Germany or France, while Southern families face a regional economy closer to that of the poorest countries, like Portugal or Greece. Southern Italians are sufficiently adapted to the agrarian setting that they would do anything to keep their children at home year after year. The fact that the poverty of the region makes it so difficult to find work and forces out-migration in search of employment is regarded as a terrible blow, not unlike the despair of the Irish who for centuries have watched their young people leave the country in search of work.

Angela Tortolli lives in Southern Italy, in a town on the periphery of Naples. She and her husband no longer have children living at home, but, she says:

> Parents want their children to stay close by them, even if they are living independently. The ideal is for the family to stay together and not migrate. When you have a very good child . . . well, you always wish he can prosper in the place he was born, but it is not possible. More than one [young person I know] has moved north, to North Italy, and often they could not find work there either.

This sentiment would not be unfamiliar to parents in Detroit or Youngstown who would like to keep their kids nearby (if not in the same house) but have to wave goodbye as their kids pack up the van and move to regions where there is a greater chance of finding gainful employment.

Bambini *Perspectives*

From the vantage point of young adults in their thirties in the Nordic countries or the United States, the level of parental devotion we see in Italian families would probably feel suffocating. It is all well and good for parents to love their children and enjoy their time together from one end of the life span to the other. But Alina, the mother who laid her wedding veil over her infant son's feet, describes his growing maturity with the kind of emotion we associate with mourning the dead. It is hard to imagine a young man in Copenhagen or Oslo feeling anything other than oppressed by this devotion.

How do Italian young people respond to it? Are they concerned about parents hovering over them? Not really. They, too, have adapted to the necessities of life in an economy and state structure that is leaving them relatively little choice. Marco Fiorello, twenty-four, a student living with his parents in Northern Italy, says, "No, I don't think that living with parents is a problem at all. It's not good to live on your own; it's better to have some company." Cesare De La Rocca, a twenty-eight-year-old college student, lives with his parents, also in a town in Northern Italy, and seems to share Marco's view. Despite this positive take, Cesare is aware of the liabilities. If you find life at home is sweet, you may develop a lack of confidence in your ability to do for yourself. It can become a crutch and in time enable a handicap.

Carla Giudice—whom we met in chapter 3—argues that being cared for by one's parents is simply a durable feature of Italian culture, an arrangement that is compatible with ideals of family life and hence poses no pressing problems:[24]

> Abroad it's normal that a person at the age of eighteen lives alone without his parents. Here in Italy, [it] is pretty rare, maybe also because we don't have universities with a campus, and usually universities aren't so far from your house, so you can return home every day. And this link with the parents, especially the mother, [is] bigger in men than in women. For example, my boyfriend lives in Turin during the week, but on Sundays his luggage with clean clothes is prepared by his mother. But I think that you can have autonomy even if you live at home with your parents. My mother wouldn't prepare my luggage.

Both the Italian government and members of Italy's left wing are more skeptical than Carla and her peers. The government is clearly concerned about the social and economic impact of the failure to launch because they can chart the consequences for sustaining a retirement system with too few young workers (the fallout of low fertility), the political friction caused by a rising number of immigrants (to make up for the small size of the native-born population), and the declining productivity of an aging society.[25]

The left-wing diagnosis is a minority view, but it is important to note an exception that proves the rule. Gregorio and his wife, Elana, express it well. The couple has two children: a daughter, who lives on her own, and a son who is thirty-two but still lives at home and has no reason to move out at the moment. Both Gregorio and his wife are political activists. When they were young, they devoted a lot of time working for the Communist Party, campaigning for workers' rights and participating in Communist cooperatives and unions. Gregorio says:

> This precariousness—they called it flexibility—is a proper precariousness. There is not flexibility at all. Flexibility means that, in case of unemployment, the state is supposed to provide me with a temporary salary or with an alternative job. If you leave me without any work or money . . . I need in any case to pay my rent, my food, maybe my mortgage, and this is not flexibility, this is precariousness. This is one of the main problems we have to face today. If we compare it with Italy's economic situation when I was young, it is definitely worse. Economic uncertainty has a bigger impact on contemporary society. Having work was for me having a permanent job—if you didn't do anything stupid. At that time, you could decide to leave your job and look around for another place. The job was totally a guarantee. We trusted in [the] future. We started from nothing, and we worked hard to achieve our goals. We trusted in our skills and capacities, day by day.

Why did this security erode? "Globalization," Elana replies.

The Politics of Accordion Families: Spain

In the last forty years, Spaniards have seen their economy shift sharply from rural to urban, the politics of the country veer from strict authoritarianism to a free and politically vibrant Spain, and the occupational structure move from one that provided nearly lifetime security to the older generation to a free fall into short-term employment and diminished wages for their sons and daughters. Very similar dynamics have taken hold in Italy, yet the diagnosis of the problem is completely different in the minds of ordinary Spaniards. Italians are frustrated by lack of opportunity, but (apart from political activists like Elana) they tend not to speak about globalization or mention the government—apart from constant grumbling about corruption and scandal. With the exception of the far-left parties, Italians rarely point the finger at corporations or special interests.

But Spaniards take it for granted that special interests are at the root of their children's problems. Rubbish contracts—the kind that give employers the right to fire at will or limit the duration of a job to a couple of years—don't fall out of the sky and land on young workers. They come from somewhere, and the ordinary Spaniard can point fingers in ways their Italian or Japanese counterparts cannot.

Alberto and Manuela Abrego have only one daughter, now in her thirties, who still lives with them. Alberto has spent his entire working life at Telefónica, the largest telecommunications firm in Spain. Once state-owned, Telefónica offered a lifetime of stable employment, well-paid, with the kind of pension benefits that could only be dreamed of by other Spaniards. Alberto followed his father's footsteps straight to this haven, starting out as an errand boy and ending up in a technical department where all his colleagues were engineers. Manuela is a homemaker. True to their working-class origins, the Abrego family lives in a modest area of northeast Spain, and their apartment is fairly humble, too. A walkup with cement floors, the home is hardly a castle.

Unlike the Japanese families who believe they have created an indolent generation, the Abrego parents know who is *really* to blame for the stagnating economy that has damaged the next generation: the government, the business elite, the global economy. That's who should be taken to task. The growing economic insecurity of Spain's workers in their twenties and thirties is the principal reason their daughter is stuck in the family home, they explain. And what, in turn, caused the insecurity? Manuela points to the relaxation of standards in labor contracts as the culprit. Before the mid-1980s, workers had longtime jobs and could depend on keeping them. These days, her daughter's generation must live with "precariousness," a term we rarely hear in this context in the United States but which is creeping into the European lexicon in countries with high unemployment and newly flexible labor contracts designed to spread employment. In practice, however, these contracts introduce short-term, fixed contract jobs where lifetime employment once prevailed. Manuela explains:

When I was young, people got independence earlier. As soon as you entered a slightly strong company, you already knew that you had [security] like a civil servant. You could search for housing in a particular area because you knew "I work here." But nowadays, you never know. Perhaps you're working one year, and perhaps on the next year you are on a different job. And with these rubbish contracts, people can never get independence. You find people in their thirties and forties at home. But it is not because they don't want to [work]. It is only because you can't leave.

Neither Spanish parents nor their adult children turn inward to discover the cause of their distress; they look over their shoulders to the government, the corporate world, elites, and other powerful actors who have shaped their options from the top down. In 2007, there were sit-down strikes in the middle of Madrid protesting high housing prices and demanding government intervention on behalf of young people on the losing end of a ferociously expensive housing market.

Eduardo and his wife, Isabella, also work for Telefónica. No better example of secure employment could be found than the jobs they had for all of their adult lives in this public utility. Yet the experience has not been repeated for the next generation of workers, even at Telefonica. Newbies must contend with short-term contracts that leave them high and dry after a few years or maybe even a few months. Eduardo and Isabella have a twenty-six-year-old son, Geraldo, who works as a freelance photographer and still lives at home. They trace his delayed departure from their home to the instability of work and the high cost of housing.[26]

During the same period that jobs began to deteriorate, the cost of housing skyrocketed in Spain, particularly in the large cities, making the move to independence all that much more difficult. Where young people in the Nordic countries have the freedom to leave home because they have a large and relatively inexpensive rental market to turn to, people like Geraldo are staring at a much steeper climb to residential independence. In weak welfare states like Spain, owner-occupied housing is widespread because it serves as the family bank, the resource against which they can borrow in the event of personal catastrophes.

But the reliance on owner-occupied housing dries up the supply of rental property and increases the cost of what remains. Young people facing many years of unstable employment cannot expect to be in the owner's market, and they have no affordable rental market to serve as an alternative: they are stuck.

Eduardo and Isabella became keenly aware of how different their son's life would be if he lived in a different kind of society when they visited Holland. It was another world. "I've been this year in Amsterdam," Eduardo explained, "and there is a rent policy for young people that you would die for. Rather than paying 600, 700, 800 euros or more [in Madrid], [monthly rent] would cost half that [in Amsterdam]. I'm convinced that Geraldo would have already left home [if he had that kind of rent]." The limited supply (and hence high cost) of rental property in Spain also creates barriers to labor mobility. If the job market grows in Valencia and shrinks in Barcelona (or vice versa), housing constraints make it difficult to move for opportunity.

Why not rally to change the situation? After all, Eduardo's generation is very familiar with the political arenas where demands can be made. If things are so difficult for the millennials, why don't they do something about it? Eduardo believes that Geraldo's generation has gone soft. They aren't able to contest the conditions leading to the diminished opportunities they are left with. He explains with disapproval:

> Young people are a little conformist these days. Perhaps because they've found everything done; they've got used to [having] things done for them. But I can also talk from what I know, because Geraldo is a boy who goes to the demonstrations for the right for housing every Sunday in Sol. He has certain interests—political, cultural, social. But of course, he is my son.
>
> But in my job, I see different guys who have contracts of one month, two months. And I see that their obsession in life is to get several months together in order to buy a mobile [phone]. And if they work several more months, then to get money in order to buy a car. Getting indebted, asking for credit. . . . And sure enough, I'm already more than fifty, but I feel surprised when I see that kind of life because I understand life in a different way. But, sure, I've also

been working for twenty-six years in a stable job; perhaps I've been a privileged person, compared to the level of precariousness that there is in these days.

Satisfied with less than their due, young men seem politically paralyzed, unable to protest, much less change their declining situation.

Cultural traditions and political history matter in understanding why the reactions to the accordion family are so different from one place to another. The long reign of authoritarianism in Spain, which held sway from the victory of Franco during World War II to his death in 1975, left deep tracks in the lives of the generation that is now at the head of Spain's accordion families.

Franco was a military general and dictator of Spain from October 1936 and the de facto regent of the nominally restored Kingdom of Spain from 1947 until his death. Deeply conservative and traditional, Franco fostered a strong sense of Spanish nationalism and insisted on the protection of the country's territorial integrity; the defense of Catholicism, the family, and traditional values; and strong opposition to Communism. Franco and the military participated in a failed coup that devolved into the Spanish Civil War (July 1936 to April 1939), during which he emerged as the leader of the Nationalists against the Popular Front government. After winning the war, with military aid from Italy and Germany, he dissolved the Spanish Parliament and established a right-wing government that lasted until 1978, when a new constitution was drafted.

After the Civil War, Spain lost thousands of doctors, nurses, lawyers, judges, teachers, businessmen, and artists, all of whom fled into exile. The Civil War decimated the Spanish economy, and Franco ended almost all international trade. The economy stagnated and become fertile ground for black marketeers.[27]

After World War II, Franco implemented a series of severe measures aimed at maintaining his control, including the systematic suppression of dissident views through censorship and coercion, the institutionalization of torture, the imprisonment of ideological enemies in concentration camps, the use of forced labor in prisons, and the use of the death penalty and heavy prison sentences as deterrents for his ideological enemies.

The Roman Catholic Church has always played a significant role in the history of Spanish education. With the success of Franco after the Spanish Civil War, the power and status of the Church was restored with the approval of the 1952 Concordat. This agreement had important implications for education. Catholic religious instruction was to be mandatory in all schools, even in public schools. Additionally, the Church was given the right to establish universities.

The control of the Church over education deepened its conservative influence over Spanish culture, but it also set up a reaction in the form of an anticlerical social movement that became an important ideological touchstone for the generation that Eduardo and Isabella represent. Even after Franco's death, the experience of living under authoritarian rule provided the template for a political culture of activism.

Mario Small's notable book *Villa Victoria* tells the tale of a political movement to preserve a Puerto Rican community near Boston. Small argues that the social capital that took root among the activists who had to fight to preserve their neighborhood rarely survived generational succession. Some children retained their parents' political commitments and became the next cohort of activists but most forgot the struggle because it was over and they didn't need to fight that battle again. The same point might be made of the living generations in Spain. For Eduardo and Isabella, politics is part of the country's lifeblood, and it is incumbent on workers and citizens to challenge the status quo when it threatens to increase the exploitation of the common man. While they see their son as a successor to them, they lament the apathy and complacency of most people in Geraldo's generation. Those bad contracts, poor prospects for decent jobs, and grown children's continuous dependence on parents are, from their perspective, a reflection of political apathy.

Gloria, the professor we met in chapter 3, sees her generation through the lens of the struggle against Franco, which fostered a rebel generation that knew how to fight for its rights. She sees that her son's predicament is not of his making; he is, instead, a victim of a relentless capitalist system. But what is worse, the capacity for developing opposition movements that was well-honed in Gloria's day has now evaporated. Her son's generation doesn't seem to know how to protest what has been done to them. Gloria says:

I think that young people are perhaps very inactive these days; they just accept anything they are told or they are obliged to do. Because, well, talking about my time, we were very combatant, and so we made a thousand complaints, demonstrations, and we almost risked our lives, didn't we? We risked an important part of our lives in those circumstances. And these days, I see young people less willing to fight.

They may not get anything, but since they don't fight, I think they get even less. Because imagine European young people united. . . . If this happened in all Europe with the participation of everybody [thinking] that we are all on the same boat—because as Brecht said, "What happens to one person may happen to you on another day"—[then we would] all feel human and collaborate and help each other.

That political edge, that desire to see the masses in the streets—we see nothing of the kind among the Japanese, the Italians, or Americans. It is a Spanish tradition for the generation that rubbed against the strictures of Franco's authoritarian regime and now wonders why their children cannot muster the energy to do the same.

Spanish Millennials

Manuel Nunez is twenty-six and lives with his parents in Madrid. He is the youngest of two sons and the only one remaining at home. His in-house adulthood is not a reflection of employment problems, for Manuel has completed two engineering degrees and has been working for almost three years in big companies. Manuel often jokes often about his situation, but his temper flares at times because his situation is not a laughing matter. Manuel says:

I think in the past they got independence earlier [leaving the parental residence]. These days in Madrid, the mean age of independence is thirty-two. That's what I heard some months ago on the radio. I think it is the highest mean in Europe. It's a little sad. It was not the case in the past. [This has happened] above all due to the prices of housing. Speculation. In the past, it was easier to buy a house, and it is not that easy these days. That's obvious.

There are other reasons as well. These days, education takes longer; young people take more time to finish their studies. Not like in the past, when there was a lower mean of people with university degrees. But these days, you may finish your degree at twenty-five, but from twenty-five to thirty-two, something happens in that gap. And I think it is the problem of housing being so expensive. Because you cannot commit, you know it is a big step, when you go to live on rent or you buy a house, you know you have a total responsibility. You know that in many cases, you have to pay much more than half of your salary. And so people take much longer to marry these days.

You are not going to live with your partner at your parents' home, are you? And so many couples have to wait to have their first house and, of course, when do they have it? Whenever they can afford it. And when can they afford it? When they have enough money. And in order to pay that money these days, you need to be saving for many years.

Julia Campos is twenty-seven and lives with her parents and twelve-year-old sister in Zarza. She has studied child education but at the moment is working on adult education. Julia spent many years living away from home, as she attended a boarding school in a different town and then went on to university. However, once she finished her studies, Julia came back to live with her parents. These days, she is biding her time before taking a state examination to teach in the public schools. Julia says:

Without good wages, well, how are you going to pay a mortgage at thirty? My God! It's really impossible. And so I think that you have to hold out here until the last minute; to say "Well I'll start saving, I'll start preparing things. And I will make the decision." In the past, it was different, it is true. I have a grandfather who is super excited about the idea that I should get married, you know? He is so excited about that idea. "My dear, are you now going to marry? But you have to marry; you are already twenty-seven." And so, of course, I spend all day trying to explain to him that I can't get married now.

I explain to him, "I have nothing to offer to a baby; my salary is very low; my boyfriend is only starting, too, because he has been [working on] his degree until two months ago, and he has only finished now." And I say to [my grandfather], "We cannot get married. We have to stay at home like this for some time." And of course, he tells me that when he got married, he had no job; nor did my grandmother, but they still got married. And he says, "My dear, it wouldn't be a problem if you had to be living for a while with your parents and having lunch and dinner with them." And of course, I say, "But if I marry, I don't want to stay in this house any longer; I want to be in my own house."

Because of course, how could I stay longer with my parents [if I were married]? Can you imagine? That would be crazy. And sure, I try to explain it to him; but no, he doesn't fully understand it, the poor thing. Salaries, because they are very low, you cannot get a mortgage really. At least for the moment. I hope in [the] future, perhaps I will.

Anna Valdez, thirty-five, is a telecommunications engineering specialist who works in the training department of one of the biggest telecommunications companies in the world. The sector has changed over the years, and in spite of high wages (compared to most regular workers of her generation), Anna feels uncertain about her professional future. She is an only child, and since she was very young, she has fought for her independence from her parents. She bought her apartment just before the sharp rise in Madrid's housing prices, and so she is also exceptional for being able to pay a mortgage despite being single. She is sympathetic, however, to her peers who she feels are unable to leave home because of a precarious economic situation and high housing prices:

In the past, a good job was one which gave you security. For example, my uncle, he's started working in a shop . . . not [as] a cashier but perhaps [as] a shopkeeper. And that was "a good job." And now the concept of work has changed very much because those jobs are considered very bad or of a low level. If you say you are a cashier in

DIA [an inexpensive grocery store], it means you work a lot for a low salary, and on the top of that, they exploit you, and it is not such a pleasant job because you burn yourself [out].

And so I think what has changed very much is the concept of a [secure job]. In the past, what happened was that you almost chose in any job when you wanted to leave. And now in the job, you are told how long you have to stay. And so in order to have a good job now, you need a mixture of quality and guarantees, and that is very unstable these days. At least in my sector.

A person who doesn't have [a] permanent income can't take the steps that would allow him to advance in his life.

Laura Fuentes is rare among Spanish youth. She moved out of her parents' home two years ago, at age twenty-five, to live with her long-time boyfriend, a computing consultant. She seems almost surprised at herself, remarking that she never expected to lay claim to this freedom so early.[28] Laura has a degree in economics and an advanced certificate in business studies. She is also currently taking an English-language course while working with her father at the family business in Madrid. Laura seems quite happy in her current job. Though she worries about the Spanish labor force, it is from the perspective of a manager trying to understand the lack of motivation among entry-level employees. Her reservations reflect a general concern she has about the fate of her generation compared to its elders:

When they worked hard, they could see some reward, and we don't. It is more difficult. Now you are not paid for extra hours. Before you worked hard in order to have more. But now you work hard and you get the same salary. Or before, you worked a lot because in ten years you could have paid your mortgage. Now you have a mortgage forty years long. You can't spend forty years [expending] 100 percent or 120 percent [of your energy]. And so you have to take it a little easier.

Spanish millennials are very different from their Italian or Japanese counterparts. Like their parents, they see structural barriers blocking their pathway. They do think being forced back into the arms of their parents is a problem, and they don't believe it is of their making.

Despite their anger at the government and business elites, Spanish parents and children see some benefits to delayed departure. The older generation remembers their relations with their fathers as emotionally distant, a mixture of respect and fear. This was particularly the case during the Franco years, when very traditional and conservative ideas about social behavior of all kinds were reinforced by the Church, the educational system, and the government itself. The climate did not lend itself to close relations but rather supported patriarchal authority and matriarchal subordination.

Today, Spanish parents want nothing to do with that old-fashioned model of parent-child relations. They want to feel close and affectionate, even as their children become in-house adults. No one seems to fear any loss of independence. Instead, parents see the silver lining, especially in contrast to their own past. "I've seen my children much at home here, very happy," explained a fifty-three-year-old Spanish mother. Her daughter, in her late twenties, sees the relationship in very similar, egalitarian terms:

> We have a more personal relationship with our parents. We can tell them many more things. I think they know us much better than their parents knew them. We may be influenced by our parents' opinion, but it is not an imposition as it was in the past. Like my parents perhaps went to buy a house, and that is something they also had to discuss with my grandparents. And I don't think that's the case any longer.

Conditional Approval: American Attitudes toward the Accordion Family

Americans are on the fence about the moral status of the accordion family. Is it something to fret over or a social evolution to accept? We are not sure whether this is a failure to launch or a social change they can live with. In general, our evaluations hinge on the *reasons* why our young people are still in the family nest and the degree of effort our children are making to move ahead in the world. If there is a positive purpose that justifies delayed adulthood, then we are all for

it. Absent that purpose, however, the underlying cultural affection for
the work ethic kicks in and creates a gnawing anxiety that our children
are taking advantage of parental largesse. American attitudes are more
conditional than other cultures, but at the extremes they can resemble
the Japanese, with their harsh disapproval and moral anxiety over who
is responsible for indolence.

Working-class Americans do not have the luxury of indulging their
children's desires for a protected period of life. Unlike the middle class,
which will bust the bank to send their children away to college, Americans of modest means keep them close to home all through their college years, expect them to work while they go to school (if they go to
school), and are often resistant to helping out with expenses, even if
the federal-government formulas for financial aid assume otherwise.
Working-class kids do not boomerang back into the family home. They
are much more like their Spanish or Italian counterparts who do not
leave home at all until much later in life.

The primary responsibility of a working-poor child in her twenties
is to take care of her own expenses and those of her children, who may
well be resident in their grandmother's home. Families at the bottom of
the economic ladder have to pool their resources from among all the active earners to keep the household above the flood tide of bills.[29] Kyesha
Smith began working in a Harlem fast-food restaurant when she was in
high school to earn money so she could buy things for herself and still
worked there at twenty-one. Her first and only child was born when she
was nineteen, and her mother looked after him while she went to work.
While Kyesha was not beyond spending her hard-earned (minimum
wage) cash on new jeans, she was always mindful of her mother's expectation that she would turn over her paycheck to help pay for her keep.
There was a lot of tension in the house between Kyesha and her mother.
One day, Kyesha packed a box full of supplies and stowed it under her
bed. When asked why, she explained that she was getting ready for the
day when she might be able to move out on her own. She was "dying
to have her own space, her own adult station in life," she remembered.
But there was no way she could pull this off on her salary of five dollars
an hour, the princely sum she was earning after five steady years on the
job. "It's easier said than done," she told me.

Immigrant children from low-income families face the same constraints. Their contributions are required for the family to manage, and as they get older and make moves toward independence, they feel the umbilical cord tighten. Their parents need to hold onto the children's earnings and sadly, vice versa. Carmen, a Dominican girl living in New York, married her teenage sweetheart, Salvador, and the couple made a point of declaring independence by moving next door in the Washington Heights apartment building filled with his parents and her aunts and uncles. But they couldn't afford food and ended up eating at the table of one relative or another every day. Salvador worked two jobs, very nearly around the clock, and made enough to cover the rent and an occasional utility bill. Carmen struggled to stay in school and keep her low-wage job, spending many years oscillating between the two. She found herself missing classes to keep her job, blowing exams because her employer would not let her go. Ultimately, the couple gave up the apartment and moved in with their relatives since pooling expenses was the only way anyone could make it.

Middle-class Americans will do a lot to insure that their children emerge into full adulthood on a pathway to upward mobility or, if not, at least on a par with the family's sense of position in the social hierarchy. That takes more parental support today than it once did, but the continuity or even upward mobility of the next generation is ample reason to support the project. William Rollo thinks it's just fine for his son, John, to travel and become a more cosmopolitan person. He wants John to have advantages he didn't have, including the freedom to sample alternative futures so that he is truly content with the choices he makes.

Of course, not every middle-class parent can insure that his child wants to follow in class-constant footsteps. Gary Mack approves of his son Bobby's choice to be a blacksmith because it insures he will become a hardworking, gainfully employed man who can take care of his family (when he has one). But Bobby's path is anomalous in a neighborhood where the rest of the "boys" are on their way to the same law schools or med schools their mothers and fathers attended, to assume futures on the same class-based glide path. Gary's friends do not think of themselves as snobbish, and some even have sneaking admiration for a blue-collar son who has walked to the beat of his own drummer. It just isn't what middle-class people expect to see in their progeny.

Middle-class families have the luxury of giving their children a platform they can use to launch themselves into the real world of adult independence at a higher level than they could manage if left to their own devices. Parents are willing to support their kids so that they can find something meaningful and worthwhile to do with their lives. Pushing them out earlier, as the working class routinely does, means foreclosing opportunities. And that's not what these parents want for their kids. They have the wherewithal to provide more latitude.

The "kid" who is working on a master's degree while living at home will generally find a better-paying and more fulfilling job than the one who has to strike out on his own at twenty-one and take what he can get. What delayed departure does is create a higher human capital mix in the next generation, by sheltering the costs of amassing advanced credentials or work experience through internships, socially worthy but poorly paid jobs. As long as they are making moves toward that higher-order future, the parental investment is deemed both worth it and morally justified. But the catch is there: it's a conditional approval.

Stephanie Phillips shares how she has struggled to define the line between acceptable and unacceptable parental involvement:

> I can't say there is a cut-off date, if I had a kid who was working in a field that they were passionate about and it just wasn't paying enough, I would help with health insurance. If they were twenty-eight years old, I think that wouldn't be right. I don't think it is OK to continually help them financially, but you want to see your children succeed, so if that is what it takes, there might be a little give-and-take. I like to think that by twenty-five, your child is financially independent.

This viewpoint epitomizes the conditional mentality of American parents. Age boundaries can be considered and reconsidered, but what really matters is the reason a child needs help. It has to be for a legitimate purpose; it cannot be just to make things easier in life. Stephanie continues:

> If I need to borrow money because I want to buy a house, I don't think that is the worst reason to ask for money. If I want to borrow

money to go out and drink, that is a huge problem. If I am thirty and want to buy my first house, that isn't a problem. But if I am thirty and can't pay the cable bill, it is a problem. It is appropriate to financially help your children but in different forms. Everybody has their own opinion of what those forms are.

Elaine Mark, the Newton resident who grew up in Zimbabwe, wanted her son to get with it and decide what he was doing with his life. She felt he wasn't making progress at the pace he should and attributed that tardiness to the scramble to make a living. Living on his own, he didn't have the luxury to think things through because—ironically— he was busy making ends meet as an independent young man. So she encouraged him to come home, so that he could lay the groundwork for a more appropriate long-term future.

The Importance of Forward Motion

While Jane and Ed Conlon really enjoy having their adult daughter, Caroline, at home, there are some parameters. She has to contribute to the household coffers by paying her parents a nominal sum, about two hundred dollars a month, to help with her keep. They don't really need the money; what they need is the reassurance that Caroline is moving toward a productive life. She shouldn't get too comfortable or think that this generosity will last forever. A little discomfort, the minor stress of parental expectations hanging over her head—all of this is good for Caroline. So say Jane and Ed. And if Caroline can handle these conditions, so that her parents don't come to feel that they are aiding and abetting sloth, the whole family can live with the absence of complete victories in favor of successful skirmishes. "I'm not ready to kick Caroline out yet," Jane confesses. Have Jane and Ed ever drawn the line and insisted on some evidence that their children are taking steps to bring closure to in-house adulthood? Well, yes. They have made it clear that forward motion, coupled with modest contributions to the family coffers, is required to justify their generosity. As Jane explains:

You have to be a contributing member of this family, and you have to do that at least two hundred dollars. So again, if the kids' decision is to mushroom and just not do anything—not work, not even for that or whatnot—then yeah, they're not allowed to stay here. It's not a free ride. They're not living rent-free.

Jane realizes that the real world beyond the front door of their New-ton house is far more demanding. There is nowhere in the region where this small a monetary contribution would be sufficient to put a roof over Caroline's head. "Where else can you pay two hundred dollars?" Jane asks. The answer, of course, is nowhere. But the point is not to cover the actual cost of Caroline's room and board. The point is to in-ject some discipline into the relationship and make it clear that there are rules.

What we see here is a compromise perspective that retains the high bar of effort but substitutes forward motion—visible progress—for the end goal. As long as a young person is making strong efforts to move toward the end point of a well-paid or socially meaningful job, efforts paying off in some movement that can be measured, then all is fairly well. Not perfect, not unassailable, but socially acceptable within the family and for public consumption.

When Caroline makes progress toward her goals, she is doing more than helping herself to a respectable future; she is insuring her fam-ily's trajectory from one generation to the next within (or beyond) the middle class. A parent who is a lawyer or a bank manager will do a lot to insure that a son or a daughter emerges into full adulthood with a biography that insures an equivalent social station and the life sat-isfactions that such a destination implies. That takes more parental support today than it once did, but the continuity or even upward mo-bility of the next generation is ample reason to follow through. And while that destination may be defined by high income or prestige, increasingly—at least for boomer parents—social significance may substitute for those qualities.

Are American parents thinking—as their Spanish counterparts clearly are—that the economy has put their kids at risk? Or are they more like the Japanese, leaning on individual character or generational culture, disembodied from the historical context that has given their children fewer options? Americans are aware of the structural forces that make delayed departure more common. But we are willing to adapt themselves and our expectations to this new reality and even find joy in it as long as our children profit from it. That tends to happen, we believe, when young people take the bull by the horns and work hard toward that master's degree or buckle down into a low-paid job that will give them valuable experience. Moving toward the brass ring is under individual control in the American universe. You play the hand that was dealt to you. It isn't possible to shape that hand to begin with, but only the individual can play it.

The problem is that not all "good conduct" is rewarded in the marketplace. An adult child can work diligently toward a brighter future, even make significant sacrifices in the name of that goal, and it may not work out. Stephanie Phillips, whose son was deployed to Afghanistan, discovered this the hard way. Though she worried about his safety, she thought he would realize the future he most wanted if he went this route. It didn't work out that way, and he came home to bide his time and try other routes. Stephanie says:

> Well, that took four years out of his life. He came back. And lo and behold, because the Army owns you lock, stock, and barrel for up to seven years, the Army called him back, and he went over to the Iraq-Afghanistan war. And that was another year out of his life. Well, now, one would think logically, if you served your time and literally have been shot at and put your life on the line for the government, that the United States would help men and women find a job within a year. Certainly that would be reasonable, especially [for] someone [who] graduated summa cum laude with a degree in criminal justice.
>
> Wouldn't you think that maybe that would be a nice lead-in for a job? It [was] not. It took another three and a half years of sending dozens and dozens and dozens of resumes and cover letters to get this job that he [finally got]. Three and one half years after he had left the Army, served honorably, put his life on the line all across the Middle East, got shot at, and got spit at by our friends, the Saudi Arabians.

America's Millennials

Newton twentysomethings who have failed to launch understand—and seem to appreciate—their parents' efforts on their behalf. They don't feel like interlopers or "parasite singles," as their Japanese counterparts would describe the situation. At the same time, parental assistance this late in life does not feel so normative that millennial Americans take it for granted. They do *not* behave as if this is the natural, inevitable progression they always expected to follow. There is an irony in this since a very high proportion—nearly 85 percent—of today's college seniors are headed home.[30] Even so, given how recent the trend is, returning home after a stint in college is a perk that should be acknowledged. Ronit Lori lived in Israel until she was fifteen. Now twenty-five and living in Newton, she has a biology research job at a local medical school. She shares:

> My pathway to adulthood has been easier than my parents'. My parents have enabled me to study whenever I want and to be free to study and not have any financial obligations while I was trying to study. Even to this day, I don't have any financial obligations, so I have time to look for a job that I really wanted, and I have a lot of guidance from them. And I think my parents didn't really have that guidance from their parents. They really did not have that financial support.

Dan Morton, whom we met in chapter 3, is working at his dream job in TV production. Dan is hoping to move out of his parents' home in the coming year. For now, he deems himself a baby boomerang that benefits from their help. By living at home, Dan can put money into his savings that will give him a head start when he is out on his own. He is more than ready to be fully autonomous from an emotional standpoint; Dan knows where he is headed in the world of work, for example. But it costs a lot to live in the Boston area, and he lacks the cash to live on his own at a level of creature comfort to which he has grown accustomed. What his parents have enabled him to do is amass a nest egg.

Peter Cohen considered living with roommates, which would have been a more grownup solution to the need to share costs. But as is true of many American millennials, he is more at ease with his parents than he would be with a total stranger, and for him returning was the only other option when college ended. Parents are better than the unknown, Peter says:

It was because I didn't have anyone to live with—at the time I [had] moved out of my [college] apartment. I didn't want to live with strangers—the independence is really important to me. I didn't want to be trapped in a year lease. How it was last year was fine. I knew I was going to stay here—I am going to be traveling a lot—I wouldn't want to have an apartment and be in Europe for a month—that was another reason why I moved home.

But living with parents is not a total hassle-free solution. Inevitably, people Peter's age are striking a compromise between the autonomy they want and the cost of other goals, like travel or a meaningful job, that cost dearly or pay poorly. Which is more important? When his parents were young, the answer was clear: autonomy first. For the millennial generation, autonomy takes a back seat to other endgames. Peter goes on:

For most people who are moving home with their parents, they probably get along with their parents or they wouldn't have moved home at all. I don't think you have to worry so much about parent-child relations—that is less of an issue—and then again, independence is huge. Without living at my home for the summer, I would not be going to Spain in the fall—thank God for that.

Conclusion

Accordion families are emerging all over the developed world because the conditions that give life to them—declining job prospects for young people, increasing (and increasingly expensive) demands for higher education, and rising housing prices—all point in the same direction: back to the homes where these young people grew up. This does not emerge in the social democracies because they draw upon the resources of the state to fill in the gaps emerging under these difficult economic conditions. Young people in Denmark and Sweden can lean on government programs for the support that their counterparts in more conservative welfare states have to find through private means. In the weaker welfare states of Japan, Italy, Spain, and the United States, that parental safety net is supporting not just survival but master's degrees or internships as well. It is helping to insure that the next generation will be more upwardly mobile than it would otherwise have been, with more education or job experience under its belt.

Despite the common causes and even the common configuration of accordion families, they signify very different moral problems in these societies. Japanese culture places a primacy on agency, on the presupposition that individuals can master their own fate and hence should be held responsible for their conduct regardless of the surrounding circumstances. Although a probing interviewer can get a Japanese citizen to admit that the country's economy has been in the doldrums for more than a decade, that the job scene has changed (fundamentally for the worse), and that there is far less available for young people who want to "do the right thing," these are not the constraints that come to mind when the Japanese try to explain why there is so much deviation from the standard pathway to adulthood. What surfaces is an explanation that this conduct is willful and could easily be otherwise.

Accordingly, the blame game is on, and the millennial generation comes up wanting. But because Japan is steeped in an agentic culture, these parasite singles cannot be at fault all by themselves. Something, someone, made them take that ill-advised fork in the road. The answer seems to boomerang back on the parents themselves: father was missing in action; mother was too indulgent; both parents sheltered their children because the parents experienced deprivation when they were young. And maybe, just maybe, Suki is walking away from marriage because she doesn't want to live the way her mother did. Young women have other options besides caring for their in-laws in silence. But what does that say about Suki's view of her parents, and what does it mean for the respect that should be accorded their marriage? Well, it is not a pretty picture. It is a picture that brings forth for many apocalyptic visions of a society in decline.

Italian parents would be stunned by such a negative portrait of the accordion family. For them, the long-term presence of children is a joy and their departure something of a personal tragedy. You know that society is going to ruin when your children have to leave you in order to migrate elsewhere for work. That is the problem, not the elongated period of their residence. Government ministers may look at the so-

cial security accounts and shudder about the consequences of declining fertility, but Italian parents have taken the presence of the *bambini*
in stride. They do worry about the dearth of employment opportunities
for their kids, but if it were possible for Giorgio to find a job that kept
him at home or, as a second choice, next door, that would suit them
just fine. The culture of familism makes sense in a society where the
state is so weak that it is an unreliable partner in the business of growing
up or sustaining a family—a society in which the family home is rarely
sold but often subdivided to accommodate new generations.

Spanish families have a political history that inclines them to look
askance at the same demographic pattern. They recognize that there
is a silver lining to their children's perpetual presence in their homes:
the erosion of the old authoritarian father is hastened by the changes
underway as the accordion family grows. But fundamentally, they are
furious at the abandonment of the millennial generation by the government, the ways in which corporations have taken advantage of global
competition to subject the comparatively defenseless to lousy labor
contracts, and the meekness of a new generation, which has not been
battle-tested on the frontlines of anti-authoritarian agitation. They look
on with approval at those hardy souls who take to the streets in Madrid to protest housing shortages or at the government's attempts to fire
civil servants to balance the budget. Militancy in the name of equity is
fine with parents; they wish there was more of it among their children
and less of the complacency that can be bought by material goods: cell
phones, designer jeans, and the like.

How does the moral status of the accordion family look on the other
side of the pond? In the United States, the agentic of the Japanese has a
familiar ring. We, too, tend to look upon individuals as the masters of
their destinies and apply a stringent test to one another: is he really trying? Are we sacrificing unnecessarily or, worse, indulging the next generation and robbing them of the backbone they need to make it on their
own? At the same time, Americans are enamored of upward mobility,
and it is important that our kids remain proud members of the middle
class or rising professionals of whom parents can be proud.

To make it that far requires more education than it once did, and
the odds are greatly improved by costly investments like unpaid intern-

ships (even if parents have to pay the rent) or master's degrees, JDs, or other advanced credentials that pile on the debt. American parents are willing to shell out to make that life possible because the trajectory of their family line matters. It isn't enough that the parents have a nice home in Newton; they want the next generation to have that much, if not more, and are willing to help cover the cost as long as they see forward motion. The minute that progress stops is the same minute that Newton parents start drawing lines in the sand, turning up the pressure for their kids to get a move on. Of course, they, too, rejoice in the close nature of the relations between generations in this modern world. In all of these societies, the distant father and the subordinate mother have faded away in favor of more egalitarian relations between the genders and closer bonds between generations. As we will see in the next chapter, this has implications for parents as well as children. Millennials aren't the only generation whose lives are changing with the evolution of the accordion family.

CHAPTER 5

When the Nest Doesn't Empty

THE SAME PRESSURES CREATING the accordion family, pushing young people back into the parental home, are elongating the period of active adulthood for their parents. Where people once began to leave the world of work at around age sixty-four, today aging adults have to earn money for a longer stretch of time, mainly to support themselves but increasingly to assist their grown children. The proportion of Americans in their seventies staying in the labor force is growing. In 1997, for instance, 4.7 percent of Americans over the age of seventy-five were still working. Ten years later, in 2007, the numbers are up sharply: to 6.4 percent. That's more than a million of what we used to think of as "old people" moving back into the labor market.[1]

The size of this crowd has increased with the evaporation of savings during the recession that began in 2008. Sitting by the hearth in a rocking chair is a fast-disappearing experience for seniors. Instead, their lives are far more active. And while they may wear their new role reluctantly, it does allow American seniors to maintain the social identity that is honored above all else in American culture: the contributing, earning adult.

If adult children require many more years of nurturance and caretaking from Mom and Dad, then parents are not transitioning to the sidelines of family life on the same schedule as they used to either. Postwar parents who started families when they were in their early twenties saw their kids out the door when they were in their early forties. Today, parents in their early sixties may have adult children in the home, who depend on them as providers and for emotional support. Because most of today's middle-class parents were older than their own parents were when they started their families and because children are relying on their parents for a much longer period of time, it is commonplace for these boomer parents to be enmeshed in active parenting for several decades longer (and later) in life than earlier generations.[2]

The cultural differences between postwar parents and baby-boom children seemed unbridgeable. But when boomers and millennials look at one another, there is a degree of recognition and common taste that is surprisingly strong. It makes a difference when, at the end of a long day at work, everyone wants to sit down in front of the same TV show. Today's millennials are filling up the arena alongside their graying parents when the Rolling Stones come to town. The Doors are enjoying a renaissance in downloads. Teens can be heard complaining that their parents, aunts, and uncles are invading their privacy on Facebook because the technology gap between generations is closing. Even Nickelodeon has noticed. In 2008, the network published a study entitled "The Family GP" that found that, as millennials become parents and baby boomers become grandparents, "today's increasingly multigenerational and diverse American families are rapidly becoming united by an expanding set of values and converging tastes."

That convergence is clear enough in the opinion polls we have about the interests generations share and the emotional bond these similarities generate: 76 percent of parents of twenty-one-year-olds say they feel extremely close to their child today, while only 25 percent of grandparents reported that they felt close to their own child. Fifty-six percent of sons share the same taste in movies as their fathers, and 48 percent enjoy listening to the same music. Sixty-four percent of daughters share a similar taste in movies as their mothers, and 44 percent like the same fashion and clothing as their moms. Eighty-two percent and 77 percent of families are watching television or DVDs together at home, respectively, each week; 41 percent of parents and kids are listening to music together; and 36 percent are playing video games together.[3]

As the millennials crest into their late twenties, their parents are a little more like friends or coequals than parents or authority figures. Rather than worrying that their children are not developing the qualities they need for independence, they often remark that they enjoy the time they have together.

That pleasure reflects the fact that boomers are not as tired of having their kids around as their own parents might have been. Postwar parents who raised the boomers in the 1950s and 1960s could afford to keep Mom at home, while Dad worked full time and pulled in wages that grew over time. American families of that era resembled the Japanese salaryman model: Dad put in long hours on the job, while Mom tended to the hearth and the children. By the time those boomers were ready to leave home, American mothers of the post–World War II generation were all too glad to put their feet up and relax. Enough! They'd spent years with their kids, and while some mourned the end of their "job," just as many were ready to spend some time on themselves and prepare for the less demanding role of grandmother.[4]

The life course was very different for the baby-boom generation. They were the first cohort in which women completed college in large numbers, equaling and in some cases surpassing the educational level of the men their age. Women flooded into the professions and began to put in many more hours on the job. Among the middle class, parents braved the new waters of dual-career parenthood just when guiding children through the increasingly competitive hurdles of childhood began to demand more of both mothers and fathers.[5] Stories began to appear regularly in the nation's newspapers about exhausted parents, frustrated nannies, and children relegated to child care, afterschool programs, organized sports, dance classes, chess clubs, and a hundred other caretaking institutions helping to make up for the time parents could no longer spend with their kids.[6]

Whether this was a better arrangement than the stay-at-home motherhood of the past became a matter of ferocious debate in the popular press and on the frontlines of the culture wars. Whatever the outcome of this referendum—and in many ways, the jury is still out—all parties would agree that today's parents, particularly mothers, are no longer preoccupied only by their children, unlike their own mothers. What impact does this have on their feelings about concluding the kind of "active mothering" they have tried to provide throughout the years before their children turned twenty? Well, they aren't quite as tired of their children as their parents were of them; they aren't as anxious to see those childhoods end. And because they are still in the labor force, with many years ahead of them before retirement, boomer parents don't think of themselves as grandparent material just yet—which is just as well because their grandchildren will likely not be born until they are well into their sixties.

The lion's share of attention in the press has gone to the changes in patterns of emergent or delayed adulthood among children. But for every millennial who has retreated to (or never left) the family home, there is at least one parent who has sidestepped a social transformation that would otherwise have happened. The boomer parent has delayed his or her metamorphosis into a senior and has now gained—if it is indeed a gain—more years of active parenting, social utility, and delayed aging.[7]

Of course, no one can stop the biological clock. All it takes to get older is a little luck. But what does it mean to be older when the child you have nurtured does not move on? Neither have you. Boomer adults have a long-term lease on a more active adulthood than would have been true in earlier generations. They may not experience the sunset years of empty nests, grandparenthood, or retirement until much later than was typically true in the past. Americans are not alone in this delayed transition. Modern Italian mothers have not given up their parenting obligations either. Long known for their adoration of grandchildren and desire to have many of them bustling about their feet, most of them hardly ever mention the idea of grandchildren today.

Globalization is reshaping every institution with which families interact, slowing down virtually every step of family life along the way by requiring more education to find a good job and more resources to buy a home. The older generation is left in a position to be helpful precisely because they are products of an earlier kind of economy. At least among the middle class, they have assets, income, and—knock on wood—good health. That advantageous profile makes it possible for them to boost the prospects of the next generation. But the costs involved are great, and for many families the only choice is to keep the kids in-house.

The Plus Side of a Full-Capacity Nest

Mutual admiration for the Rolling Stones may be one reason for the compatibility of these generations, but there is more at work here. Boomer parents are looking for a different model of parent-child relations than the one they experienced in their youth. When they look back into their teen years, many of today's parents don't particularly like what they see: distant fathers whom they respected or feared but didn't feel close to and mothers overly invested in their children or perhaps just unhappy to be abandoned in suburbia.[8] That model is history now, but what took its place has durable implications for the way that older adulthood is experienced. Today, accordion family life is building a foundation of closer relations between parent and child, one that can blossom into a more egalitarian relationship and move past the authority relations integral to life with younger children, no matter what the generational culture.

Grown children in the home introduce other benefits, including new ideas and experiences that make their parents feel younger. Millennials make the home atmosphere more exciting, adding an electricity that their parents appreciate for shaking them out of routines. Boomers learn about new trends in popular culture or how to operate the latest high-tech inventions—from iPads to Facebook—from their progeny. All that comes to a halt, temporarily, when the younger generation goes off to college, but it resumes if and when it boomerangs back. This is the same stream of influence that commentators noted when Barack Obama ran for president: twentysomethings urged their parents to vote for him, and older voters took a second look as a result.[9] Children are innovators, and they push that stream of knowledge toward the older generation, which makes their parents feel more "with it." And what could be more appealing to the boomers, who made the whole idea of being "with it" something close to a brand?

Jane Miller lives on a quiet street near the center of Newton. She is American through and through, but her grandmother came from Italy and conveyed some of that "family feeling" down through the generations. Jane has her own cleaning business and, in addition to her own children, has also raised foster children. Her son Jacob is twenty-six and lives at home, where he has the whole third floor of Jane's house to himself, "like an apartment." He has a well-paid job servicing vending machines. Having Jacob around seems to have slowed Jane's biological clock, she says:

When Jacob and his generation stays in touch with my generation, it makes *them* old. They make *us* young. Because we hang out with those kids a lot. Jacob will come down and go, "Movie night?" One night a week they all used to pile in here, there would be like twelve of them or fourteen of them. We'd make bowls of popcorn, and they would by lying on the floor or sitting on the couches, and sometimes we'd watch a cartoon. Tim loves cartoons; [that's] my son-in-law. He is six-four, a great big guy, and he loves cartoons. And we watch movies, family movies, or sometimes we'll all go to a theatre. We did it a week and a half ago: we went to see the *Pirates of the Caribbean*. Jacob and his girlfriend, my niece and her girlfriend came down from New Hampshire, my husband's other niece [who is] like our daughter, our daughter and her husband and their teenaged daughter, she's fourteen, she came, and we took a whole row, and we went to the movies. So we like to do that, and we like spending time together as a family.

In earlier generations, Jane might have felt she was an elder by this time in her life. But the presence of her grown son and the friends he invites into the house introduce a note of levity and enjoyment to her life.

Her Newton neighbor, William Rollo, also feels younger now that his son is home. John brings new ideas into his dad's orbit, William says:

> One of the things that I enjoy is that you have the younger person with more contemporary ideas, and you get exposed, keep in touch with things, have discussions about it—it is very interesting seeing someone involved in their ideas and their interest, that's fun.

The return of boomerang kids may even affect the way parents eat. Accustomed to preparing meals for four or five, empty-nest parents may stop cooking in favor of expedient take-out meals. They put a lot of thought into nutrition when they were raising growing children, but why bother for just one or two? Lucy Tang, a Newton resident who hails from Taiwan, works for a health-care company as a nutritionist. Even though her business is healthy food, in the absence of her kids, she stopped thinking about what she was putting on the table. But when they returned home, there was a reason to be interested again, and the kitchen has turned out to be the place where Lucy bonds with her kids. "We sit in the kitchen," she explains, "we have a nice meal, we have nice conversation, enjoy the laughs."[10]

While friendship across the parent-child boundary appeals to both genders, it is perhaps even more important for fathers than mothers.

Accustomed to having male friends in their adolescence, men often lose the knack and defer to their wives to organize a social life. Women are better at preserving all-female friendship circles, hence, in their maturity they have the best of both worlds: girlfriends and friends who are couples. But men may find themselves more isolated from male companionship, not on the job but in the off-hours, and their sons may fill that gap as they get older. Plus the authority that comes with the job of being Dad is no longer so necessary. If Mom hates science fiction movies or can't stand the bloodshed in the latest shoot 'em up, the boys can go off together and hang out to their hearts content.[11]

Gary Mack, a middle-aged Newton resident, finds the presence of his son, Bobby, a tonic for his reservations about getting older. The father has, in a sense, acquired a new friend whose interests and experiences shape his own. What was once a top-down relationship has now become something more egalitarian, and that has real benefits for Gary:

> I enjoy Bobby being in the house, and I think it's a good thing. He is a very sweet, pleasant, friendly guy, and he likes doing many of the things that I wish I had liked doing when I was his age. So it makes me somehow feel a lot younger, being able to revisit some of the hobbies and skills I never explored when I was younger. Things like metalworking, welding, that sort of thing. His presence here in the house for me is quite enjoyable.

The importance of these bonds between generations may be even more pronounced when the parents' marriages have dissolved. Lily Heller is divorced. She loves having her son at home but is concerned that he may feel obligated to keep her company, something that cannot become his responsibility. "He graduated college last year, although he plans to move out in the fall," she says. "I essentially said to him, 'You don't have to feel like you have to be here because of me. You are supposed to go on.' But I think he feels like he is the protector."[12]

Money Matters

Low-income families, including the record number of foreign born in the United States and Western Europe today, are very familiar with one of the most valuable aspects of the accordion family: the capacity to

pool resources and cut expenses by "doubling up" the generations under one roof. From the perspective of the millennial child, this can be a
dubious proposition. On the one hand, it provides for a higher standard
of living than she could afford on her own. Kyesha Smith, the young
African American woman we met in chapter 3, could not possibly have
afforded a decent apartment or child care for her son when she was
twenty-one and trying to make it on her minimum-wage job at the
Burger Barn on Harlem's far west side. As she edged toward twenty-five,
that dependency was irritating to her in the extreme. She fought with
her mother for control of her son. She resented having to turn over that
pay packet. Every spring, when the time came for income-tax refunds—
which she looked forward to all year since it was like a forced savings
account she could spend on big-ticket items—her mother would be
waiting at the mailbox for her cut. The idea that Kyesha would be stuck
in this infantilized limbo forever was depressing beyond measure.

But from her mother's point of view, Kyesha's contributions to the
household were not only necessary to keep them afloat, they were a
legitimate transfer in light of what the young lady was getting in return: free child care, the freedom to go out at night and keep up a sem-
blance of a social life, a roof over her head, and food on the table. "It's a
bargain," her mother would explain in her testy way. In truth, though,
Dana was getting a bargain, too. A longtime recipient of public assistance, Dana never had enough money to make ends meet. In addition
to Kyesha, her oldest child, she had three other dependent children on
the family budget, including a very sick two-year-old, who was younger
than her grandchild. Kyesha's earnings brought in much needed cash
income, which could be used in ways that food stamps could not. The
dependency in this household ran in both directions: Dana needed Kyesha at least as much as the other way around.

In good times, this kind of accordion family is common mainly
among the poor and working class. It is an adaptation that has spread
like wildfire, climbing well into the middle class, during the Great Recession of 2007–09. More than 49 million Americans now live in a
household that consists of at least two generations of adults.[13] The accordion opens up to receive the job seekers who cannot find work, the
divorced mothers who can't afford rent, and the sickly grandmother

whose family does not have the resources for nursing-home care, as well as the boomerang child whose delayed departure is occasioned more by the desire to launch at a higher level than a freshly minted BA will permit.

Economic downturns remind us of how important the family is, all around the world, as a buffer against the ups and downs of the market. Yet it has always been there, waiting in the wings to absorb the catastrophes big and small, the "welfare state of the first resort" to which people turn when they are in need. Most of the time, we think of that help as cascading down. Among the middle class, parents tend to be the ones with more resources (real estate, savings accounts, steady paychecks, and patience). But Kyesha's story alerts us to the fact that the resources can flow the other way. When we look at what it means for the nest to remain full, we have to recognize that it sometimes translates into economic support for the parental generation long before they are elderly.

Stephanie Phillips's appreciation for the benefits of a full house was reinforced by the help that her son gave her when she was down on her luck. Her son entered the Army after he finished college, in part because he couldn't find a job. His deployment to Iraq coincided with a bad patch for her, she remembers:

> And all the good he's done [for me]! There was one time when I was unemployed when he was overseas, and he sent me $2,000. This is probably a month or two's salary. Because he knew there was a need.

Stephanie is helping him now, but he was there for her when she needed it. In Stephanie's family, this kind of reciprocity has been the rule rather than the exception. It has pulled the generations closer, into something more like bonds between equals than the kind of top-down relations that have been the norm between parents and children. She adds:

> People ask, "Don't you charge him rent?" "No, he's my son, he's my child." I've given money to my daughter, and she says, "Oh, I don't like to do this." You know, when I was forty-three, I was going through a divorce, my husband had left. My mother reached in her pocket-

book and said here. The bills would come $5,000, $10,000 from the lawyer, and this was a divorce [my husband] had prompted. Mother said: "Here, just do it, I have it here. It's just fine." And I thought, "I don't know what I would have done if she hadn't helped me out." I had absolutely no way to pay the legal fees, much less pay the taxes. I can't imagine how I would have survived with this house and the two children. I can't imagine. And I couldn't pay her back.

All the way around, as Stephanie sees it, this is what family is for. Its purpose is to draw a fence around the people who love and care for one another and insure that they protect one another. It is a launch pad for the family mobility project, but it is also the haven in a heartless world, one that knows no limits just because its younger members are in their thirties. Most of all, it works both ways: the assistance flows up and down, depending on who has and who needs. That's ideally how families work. As she explained to her daughter: "Maybe someday, sometime in your life, you'll have a chance to help somebody else out. That's what you do in the cycle of life."

Still Needed after All These Years

Newton parents remember the atmosphere of their children's teen years with great fondness: Kids rushing in and out. Soccer games on fall weekends; cheering from the sidelines at science tournaments. Chewing their fingernails while waiting for those fat envelopes from the college admissions offices. But with the frenzy comes the obligation for surveillance and all the discomfort that goes with it. It's 3:00 a.m., where is Johnny? Janie wants a supply of birth control pills. Is that the right thing to do?[14] Suburban parents are particularly ill at ease because their children are behind the wheel of a car after the age of seventeen and have to be trusted not to do stupid things. Many a Newton parent has woken up on Sunday morning to read in the *Boston Globe* about Saturday-night tragedies, most of which involve drunk driving on winding roads on the peripheries of these affluent suburbs. In the high school years, parents drill into their children the importance of buckling seatbelts, and give them money to keep for cabs, just in case their friends have had too much to drink.[15]

For the most part, the adult child is past all of that. Twenty-five-year-olds can make dumb mistakes as well, and most accordion parents find themselves sleeping uneasily until they hear the key in the door, but the level of surveillance required diminishes as the boomerang child ages. As a result, in-house adulthood permits parents to enjoy the more pleasant aspects of parenting without having to engage in the more tedious aspects of discipline and surveillance.

Surveillance and discipline are obligations parents undertake during their children's teen years, but these responsibilities are not emotionally satisfying. What *is* gratifying is the feeling of making a difference, being of use in guiding the next generation. The empty nest feels silent and foreboding at times because that sense of emotional connection through advice and counsel diminishes. Dropping that last kid off at college is a sharp shock to the identity of mothers and fathers whose lives have revolved around their children for twenty-five years or more.

In recent years, boomer parents have been subjected to a withering critique by pundits for devoting themselves to grooming the next generation. Decried as "helicopter parents," hovering neurotically over their kids' academic, social, and athletic lives, the middle class has been hammered for being unwilling to let go.[16] Yet the landscape of emergent adulthood has become a fiercely competitive one, with opportunities to attend selective colleges and professional schools ever-more sought after. Entire industries have emerged to prepare the millennials for the scramble they face when they try to squeeze through those crowded bottlenecks. On the other side of the hurdles lies greater affluence and prestige, but jumping over them involves devotion and no small amount of parental guidance. To pretend otherwise is simply naive.

To move a child along that pathway requires a huge commitment that involves more than money; it requires endless supplies of advice. When an adult child boomerangs back into the household, turning on the advice spigot is like discovering old muscles that can be coaxed back to life. It can be painful at first, but after a while there is a certain joy in recognizing that they still work. Parents *are* still needed after all these years. For American families, the accordion family creates the environment in which that familiar role comes back to life, particularly since it is defined as a temporary (even if elongating) period whose purpose is to prepare the twentysomething child to launch into a marketplace that is so crowded.

This is a new way of thinking about the role of older adults whose job is no longer over when they ship their eighteen-year-olds off to college but resumes in a slightly different configuration when they boomerang back. In Japan, however, the accordion family is not exactly new. It is more of a throwback to the past. Having already seen the rise of the nuclear family against the backdrop of an Asian tradition of three-generation households, the Japanese must think simultaneously about the value of the old ways that saw grandparents living with two younger generations and the complexities of the accordion family, which subtracts the oldest of the old but adds in the younger generation for many more years than was true in the past. Moreover the role of the younger generation has changed. Young married women, once caregivers to the older adults in the household, are now receiving help (from their parents) rather than giving it.

Ikuo is fifty-nine years old and lives with his wife and his twenty-three-year-old son and twenty-seven-year-old daughter. He works as an engineer for an automobile manufacturing company. As is true of many Japanese his age, he has his reservations about the accordion family. He thinks that it may be "neither good nor bad," that what matters is the quality of the relationships between parents and their adult children. What he *is* sure of is that there are benefits of coresidence across three generations, the traditional Japanese pattern. Children get something out of the presence of their grandparents. There are opportunities for socialization across the generations, Ikuo says, that cannot come about any other way:

> If a young person stays at home [and gets married] and has a child, having a grandmother is beneficial since the grandmother can provide a different type of education from that of the mother. If there are a greater number of people at home, children learn from that experience.
>
> It is important for children to learn about society. For example, if there are three children at home and they have a quarrel, they will

split into two against one. So, one of them will be in trouble. They learn they should be on good terms with everyone. This is an often-said story. If the family is larger with people from different generations, children can learn about the system of society firsthand. So I think it is good in terms of education.

At fifty-two, Masato lives with his wife, his twenty-three-year-old son, and his eighteen-year-old daughter. An admitted traditionalist, Masato is no fan of the nuclear family. From his perspective, it is, well, atomistic. Nuclear families, he thinks, incline people to ignorance because people get no firsthand understanding of the whole life cycle. A return to the ways of the past would be better for everyone, he argues:

> Parental influence will decline if family members live on their own, like the nuclear family. It sets people free. But if young people live with parents, they can observe the process of aging of their parents. When they have children, there will be grandfather and grandmother nearby. In the sense that there are influences between generations, I don't think it is all bad living together. It's not that there are only good aspects, but it's not entirely bad [laughs].

The Social "Retardation" of the Aging Parent

From one perspective, the accordion family is a parental fountain of youth. Aging itself is not what makes people feel old. It is the loss of a valued social role that matters most. Asian societies traditionally venerated the elderly and hence the move toward the sunset of life was a positive transformation. In Japan, age and importance go together; they aren't considered mutually exclusive.

In the West, we may be ambivalent about youth, but we know where we stand on aging: we don't like it. Millions of dollars are spent trying to avoid the ravages of wrinkles, paunches, and grey hair—anything to avoid the inevitable. Even so, with age comes declining energy, a desire for some peace from the Sturm und Drang of tempestuous teenagers or the pitter-patter of tiny feet attached to babies that need diapers changed. Grandchildren are the answer! They provide all the joys of those remembered childhoods without the trouble. However, declin-

ing fertility and the advanced age at which childbirth takes place mean
that many an aging boomer will not hold their grandchildren anytime
soon. And unless they live to very advanced age, they will not know
them for long.

Paolo Trosso lives in Sant'Antimo, an Italian town of sixty thousand
inhabitants. Situated in the inner suburbs of Naples, it is considered a
district of the city itself. The Trosso family lives in a detached house
that has two floors, although the whole family—Paolo, his wife, their
grown daughter, her grandmother, and her grandmother's nurse—live
on the first floor, which looks like a big apartment full of furniture and
knickknacks. Paolo and his wife, Cinzia, are not voluble, but when they
do express their emotions, they reflect on how much they wish their
daughter would marry and begin to raise a family. "Maybe it's egotisti-
cal," Cinzia comments, "but I would prefer that she started a new family
because I would like to enjoy some babies born by my daughter's marriage." Sadly for them, nothing of the kind is on the horizon.

Maria Moreno, a middle-aged woman from El Pilar, a working-class
neighborhood in northern Madrid, might be expected to feel much the
same way. After all, Spanish grandparents have been as much a fixture
in the family as they are in Italy. But for Maria, there are limits to the
romance with three-generational family life. Maybe it isn't such a good
idea. The modern way, which inserts babysitters or child care where
grandparents used to be seems to her like the way to go:

> Honestly, I think grandparents should be there to enjoy a little of
> their grandchildren. But taking care of them daily, [I am] not so
> sure I think it is good for children to be so long with their grand-
> parents. They should be with their parents. [Parents] have to be
> sufficiently mature as to be responsible for their children. [It is one]
> thing if a child is ill one day, and the grandfather takes care of him.
> But I see in my neighborhood old men, who are older than seventy,
> almost in their eighties, with the children all day. And I think, hon-
> estly, that that is a cruelty [on the part of] the parents.

Many boomer parents will never find themselves in this role at all
or, if they do, it will come very late in life. That is a profound change
in countries like Japan or Spain. Americans also have come away from

many decades of increasing the lifespan with the expectation that we will spend years in the role of the kindly grandparent.[17] But if the millennials delay childbearing, as the boomers did before them, only those who live into their late seventies are likely to spend a long period nurturing their grandchildren. For some, this is a cross to bear; for others, it matters less and less because the span of their active lives as parents is elongating.

The Downside of Prolonged Parenting

It is tempting to see nothing but the upside of the accordion family and attribute whatever strain it produces to the economy that surrounds it, not to the forces that brought it into being. For affluent families, the inside of the accordion is often unproblematic and even a source of great pleasure. But not always. Active parenting for a prolonged period of time produces burdens for the caregivers, now in their sixties and still in charge of a household while, in earlier generations, they would have been finished with these chores fifteen years earlier.

Claudio Pirelli is twenty-nine and lives in Southern Italy with his mother and brother. He works with his brother at the commercial office their late father created. Claudio wanted to work in informatics in Bologna but was unable to find a job and returned to his parents' home. But when asked about household chores, he says: "This is my mother's responsibility. We are out for work all the day long."

Ricardo Morra, whose son Alesio lives at home and practices his trade as a freelance photographer, wondered aloud whether he and his wife should help their son set up his own place. He would have more privacy, and they would be disturbed less often by his irregular hours. But what would Alesio do with his laundry? Ricardo remembers:

> Three years ago, I said to [my wife], "I think it would be convenient [to help him pay rent on his own apartment.]." And besides, since he is photographer, he works with people who have no hours, right? Because sometimes he has to do photos early in the morning and so on. And he works with people who are in his same conditions, and so I think that if he goes living with people who have his same hours, that way one may arrive home at seven [in the morning], the other at five.

But she said no. She said that if he left, that was with all the consequences [of doing his own laundry, etc.]. Now he spends long
time with his girlfriend. And of course, he comes back and brings
his dirty clothes. Now they've been in the International Festival
of Beniccàssim, and it's been the same—he has arrived with lots of
dirty clothes to be washed. His mother has put it into the washing
machine. What she says is that she doesn't want to be like those
mothers, but I think it is unavoidable; unless the guys are very autonomous, capable of self-management, as I say. But no, those must
be very few.

While boomerang women are just as capable of sloth as their brothers or boyfriends, there does seem to be a gender problem afoot here.
Young men seem far more likely to drag their feet when it comes to
striking out on their own, and they seem less inclined to worry that they
are putting their parents, especially their mothers, to a lot of trouble
when they remain at home for prolonged periods. Why? In many respects, the transition to the accordion family has been a more profound
shock to the role of men than it has been to women. In many countries,
including the United States during the 1950s and early 1960s, it was
perfectly acceptable for a girl to be dependent; she was not expected to
be otherwise. It has never been truly acceptable for her brother to do
the same.

In the past, tradition dictated that women were expected to go
straight from living with their parents to marriage. It was unseemly for
them to live on their own. Independence of the kind that the women
of *Mad Men* exemplify was new in the early 1960s and vaguely dangerous. Absent the supervision of parents or husbands, the taint of sexual
promiscuity hovered in the background. Men never suffered from that
suspicion; they were expected to be sowing their wild oats. At the same
time, men were (and still are) expected to don the role of provider and
could not avoid the label of "childish" or worse if they were not making
strides in that direction.

Although there are many exceptions, it seems that accordion families in America have an easier time working out the details with their
daughters than their sons. Sons seem slower to mature, and parents

worry more about whether they will be responsible. Compared to their fathers, young men in accordion families seem to have fallen behind on the calendar of independence.[18] Young women—compared to their mothers—have accelerated their movement into the competitive world of careers, even at the expense of their "other career" as mothers.[19] Samantha Mason is a divorced mother of three—two sons and a daughter—who lives in Newton and works in a Boston-area library. She grew up in the South and moved out of her parents' home right after college, when she was twenty-two. She got married that same year. Samantha's two oldest children have finally moved out, but the youngest one, Justin, who is still in college, has been living with her during the summers. Justin likes to go out and enjoy himself without giving her a detailed account of his plans. It is hard for Samantha to accept that unbounded freedom; she has to bite her tongue to avoid raising the suspicion that she doesn't completely respect his autonomy:

> I've gotten a lot better, so we really don't live in conflict, he and I, but I have to every once in a while catch myself and say, "Wait a minute leave him be, you trust him, you know him." If he's going to go out and stay till four o'clock in the morning, don't waste any sleep over it. He's an adult, and you've taught him, and if you haven't taught him by now, then it's all over anyway.

Gloria is a university professor of French language and literature in Madrid. She is extremely thin with brown eyes, pale skin, and straight, dark hair, which falls just slightly below her ears. She speaks softly and slowly and, as befits a professor, she enjoys giving long descriptions of her family laced with quotes from authors. Gloria's husband is a French sculptor. They have one child, now thirty-three years old, who lives with them and is finishing his final project for a degree in architecture. By her own admission, it has taken her a long time to develop the confidence she needed to let him make his own decisions. Only in his thirties has she come to grips with her son's identity as an in-house adult:

> If he calls me and tells me where he is, I'm delighted, but I don't put any pressure, nor am I thinking every moment, "Where will my son

be?" Because he must already know what he is doing. Until a certain age, yes, I have been very jealous of all his friends, of everything. And I have tried [to see that] certain friends that I considered were not [good for him] .... I'm sorry, perhaps I've exaggerated, but I have tried as much as I could [to make sure] that he didn't see them. Right now, I would tell him to see whomever he wants to see and that he does whatever he wants to do because it is not in my hands, and I won't be the person who is going to tell him what he has to do.

The labor market has reversed young men's life chances in profound, possibly irreversible ways. For women, there is, if anything, more opportunity today than ever before, relative to the past. While girls remain in accordion families, their alternatives are of more recent vintage, and the perception that they are suffering from economically induced setbacks is more muted. Adult men still at home are perceived to have suffered a more dramatic reversal of fortune, and their parents—especially their mothers—may be inclined to view them as more immature than their female counterparts, who may be tied just as tightly to the apron strings. Perception tracks reality in important ways. In the twenty-five to thirty-four age group, 22 percent of American men are living in accordion families, compared to 18 percent of women.[20] The gap may be partially attributable to the way in which the economy has compromised the labor-market options for young men while opening comparatively more opportunity for their sisters.

The mother who has taken up the household obligations that come with hosting adult children may love them and even take joy in having them near. But she can also be exhausted by the responsibility. Gema Santiago is sixty-nine and lives in a Spanish village with her husband and adult daughter. Gema's oldest daughter died in her teens; and her son is married with children and lives on his own. Because her other daughter remains at home, Gema feels useful, but she is also tired. She would like, someday, to reclaim her time for herself:

Parents get to an age in which they would like to liberate themselves from their children, right? You also want to live your own life. You want to have a life and to liberate yourself, being able to say, "Well, they are already settled, and they can follow their own path now." To have your own freedom. In a way that if we want to go out, that's fine. If they are studying at home, you don't go out so easily.

What stops Gema from going out anyway? After all, her daughter is twenty-six. Surely she doesn't need constant companionship. Gema is uneasy, though, perhaps because of the trauma of losing a child, which understandably leaves her more skittish than many accordion parents. In truth, though, she knows only one way to be a parent, and it has little to do with her daughter's age. It has to do with the responsibilities of motherhood:

> We are not going to go out. If something happened to my daughter while I'm partying, I would never forgive that to myself in the rest of my life. And so I never go out. I prefer to stay here.
>
> Her father [drives her] to the school to prepare for the public examination. Because she comes back from work, and she would have to take the car and drive; and she is getting up around eight in the morning in order to go out to work; and she would have to come back and then take the car to go to Cáceres, which is quite a few kilometers. And so her father used to go with her so that she could sleep and be more awake.
>
> He waited for the two hours that the courses lasted, and then they came back. That's why I say that parents . . . there are some who make more sacrifices.

Veronica Flores's daughter still lives with the family in Zarza de Granadilla while she pursues her studies in accounting. While Veronica loves her child, over time the feeling that her own life is cramped by her daughter's presence has been growing. Her son's life may cause her similar problems in the future. For now, she says, the friction surrounds her daughter's desire for a private life (without a place of her own) and her mother's appetite for privacy:

> I am forty, and my children sleep next door. And so she's also deprived me of my liberty, and she hasn't realized, they've got into my

house, and they've taken our liberty. Sometimes when my husband and I wanted some intimacy, we had to go out because children have invaded [the house]. She has, in that sense. [My son] has a girlfriend, but he doesn't bring her [home] for the moment. He is going to turn twenty, but she [has been bringing] her boyfriend home since she was eighteen.

It's the only thing that has gone wrong. But at the same time, you don't know how to act. Because you can find [yourself with] two enemies. When I protested, [she and her boyfriend] both got cross, and she didn't come home for fifteen days. And that situation also hurt me. So either you leave them or . . . I don't know. And at the end, you think: All right, whatever.

Coming to a crossroads that no generation before has faced exposes parents to uncomfortable decisions and potential conflict, particularly if they lack the space to simply let their children come home and do what they want out of their eyesight. For many families, this is not possible, hence they have to come to grips—or squirm uncomfortably in their chairs—when their desires or moral sensibilities about who sleeps where conflict with those of their adult children.

Personal behavior is not the only source of friction. Money enters into the equation,[21] either because expenses are outrunning parental income or because parents come to feel that they are being taken for a ride. This is surely an issue where Veronica is concerned:

What need does my daughter have to marry in order to go to bed with a man or to do her own life, if she's already doing it here? She has her job; she has money because she manages the cash desk exactly as I do. She goes out with him, and she can buy whatever she wants: a T-shirt, some trousers, whatever. She lives with him, sleeps with him, and she's at home. She has no hurry to marry. And I say to her, "Get a mortgage, and you make your house." "No, no." Why would they want to invest or to spend money or to become indebted? They can do it little by little. I think that's fine. But in the meantime, parents . . . you notice [the expense of] sustenance. Because it's all right with her, but I'm also giving money to her boyfriend.

Even when there is no disagreement about what is appropriate behavior under the parental roof, there can be tensions that stem from
parents' needs for autonomy from their children, as much as the
reverse. While Ricardo, whom we met earlier, seems to have a good relationship with his son, he sees his son's continued residence with the
family as a little strange:

After a certain age, I think it is a problem. Parents need, when the
moment arrives, their own space and privacy. I haven't had the time
to live that, but I talk to colleagues and other people, and they feel
like being on their own, too. And when you go on holiday, we [par-
ents] are very silly, in general, and we leave the fridge full, we just
[add] complications. It is not the same [as] a couple who says, "Let's
go for three days wherever," and they have no other worries as when
you leave your child at home. And even life together: I think it is
better to be separated for daily life after a certain age.

Ricardo loves his adult kids, but he longs for more—not less—of a
generation gap than what he is experiencing today. He has a good relationship with his son but feels the young man's perpetual residence
with the family is peculiar. It might be better if the boy would move
out, he says:

There is nothing positive about [the delayed departure of young
people from the family home]. I think it is a problem. I'm not the
kind of parent who likes being with his child all day. That kind who
go on holiday together and go to the cinema together. From time
to time, we go out for lunch together; and sometimes we go to the
cinema. But it is not something I'm very enthusiastic about. Even
going on holiday [together] is something I don't like. And I haven't
done it for seven or eight years. Because he doesn't enjoy it either.
We have a different life rhythm, and he is into a different story.
There is one generation or two, which are going to be mashed. And
parents . . . the couple also would like to be alone and have their
own life.

That's the way I see it. Perhaps it is an excess of selfishness on my
side. But I think it is going to be very problematic. Because I think

that there are a couple of generations who are going to have it very difficult to get access [to housing], unless they decide to emigrate [somewhere where housing is cheaper].

The accordion family is not for everyone. But for those who see the downside, the structural problems remain. Wanting privacy and the freedom to return to a kind of carefree, pre-child life, is fine for those who have the means to set their children up somewhere other than their own home.[22] The wealthiest Americans—and their counterparts overseas—are doing exactly that when they subsidize their adult children's rent, health insurance, tuition fees, and the like. That is not an option for those of modest means. The less affluent cannot avoid the presence of the millennials under their feet.

The Retirement Squeeze

Middle-class parents are already facing an uphill climb to save for retirement, for future medical care, and perhaps for the support of their own aging parents. If the next generation cannot support itself, cannot manage the costs of independence, their families are faced with tough choices. No one wants to think of the generations as competitors, but since they are turning to the same pot, families are, in a very real sense, facing trade-offs. Savings accounts raided to pay the ever-escalating tuition at private universities will not be there when the boomer generation can no longer work. Jane and Ed Conlon of Newton, who have three kids, shared their thoughts:

ED: Whoever wanted to go, you got a year of college, and then [my parents] stopped. We, on the other hand, have borrowed, stolen.

JANE: Well, we haven't stolen.

ED: Well, taken from our—depleted our retirement savings.

JANE: But we've depleted our retirement to give our children college educations. Well, we haven't paid fully. They are still taking out loans.

ED: Yeah, [our daughter] took loans, and the second one took the money. You can put this on tape. He peed it down the toilet because he didn't do too well with it. And the third one, we're struggling to come up with the money to give him as much as we can so that he doesn't have to have the tremendous loans. But even [our daughter], $50,000 in loans compared to almost $100,000 we gave her.

If a generous welfare state were standing in the wings, perhaps these risks would be unproblematic (or unnecessary to take, as the state might subsidize the cost of higher education or housing). But in the United States, as elsewhere, pressures are building in the opposite direction: to cut the cost of government.[23] Boomer parents are squeezed in all directions. Their own elderly parents need their help, and so do their grown children. But there is only so much to go around and still provide for the looming retirement of the boomers. It is not a sustainable situation.

The squeeze may be even more serious in Japan. When we look at the demography of the freeter population, we see that it is no longer so young. Today, freeters are getting close to the age when they will be dependent on their parents' retirement monies. If the current situation does not change, predictions are that the number of freeters thirty-five years and older will triple to 1.5 million by the 2020s. Because their earnings are low, this outcome would have some serious fiscal consequences: approximately 1.4 trillion yen annually in lost tax and pension contributions.[24]

Hiroshi, a fifty-six-year-old salaryman living with his wife and twenty-two-year-old son, is worried about a related issue: how will his child survive if he burns through everything that remains, including whatever inheritance there is? Hiroshi explains:

> [As long as children] are under the protection of parents, they cannot acquire the abilities to be independent. Parents will die eventually. Even if parents leave some inheritance behind, the child without any ability to be independent will be forever sponging off his or her parents' economic power. Eventually, children will eat up whatever is left. They cannot continue to live like that forever. That will be worrisome. . . . It is worrisome for parents that their children cannot be economically independent. They must have a feeling that they want their children to work and become independent as soon as possible.

The problem plays out in the confines of the accordion family, but for some, it is taking on a larger significance when they multiply their personal situation by the number of families they imagine are in the same fix. Alonzo, an Italian retiree, has a lot of spare time these days. Even so, he keeps busy puttering around his house, fixing sinks that have blocked up and roof tiles that have fallen off. His seems to lead a bucolic existence, but when Alonzo dwells on the long-run situation of his country, that satisfied patina disappears in a hurry. He thinks there are some serious problems on the horizon,[25] and the accordion family is a bellwether for them:

> If you consider a forty-year-old child today who worked in snatches, how will he manage? And our society is more and more an elderly society. If all people have [started] working when forty, if they pay their [social security] contributions, you are almost safe. But in fifty years, all our children will be seventy to eighty years old, and if they don't have anything now, can you imagine that time? Our society is getting worse and worse. In a few years, it will be a poorer society, uneasiness will increase and criminality, and we will have a tremendous difference between rich and poor people. This is already a very serious and bad situation!

Conclusion

The accordion family is rearranging the entire landscape of human development in the advanced post-industrial societies, not just the part that defines the social role of the in-house adult. Because the change seems most transformative for the millennial generation, we focus attention on how adolescence is growing longer, why the Spanish blame the government for this debacle while the Japanese look inward for the source of a worrisome trend. Yet youth are not the only part of the social universe that is changing in the face of globalization. Their parents, the boomer generation that saw so much social change in its early years, is poised for one more mega-change: the one that keeps them active as parents into their sixties and, potentially, sees their experience of grandparenthood cut very short. The consequences of delayed aging, not in the biological but social sense, have yet to solidify. We see men and women turning to examine their experience, unsure whether it is entirely a plus or a minus, often opting for a muddle of both.

At the same time, they are grappling with what mature life is supposed to be like in an era when we are living twenty years longer than was typical only two generations ago. For those with resources and social roles that are a source of pleasure, the new elderhood is a boon. For those who are low-income or who face conflict and disappointment in the sunset years, it's another story. Several years ago, Japanese doctors began to diagnose their older female patients with a rash of "Retired Husband Syndrome." Long accustomed to living gender-separated lives, wives in Japan are finding the stress of their retired husbands' presence in the home unbearable and have come down with physical symptoms, including stomach ulcers and rashes. These women, "feeling chained to the tradition of older women remaining utterly dedicated to their husbands' well-being," are having difficulty dealing with spouses who, cut off from their prior, work-based social networks, hardly leave the house. Specialists in treating RHS have emerged, urging therapy for the wives and "retraining" for husbands that includes instruction in how to shop, cook, and clean for themselves.[26]

Under these circumstances, the presence of adult children in the household may be a blessing for the way it provides distractions from RHS. Or it may just add to the pile of laundry and the feeling of many older women that they are trapped by the obligations they feel to serve others. The Japanese situation illustrates the complicated context in which the accordion family has emerged. It is but one of a series of profound changes in developmental patterns affecting the entire life course.

CHAPTER 6

Trouble in Paradise

SOME CULTURES HAVE ADAPTED and even found a silver lining in the accordion family. But if other choices were possible, we probably would not see the accordion opening up this far, this often. After all, in more prosperous times, when labor markets were more welcoming of new entrants, young people all over the developed world left home earlier, married sooner, and began raising the next generation in short order. The average age of first marriage for men in the United States has moved up from 23.2 in 1970 to twenty-eight in 2009. Japanese men married at twenty in 1970; by 2008, they were waiting until the age of thirty. The same pattern holds for women: they are marrying later than ever before.

What if there were no financial pressures in the mix and young people had complete freedom to decide where to live? We cannot be sure that they would jump to live on their own or marry young, as they did routinely in the 1950s and 1960s. It is possible that the millennials would cleave to their parents' home anyway. But this seems unlikely. When we look at Denmark and Sweden, where there are few financial constraints on residential independence, we see the same rush for the door that was typical of the baby-boom generation, which came of age in more prosperous times in most parts of the developed world.

Surprisingly, while the generous provisions embodied in the Nordic welfare state underwrite the residential independence of the generations—young, old, and everyone in between—all is not well, not even in this paradise.

Nirvana in Northern Europe?
To understand why young people in Sweden and Denmark can buck the trend producing accordion families in the rest of the developed world, we have to examine what the state provides. Globalization has

had a very similar impact on the economies and labor markets of these two countries, leading to sharp upticks in youth unemployment and increasing demands for the credentials that come from higher education. Pre-tax inequality—the gap in earnings between the best paid and the least favored—is very similar as well. Yet the political compact that governs the Nordic social democracies intervenes through heavy taxation, generous redistribution, and universally available, high-quality services to produce egalitarian societies with much-reduced levels of stratification.[1] Accordingly, Swedes and Danes look to the state from cradle to grave for virtually every support that, in countries like the United States, is the responsibility of the family. Young people are able to maintain a high level of independence and autonomy because Nordic social policy provides the resources for them to live as adults even when they cannot earn their own keep.

The Nordic model of social policy emerged in the context of World War II. Sweden started with the introduction of universal old-age pensions and equally universal child allowances in the 1950s, and compulsory and universal employee benefits (unemployment, disability) followed. Social-security provisions were further improved and extended in the 1960s and 1970s. The extension of the maternity leave to a parental-leave policy was part of this development as was the expansion of social services for the elderly and then for children.[2] This largesse is financed by direct and indirect taxes and by contributions from employers and employees.[3] In 2003, Sweden spent 31.3 percent of GDP on social protection (down from a high of 38.6 percent in 1993 and 1994) and still holds the record for the highest proportion in the European Union and the Organisation for Economic Co-operation and Development.[4] Denmark's path to social democracy differs in some details, but the broad outlines are very similar.

These Northern European states enjoy very low levels of income inequality as a result. Pre-tax, they don't look very different from highly unequal countries like the United States or the United Kingdom. Post-tax, it's another world. Accordingly, there are relatively few "have nots" or high-income "have alls," and this leveling promotes a degree of social cohesion and support for government intervention to guarantee redistribution, as well as an almost unparalleled level of generosity in underwriting social services.[5]

In both countries, commitments to gender equity are deep and enduring. For example, the Swedes insist that new fathers go on work leave to take care of their children; Sweden also legislates against wage differences between men and women. Generous family allowances subsidize the cost of raising a family and avoid all the penalties that households in weaker welfare states incur when mothers and fathers try to combine work and family.[6]

What do all of these social policy provisions have to do with the accordion family—or rather, its absence—from the Nordic landscape? Social policy matters enormously.[7] In countries with a weaker welfare state, the family is the buffer between young people and the relentless market pressures that can reduce their options. Predictably, adult children from high-income families are advantaged because they can bide their time in their childhood homes and land internships that yield references or work and save enough money on rent to book a plane to Spain to experience life abroad. The most dedicated, who easily pass the work ethic test, will take jobs, no matter how poorly paid, where they can build up experience that might, in time, pay off in upward mobility. Those whose families cannot help them have to take what they can get, particularly if they live in a country where the state does not help students with financial aid or subsidize employers to hire them as apprentices. This is where inequality and the path to adulthood intersect in a weak welfare state, in the form of differential opportunity and the uneven ability of families to help.

In the Nordic countries, there is little need for the family to be a cocoon for twentysomethings. Or perhaps it is more accurate to say that the state serves as the backstop that shields Swedish youth from the harsher side of the market economy. The state is absorbing the financial strains that countries like Japan leave to private means to shore up.[8]

Though Nordic countries are generous to their citizens, in recent years they have begun to worry more than they once did about the damaging consequences of long-term unemployment. People out of the labor market for months on end—including an increasingly large proportion of the country's young workers—are at risk for being unable to resume their careers. Accordingly, though the Swedes and Danes are generous—far more so than virtually anyone else—to citizens and immigrants down on their luck, they expect concrete efforts to find new jobs, seek training, or further education. Sitting around at home is not an option, and those who pursue it risk the loss of almost all but the most meager benefits. For those clearly trying, though, the cushion is much softer than what they would find almost anywhere else in the world. This so called "active labor-market policy," has now been augmented by what the Nordic countries term the "flexicurity policy," a creature of a more conservative time that makes it far easier for private firms to fire workers, thus pulling Sweden closer to the liberal model of the United States. Yet the state continues to provide lengthy and generous replacement income for those on the wrong end of a pink slip as well as far more extensive investments in retraining facilities, state-subsidized employment in the private sector, and job-search services of the kind we have never seen.

The pace of globalization has been relentless all over the world and has taken its toll on the character of the youth job market, even in the progressive Nordic states. They remain part of an international trade system that creates downward pressure on wages and working conditions from low wage countries like China and India. Just as we see the evaporation of lifetime employment guarantees in the weak welfare states, so, too, do we see diminishing job quality in the Nordic countries. As Thomas Cook and Frank Furstenberg explain:

> In economic hard times, young workers are the first to be fired since they are not as immediately productive as experienced workers. International competition is probably forcing businesses [to] be leaner, requiring investments in the next generation to be justified economically and not as contributions to the state and its citizenry. Jobs do not last a lifetime anymore, and to be apprenticed in one trade is no guarantee that the same trade will exist when one is 55. The central dilemma of the Swedish system is retaining and developing quality jobs with good prospects for those who do not go to university. . . . Even so, the state of affairs is better than elsewhere.[9]

In 1987, 71 percent of Swedes age twenty to twenty-four had a job classified as steady; in 1998, when the recession was over, that rate had dropped to 54 percent, and the disposable income available to young people was lower by about 25 percent.[10] Deterioration in youth employment has accelerated in more recent decades. In 2007, unemployment for those between the ages of fifteen and twenty-four was 18.9 percent in Sweden. In 2009, that figure jumped to 25 percent, well above the European Union average of close to 20 percent.[11] Even in a country that is famously egalitarian, the impact of job instability was unevenly distributed. Young people who failed to complete high school experienced more than four times the unemployment of those who did.[12]

To varying degrees, these conditions have afflicted most of the "first world" economies. From Japan to Spain, from the United Kingdom to the United States, we see deteriorating labor markets, especially for young people. As the new entrants to the sweepstakes, they are unable to protect themselves from the changing nature of contracts as they shift from full time to part time, as wages slip and unemployment grows. These are the forces militating in the direction of the accordion family in the weak welfare states.[13]

Yet the predicament caused little economic hardship, given Denmark and Sweden's generous support of the unemployed,[14] and it did not lead to the spread of accordion families. Nordic social policy made that response unnecessary since, typically, unemployment benefits are extended to everyone who has been in the labor market, even if they have worked for only a short time. It provides for up to 80 percent of the salary earned before becoming redundant, which is far more generous in all respects than American unemployment benefits. Moreover, there is a basic unemployment benefit for those with very little employment experience. On the one hand, this provides a platform underneath young people that they lack almost everywhere else. On the other, it is less generous than it once was. Today, Swedes on the basic benefit receive about 320 kroner (about $44) per day, which falls short of the cost of living and makes it imperative for young people to remain in the labor market.

These provisions make it more likely that unemployed or underemployed young people can live on their own if they take on roommates or find other ways to practice income pooling. This is particularly possible because the state provides for a supplementary benefit—beyond unemployment compensation—that is designed to close the gap. The rate at which young people ages twenty to twenty-four depended on this benefit doubled in the 1990s (from 10 to 20 percent) while remaining steady for other age groups, which suggests that Swedish youth are struggling to find good-paying jobs, just as their age mates are in other countries. But since they get help from the state, they can be less dependent on their families and more likely to be residentially independent.

Generous support of higher education, vocational education, and training/work study programs also helps to insure their residential separation. In the 2004–2005 academic year, more than 45 percent of young Swedes were enrolled in a university or college, made possible in part by study grants and loans available to everyone.[15] Higher education is free of charge, both for Swedes and for foreigners, for a very long period of time.[16] A Swedish student older than twenty can receive financial aid for studies at "folk high school,"[17] in municipal adult-education programs, and in other forms of upper-secondary education. Amazing to Americans, financial aid is available for students all the way up to their fifty-fourth birthday, though the amount declines after they turn forty-five. If a student has custody of a child or children, he or she may qualify for an extra child allowance. This grant is payable until the calendar half-year of the child's eighteenth birthday. The size of the grant will depend both on the number of children and the student's "study tempo."[18] Every Swedish student is entitled to twelve semesters (six years) of allowances and loans.[19] Denmark (and Finland, for that matter) follows a similar policy pathway.

This helps to explain why so many young (and not so young) Nordics are in college or university. But we see prolonged periods of higher education in countries like Italy and Spain, where the accordion family abounds. Why hasn't this household structure developed in Sweden? The answer, according to Cook and Furstenberg, is that Swedes have other housing alternatives:

> The vast majority of Swedish students live in dormitories or lodgings, reflecting the high national value placed on being independent and leaving home. This early exit from home is made possible by housing policies dating back to the 1930s that sought to increase the then-low Swedish birthrates by subsidizing the amount of housing available and even the space per house. As a result, housing is more available than in Italy and at prices that are more affordable locally.[20]

By age twenty, most Swedes and Danes are out of the family home for all or most of the year, whether they study at a university or not. Because these countries have large stocks of rental housing, their youth have many more alternatives than, say, Italians or Spaniards, who (as noted in chapter 2) are forced into an owner-occupied market. Moreover, Nordic youth are supported in their efforts to strike out on their own by generous housing allowances for those who do not earn enough to afford a roof over their heads. Swedes between the ages of eighteen and twenty-nine without children can obtain a housing allowance if they have a "low income." The amount they can receive depends on how much they earn, housing cost, and the size of housing.[21]

Romance, but No Rings

These resources also enable Nordics to maintain more unorthodox or informal family-formation patterns. Most people leave home right after high school; they live alone or live with romantic partners. The strength of the Scandinavian welfare state may be weakening other kinds of social bonds. They do, eventually, marry, but both Danes and Swedes tie the knot very late in life. "By age 25, most Swedes have been in stable cohabiting relationships that are in some respects like experiments in marriage," according to Cook and, "though marriage itself occurs on average at age 30 for women and 32 for men."[22]

While most people in the Scandinavian nations get married eventually, the proportion of people who never marry has been slowly increasing over the years. In 2001, 17 percent of all fifty-year-old women in Sweden and 25 percent of all fifty-year-old men had never married. This can be compared to their share of unmarried counterparts from twenty-five years earlier; 7 percent and 13 percent, respectively. However, most of this new group of never-married fifty-year-olds either are currently living in a cohabiting relationship or have done so earlier in life.[23]

THIS CASUAL ATTITUDE toward matrimony does not stop children from arriving. Many couples marry between the first and the second child.[24] Marriage is not required in order to become a parent, and no stigma is attached to giving birth outside of wedlock. It is a testament to the strength of the labor market and, even more so, the generosity of government benefits that Swedish women have the largest families in Europe. Even though the average age at first birth is 28.5, Swedish women have 2.1 children compared to Italy's 1.3.

The patterns of family formation Americans associate with the poor—single-parent households, cohabitation, and out-of-wedlock childbearing—are very common across the classes in the Nordic countries. In the United States in 2007, nearly 40 percent of babies born were to unwed mothers either on their own or in relationships of short duration, and the majority of these mothers were from low-income families. In Scandinavia, unwed parents are plentiful among the vast middle class. In Sweden, about 55 percent of births occur outside of marriage, which is higher than virtually anywhere else in Western Europe. In Denmark, that figure (as of 2007) is about 46 percent,[25] but most of these families are composed of two cohabiting parents, living in consensual relationships, and their biological children.[26]

Compared to the United States, non-marital unions in Scandinavian countries are more stable and more likely to transition into marriage. The situation in America is due, in part, to the problems that poorly educated American men have finding employment, which makes them less desirable husbands, even though couples (and women in particular) are keen to have children. Sociologists have identified the growing rate of "multi-partner fertility" as a consequence of the increasing inequality that is leaving the low skilled, and increasingly the working class in the United States, out in the cold economically and ever more entwined in patterns of non-marital births.[27]

The strength of the welfare state in social democracies provides families with a safety net far more generous than anything we see even in the wealthiest of the "liberal states" like the United States or United Kingdom, not to mention the more conservative states of Italy or Japan. So stark are these differences that we can speak of these Nordic countries as places where adults in their twenties and thirties face few constraints on where they live. They are not forced into accordion families, and hence the phenomenon is almost unknown. Yet no country in the developed world is immune to the pressures of globalization. The Nordic countries are no exception.

Weak Connections

Scandinavian countries have found ways to protect their citizens and foreign residents from the ravages of globalization to a degree that is remarkable. It costs them in tax dollars, to be sure. And they are backing away from some of the most generous policies, having concluded that prolonged unemployment is unhealthy for the country as a whole and for immigrants in particular. Relative to the United States or the more conservative countries like Spain or Italy, it would seem the Nordics have figured out how to avoid the pressures producing accordion families elsewhere.

Ironically, the strength of the welfare state has loosened the bonds between the generations, something that wouldn't come as much of a surprise to those who have become acquainted with the bleaker side of Scandinavian life depicted in the works of novelists like Henning Mankell and Stieg Larsson. Mankell's fictional detective, Kurt Wallander, is depressive, divorced, with few close friends, and a tendency to over-indulge in alcohol. Over the course of Mankell's series, Wallander becomes increasingly disillusioned with both police work and what he perceives to be the disintegrating society that produces the gruesome crimes he investigates. Larsson was a journalist and political activist who worked to expose right-wing extremist organizations in Sweden and was passionately concerned about violence against women. The heroine in Larsson's wildly popular Millennium Trilogy—the series that has inspired the film versions of *The Girl with the Dragon Tattoo* and its sequels—is a reclusive, tattooed hacker whose childhood and youth were marked by abuse and brutal sexual victimization at the hands of her state-appointed legal guardians. Hardly depictions of an evolved society.

For better or worse, the economic dependence of Italian or American millennials on their parents reinforces the ties they share. In the Nordic countries, the autonomy the generations enjoy from each other—the many ways in which they do *not* need to lean on each other—seems to have created some misgivings. People everywhere would like to believe that "love is enough"; that if financial dependence were not part of the picture, sheer affection would guarantee the solidarity we expect between generations, at least within families, if not across whole societies.

Surprisingly, this does not seem to hold. For many Scandinavian parents, the insertion of the state—through the direct provision of benefits to young people—means that they define parenting as ending when their children turn eighteen. After that, young adults are on their own, both financially and emotionally. If this was just taken in stride, it would not cause distress at all. Instead, Nordic parents and children are asking: do we need each other enough?

The issue arises particularly in families that can look across the European landscape and see how different their culture is from the norms in other societies. Robert Jensen is a middle-aged Dane and the father of two sons, twenty-nine and twenty-four, who live on their own. Robert has relatives in Spain. He notices how different the emotional temperature is in their households, and that makes him wonder whether something is dying in Denmark. He asks: "Are we losing something that the Southern European family pattern has? Maybe, compared to my cousin that lives in Spain. They all come over for dinner on Sundays, all the family members across generations, because they are having paella, and they are going to talk to each other. I think we are missing something."

It's not that Danish children don't love their parents and vice versa. Love may simply not be enough to insure the cohesion between generations that develops when the reliance of young people on their parents is stronger. Without some level of interdependence, parents and children may drift apart because they don't need each other as much as in cultures where love and dependence, affection and constant infusions of help and material support, are intertwined and help to reinforce each other.

Where does this brave new world of family structures leave more mature Danes and Swedes when they think about whether they are content with the transitions they have witnessed? Just as Nordic millennials have raised questions about the direction of social change, so, too, do many of their elders.

Robert wonders whether his society will wise up and try to recapture something precious they have let go:

I wonder if at a certain time, people will go back to basics. Maybe in ten years time, it will be in style to spend time with your family.

I think this might happen. Some sort of reaction to all this. Families where everybody sits down around the table every Sunday and don't focus on each generation realizing their own needs and [that they each have] so many things to do.

But Robert doesn't know whether that really will come to pass.

Frederick and his wife, Anke, live in Aarhus and have two children. They cohabitated for several years and then married when Anke's son, Gunner, was six years old. The daughter they share is now in her mid-twenties. Their children live fairly close by, and so Frederick and his wife see them regularly. When Frederick compares his own culture with that of Southern Europe's, he reflects uneasily on the loss of intimacy Scandinavians feel and wonders if they aren't fundamentally selfish:

I think [people in Southern Europe] are more secure because of their families and that structure. They know where they belong; they aren't just sent off to manage on their own, they take care of each other, and that gives them a certain level of safety, even though it might also make them dependent on others. But in that way, it is a good mentality; people are incredibly open in Italy. People aren't like that here. Then again, this might have something to do with the selfishness.

Anya is divorced and lives with her new partner in Simrishamn, a small fishing community. She works as a head manager in church administration in town, and her children live and study in Lund and Halmstad. Anya married at the age of twenty-eight but has worked and provided for herself since she was about twenty-two. She had her first child when she was thirty-one. Anya says:

[Children] always want to free themselves, but I heard [from] someone who had been down in South America and came home with big eyes and said, "So nice, there the generations do things together," and we don't in Sweden. We have dancing for sixteen-year-olds, we have dancing for thirteen-year-olds, for seventeen-year-olds, for nineteen-year-olds, and then up, but we never dance together. And we have parties apart.

We isolate ourselves from each other. Older people don't count. In Southern Europe, the older generation . . . you can go to them and ask advice, they have like a life wisdom that the young don't have, and I think we have to go back to that. We see older people, [and we're like] "Get them out on the ice floes. Away." Then they're not seen, so I don't need to be afraid of getting all those wrinkles, but then I can pretend I don't have them because that's what's important.

It's the surface again, in a way: it's so empty, and I think it has to change.

Anke is twenty-four years old. She grew up in Silkeborg, a city about fifty kilometers west of Aarhus, with her Swedish doctor father and Danish mother. She currently lives with a roommate in Aarhus, where she moved about four years ago to enroll in university. However, after beginning a course in medicine with the aspiration of following in her father's footsteps, she switched to pursue a teaching degree in order to become an elementary schoolteacher. Anke, too, is unsure that the virtues of the Nordic way of life are worth the emotional price its people— particularly the elderly—pay. "I think [Southern Europeans] look more after each other," she says. "We send the old people to retirement homes, and then they can sit and wait for us coming to see them every Sunday."

Mathilda Tjelden is a twenty-two-year-old woman, and in the years since graduating high school, she has spent some time traveling around the world, most recently to West Africa. Between trips, she has generally lived at home with her parents in Vejle, a city close to Aarhus, and worked a number of jobs, including as a waitress, in a warehouse, and in telemarketing. She stays there now as she prepares to start university in a few months to study philosophy. Even though her ties to home are more durable than most of her age mates, she laments the anomic nature of her society:

> In comparison to other [cultures], I think that Danes are a bunch of rootless creatures. [This is] due to the fact that we leave home so early but also due to the fact that we are individualists. I don't know whether it would be different if we didn't move out so soon [from

home]. I mean, if there was a bigger acceptance of the family; that would make it possible to accept one another. I mean, here [in Denmark] people don't easily accept each other. People hold onto what they think is right. Everybody thinks that there was something wrong with their childhood, and something was missing. Maybe if you stayed with your parents for a longer while, you wouldn't feel like you didn't get enough love.

Christoffer is fifty-two and lives with his wife and youngest son (seventeen years old) north of Copenhagen in a town called Hillerod. He is an administrator with a trade association with offices in downtown Copenhagen. His older son, Simon, lives independently in Jutland, where he is studying. Christoffer is worried about how Danish families are faring in an era of individualism. "It's not that children don't love their parents," he explains, "and vice versa." Christoffer is just not sure how much they *need* each other. The primacy Danes place on independence translates into emotional distance and so, he sees, parents and children spend their time with anyone and everyone other than members of their own families:

My opinion is that the family [ties] all in all [aren't] super strong. I think that everybody would tell you that the individual generations are far more selfish, and there really isn't a lot of space for the family. Of course, young people would tell you that they like their parents, but they just don't have time for the family. And my generation would tell you that they need to realize themselves [by going] to Australia or something like that.

Christoffer and his wife would not consider doing what Spanish or Japanese families routinely do to protect their kids from the ups and downs of the labor market. He finds the idea of the accordion family almost inconceivable. Yet Christoffer thinks his attitudes have cost his society something. He describes it as hollow and internally disconnected:

We have certain occasions where we meet and get together across the generations. But we don't have those large families like they do down south. But then after all, I think we still as a family enjoy [be-ing] together. I would think that Simon would also think so, but then it isn't like we get together every Sunday or something like that.

This is not a generational problem. Christoffer doesn't think he is very different from his parents, nor does he think his children would warm to the idea of multigenerational solidarity. It's a Danish trait, and they are stuck with it. They don't make time for one another because it just isn't a high priority. Christoffer continues:

I think there will be less getting together in the future, and this is not only my children's fault. They are not the only ones that don't have time; it is also Inge and I. When I take a look at the stuff we do, well, when we sit down in May we might be able to schedule an ap-pointment with some friends sometime in August. Then we might have one free weekend in August, so when things are like that. It is hard to get time for family.

But if you are trying to make spontaneous plans to do some-thing with us in three weeks, we would say: "In three weeks, are you crazy? Saturday we are doing this, and Sunday we are doing that." And I think we are only getting worse.

Of course, it is quite possible for the interdependence that comes naturally in Spain or Italy to flip over into infantilization or emotional suffocation. In chapter 3, we saw plenty of examples in which adults in Japan resented the intrusions of their parents and many instances in which Japanese parents developed a powerful antagonism, bordering on disgust, for their dependent children, matched only by their self-criticism for producing the freeter generation. Newton families were largely content with the accordion arrangement as long as their adult children were making progress toward a high-status future. But woe be unto the twenty-five-year-old who appears to be going nowhere.

Clearly, the multigenerational household has its emotional limits. But these negatives are the unbalanced version of intergenerational ties that build in a society where the mothers and fathers draw genuine emotional satisfaction from their children, which they express in care and support. Adult children return the favor, not only when their parents are elderly and need help, but in their twenties and thirties when they crawl out from under past conflicts with their parents into the equanimity that characterizes relations between adults, even if they are still parent and child. Mutual need sustains mutual affection; they can be hard to pull apart.

When the state steps in to cure the need, financial security increases, but the bonds between parents and children atrophy.

Family Formation

Does the presence of strong welfare states in the Nordic countries make men and women more independent of each other and hence less likely to marry? Or is the high rate of labor-force participation one of the reasons why we see a lower rate of marriage? Either way, goals that most liberals would embrace—protection from hardship and equal economic opportunity for women—seem to be associated with a lower rate of marriage as well as a high rate of residential autonomy for young people. Is this a problem or just a change? Scandinavians have mixed views of these trends. Social changes in marriage patterns swept the region several generations ago. Today's youth seem to have their doubts about the wisdom of this transformation, perhaps out of dismay with what the looseness of family life has bequeathed to them.

Wedding customs reflect the new generation gap. Older Scandinavians were very casual about the ritual side of marriage. It seemed to matter little to them whether it happened or when, and they often pulled on a pair of blue jeans and hopped a streetcar to tie the knot at City Hall with no fanfare, no celebration. The resurgence of the fancy, expensive, "white wedding" among today's millennials is evidence of a change of heart. Elders look on in stunned surprise as their children plan for nuptuals that rival an American society wedding.

Christoffer married young, yet he feels his attitude toward marriage was in some respects more practical than that of his children's generation:

> The younger generation looks a bit differently on [marriage]. On the one hand, they would say, "Oh, we don't care so much about whether we are married or not." But then on the other hand, when people do get married they are about thirty-three or thirty-four,

and then they goddamn spend one hundred thousand kroner, or something like that. I think that is quite a paradox. I guess it is sort of a symbol of status. It just keeps going.

In my generation, we probably had a stronger desire to marry, [but] we would never dream of spending one hundred thousand on the wedding. You would think that was way too much.

Sven grew up outside of Copenhagen in Roskilde with his parents and two younger siblings. Now twenty-eight, he has returned to the city of his youth to work in the Ministry of Social Affairs, using his training as an economist. Sven recognizes that attitudes toward marriage—or at least toward wedding ceremonies—are changing, albeit unevenly, in his generation:

> There are people that want the whole big thing, the big white church wedding, but then there are also the kind of people that want to make things a little less formal. People [choose] not to get married because they think it is an unnecessary hassle or a pointless ceremony or because they don't want to commit themselves.

He doesn't think marriage is important as a statement of commitment for a couple. It matters only when children come into the picture. "Marriage means something if you have kids," he says. "Then you are stuck with each other. Then you really have something together. But the thing about getting married isn't so important."

Nadia is a forty-nine-year-old woman who lives in an apartment in the center of Copenhagen with her husband. They have been living together for twenty-seven years, since she was about twenty-one, but they only married twelve years ago—largely for financial and legal reasons. They have one daughter, Jamilla, studying at the University of Copenhagen to be an urban planner. Jamilla left home when she was about twenty-two and moved just around the corner to another apartment in their building complex. Jamilla says:

> More people get married today. . . . I think it has something to do with the romantic wedding. [At first] it isn't in style, then it is.

I think it is because people don't think that everything is perfect, and then people want to do [things] differently [so that it is perfect].

Saskia is a middle-aged widow living with her son. She still works, as does her son, who has a job in a furniture factory. She is among the few Danish parents with children still living at home, which seems to happen only in rural areas where the land passes between generations. Saskia and her son get along well and rarely experience conflict in the house. As a widow, she has had some time to contemplate her future and, in hopes of finding someone new, has started dating. She would be the first to admit, however, that it is hard to find a partner after many years in a happy marriage; no one quite measures up to her late husband. Yet back in the day, when she first married, weddings were quiet, simple affairs that often were so low-key they didn't involve family members other than the couple. Today things are different, and that puzzles Saskia:

> There are some people who marry and it has to be so grand. That is the Denmark of today. Weddings are very expensive! The wedding I attended last Saturday probably cost about sixty thousand kroner. That is a lot of money.
>
> When I got married, my mother paid for the wedding. I don't think the parents of the bride pays anymore.

Why this sudden change in a direction most would associate with tradition rather than modernity? It could simply be fashion. Scandinavian newspapers display elegant tuxedos and gorgeous dresses that may simply appeal for their luxury. Equally possible, we may be in the midst of a generation gap, a symbolic marking off of millennial culture in ways that make it distinct from their parents' culture. Generational change is common enough, and there is no reason to think that cultural preferences only run toward a more informal, blue-jeaned transition. It can just as easily run in the direction of romance and opulence.

As sociologist Andrew Cherlin has pointed out, we see a similar drift among low-income and working-class Americans refraining from marrying precisely because they cannot afford the fancy white wed-

ding. Why not revert to the informal customs of the boomer generation? The answer, Cherlin says, is that marriage has become a status
symbol; a marker of arrival. If you can't afford the marker, you don't
marry.[28] In the past, that would have meant that you don't have children either, at least not until the rings are on the right fingers. Today
the strictures against out-of-wedlock childbearing have largely eroded
in the United States, as in the Nordic states, and hence we still see a high
rate of non-marital births to cohabiting couples. Whether they marry
or not is, however, another question.

Just because these trends have emerged in Scandinavia and the
United States does not mean we fully accept them in either society. We
need not review the culture wars that have raged in the United States
over cohabitation and out-of-wedlock childbearing since they are well
known. We think of the Nordic countries as laissez faire where these
issues are concerned. But this masks some behind-the-scenes reservations that Danes and Swedes express about the direction their society is
headed, about the distance they feel opening up between generations,
between groups, and between individuals, and it lends itself to a different interpretation. Young people whose parents didn't marry at all or
not until late, who have grown up with high divorce rates, may be re-
asserting a more traditional culture because the pendulum swung too
far in the other direction. If that is the case, it won't be because there
is stigma attached to being a child of unwed parents since, manifestly,
there is none. Nor is there social disapproval for cohabitation; it is the
norm, and it is embraced. What may be under construction, not yet
completely codified, is an increasing desire for more stability and tradition, which marriage has long represented in other societies.

Palle, a twenty-six-year-old man who lives independently in Copenhagen, where he is a student, exemplifies this attitude when he
says:

> I think I would [get married] more as a provocation toward my
> family. They are so darn untraditional. They are a part of the 1968
> generation [hippies, the rebellion of the youth]. I think since we live
> in a globalized world, it is important that we celebrate our own tra-
> ditions. And this is a part of that . . . a church wedding.

This transition may represent the long-term outcome of some of the confusions that come to roost in adults who grew up in households that are, by traditional standards, unorthodox. Henrik, a fifty-three-year-old teacher in a local elementary school, lives in a typical yellow Danish house in Greve, south of Copenhagen. Full of winding little paths, a stranger can easily get lost in Greve, which is why he meets newcomers at the train station. Henrik lives with his wife, Hette, who is not the mother of his children. She has children of her own who live with them. Henrik has three daughters who lived with their mother until they were on their own. He retained his ties to his girls, even though he didn't live with them, but the ease with which he let go of them after they were eighteen suggests how much the Danes value independence over sustained emotional ties. Henrik says:

> I mostly missed them for the first months, and then it wasn't that hard after that because we got used to being on our own. I don't feel bad about that. That is all right. We have more freedom to do what we want, and we aren't tied up in the same way; we can do what we want.

When asked what about the children would be different if they lived at home longer, Henrik observes:

> I don't think they would like to. I think it is a natural thing for them at some point—they want to move away from home. It isn't like we have been on bad terms or had some conflicts. They have just felt that they were ready to leave.

Twenty-seven-year-old Henne lives with her boyfriend in a two-room apartment in Amager, Copenhagen. Her boyfriend is Dutch and works as an in-country manager for a Dutch company in Denmark. Henne's kinship tree has many branches, reflecting the complexities of family ties not unusual among Danes of her generation. She has a younger sister on her father's side and one on her mother's side. Both her parents have new spouses. She describes hers as a very modern family, referring to the several marriages:

I actually lived with my mother until I turned fifteen, and then until I turned nineteen, I lived with my dad. It wasn't that long, but I have a very close relationship to my father. We lived together for those years, we [have] very similar personalities, and we are sort of bossy, to be honest. I think I found out that I was ready to leave home, and I think that was what was best for our relationship. It was time to go.

Many Danes are at ease with these arrangements. They are aware that they are more distant from one another than would be true in Spain or Italy, and at times they lament the lack of closeness in their families. But alongside the underlying concern about whether this is the best way to arrange their intimate relations, they are also wary of too much closeness.

Jannie's daughter, Christina, didn't live with her when she was a child. She lived, instead, with her grandmother, who had an apartment in the same building as her mother. Jannie saw Christina on a regular basis but in a sense didn't raise her. Jannie still lives in the apartment building with her husband, the building janitor, to whom she has been married for twenty-two years. She doesn't feel the desire to be closer to her child or the rest of her family and doesn't really understand why other societies find it worthwhile to develop such strong bonds. To her, this seems like too much emotional baggage. One of the reasons her first marriage broke up was that her husband, an immigrant from Yugoslavia, wanted close intergenerational ties, and Jannie could not stand the idea. It invaded her private space. She remembers:

I sometimes wonder why people take so much care of their family in other countries. I don't know if it's because they have nowhere to send their elderly family members, or if it's just because they care. [Denmark] is another culture. Christina's father is Yugoslavian, and he wanted the same thing [as they do in Spain and Italy]. I got married to him, and that only lasted three months because he wanted us to move in with his parents, and I just couldn't do that. I wouldn't want to live with the brothers and sisters.

You'd have to wait on everybody and [have] people around you all the time. I think it is more than enough to have my in-laws over. I don't really see why families should live together. I don't see how you should have any privacy.

Birgit lives in a small village on the island Mors, situated in a fjord at the northern part of Jutland. She is a fifty-five-year-old widow living alone in a large house and has three adult children, none living with her. Birgit has travelled in Eastern Europe, where she saw how the generations depend on each other and live together because space is at a premium and resources will not stretch to accommodate individual households as it does in her country. "In Poland," she explains, "often the children live upstairs and the parents live downstairs in the house, and then they eat together." Such a practice would be very rare indeed in Denmark. Birgit reflects:

> We are more selfish than people in other countries. We are self-sufficient a lot of the times. And I wouldn't like [living with the family] because I have a job, so I wouldn't like to live with my children and grandchildren; I need my space. I love to see them. But I also like when they go home. I don't know, I think it is a very personal thing.

Birgit would like to find a way to spend more time with her adult children, especially now that she is alone. But she doesn't go out of her way to make it possible, and neither do they. Everyone seems to be busy, according to Birgit, with higher priorities:

> There are so many things we have to do, and sometimes we don't have the time or the energy to take care of the family, and I think it has something to do with the fact that we have all these possibilities. And I know that my own children have a lot to do with playing soccer and handball.

All in all, she values her independence and privacy over more intimate contact. She likes to see her grandchildren, but she "wouldn't like to have them living here." She concludes:

> I want to live my own life. So there is a balance. I understand the places where people live with their families, but then I suppose the [grandparents] have more time to take care of the grandchildren, or someone else in the family does. I think the reason why [we don't live together] is because we are working.

I think in those countries [where families are closer], people have more adventures with [their] families than you do with friends, like it is in other social relations.

Birgit prefers the lateral ties with friends to the vertical links between generations.

Conclusion

We are inclined to think that there is a right and wrong way to organize family relations and intergenerational bonds. It is hard to avoid the temptation to shake our heads when encountering a society in which family relations are either far more distant or, in the case of Spain or Italy, much closer than ours. In either direction from the United States, we see divergence in how parents connect to their kids. The Nordic states have developed more distant relations, partially by dint of cultural temperament and partially because the generosity of the welfare state means that the kind of reliance adult children in the United States have on their parents—particularly in the middle class—is not necessary there. Scandinavians have the state to help with education, housing, elder care, and virtually every other aspect of modern living that, in other countries, requires an intergenerational social compact.

For those who live in societies where this private safety net is fraying at the edges, taking on more burdens it can comfortably handle, it is only natural to admire the security and flexibility that the Nordic countries provide for their citizens. And even if those social democracies have started to reign in the cost of the welfare state and introduce more conservative policies that hold individuals responsible when they find themselves unemployed, they are still remarkably generous by American standards, much less Japanese standards. This would seem an admirable solution for families straining to provide for their adult kids, raiding precious reserves parents have set aside for their retirement. It seems the perfect solution.

And in many respects, it is. Still it is not clear that the social relations they have evolved are making Scandinavians all that happy, and the nirvana we might expect among them has its own complexities and sharp edges.

CHAPTER 7

The Birth Dearth and the "Immigrant Menace"

JAPAN HAS ONE OF THE WORLD's lowest fertility rates. In 2008, Japan's population fell by a record 51,317. The shortage of children is so severe that the government has created a cabinet position to deal with the problem. Local authorities took to hiring matchmakers to encourage young people to find their soul mates. When they were unable to get satisfaction from private matrimonial agencies, authorities took matters into their own hands and began to set up municipal matchmakers.

The Japanese are attempting to stave off a demographic imbalance of frightening proportions. A 2009 article in the *Independent* says:

> If current trends continue to 2100, the number of Japanese will have halved and many vibrant cities will be ghost towns haunted only by the elderly because the country has the longest life expectancy on the planet. This estimate is based on the 1997 fertility rate of 1.39 children per woman—well below the 2.1 replacement level that a country needs to keep the population from falling.[1]

Despite the severity of the problem, Japan has so far rejected what seems like an obvious answer: allowing mass immigration. According to some observers, the refusal to entertain this solution derives from a commitment to the "racial 'purity'" of a population in which foreigners account for only 1 percent."[2] To be sure, the United States waxes and wanes in its enthusiasm for immigration and, as we have seen, even the famously liberal Nordic states are experiencing problems with assimilation. Nonetheless, Japan stands at the extreme end of the continuum. The United Nations claims Japan needs six hundred thousand immigrants a year, but in 2009, Japan accepted only thirty-six refugees and tightened its restrictions on entering the country.[3]

176 THE ACCORDION FAMILY

In almost all of the countries that have experienced growth in the proportion of accordion families, the subject of delayed adulthood sparked diatribes about immigrants. What is the connection? Native-born Europeans understand that one consequence of their children's long stay in the household is that they are not marrying and not producing the next generation. As a consequence, the next generation of these high-immigration, low-fertility societies is far more diverse than it ever has been. The prospect of a society that looks different is not always welcome.

Marina Tessiore knows this problem from the inside:

> Yes, I think [people having fewer children is] a problem, also because immigrant people don't stop [having children], and so one day they will be more than us. But I understand that nowadays having many children is hard.

Now 5.8 percent of Italy's population is composed of the foreign-born, most of whom have flocked to the region where the Tessiore family lives, the most prosperous part of the country. Here, immigrants account for nearly 8 percent of the total population.[4] When children come out to play in the parks, it is the sons and daughters of the immigrants that Marina sees. She has only one grandchild at an age when her mother had a dozen. Her counterparts in Spain would see much the same on the playground. In 2008, one in five Spanish births were to foreign mothers (20.7 percent) and increased 15 percent in just one year.[5]

In countries that do admit immigrants (whether legally or illegally), the newcomers often have children at a much earlier age. Both Spain and Italy have below "replacement level" fertility among the native-born[6] but much higher birth rates among the immigrant communities in their midst. Immigrant mothers have more children, and among immigrant families completed family size typically outstrips that of the native born. The resulting gap can produce new and acute anxieties about who owns the national culture.

Japanese parents are keenly aware of the problem of low birth rates, not only in their own families but for the society at large. Kana, whom we met in chapter 4, lives with her thirty-one-year-old daughter. She complains about how women are less likely to consider starting a family when society won't help them with the expense of doing so. From Kana's perspective, the problem of declining fertility is a matter of "basic human rights," meaning the rights women should have to pursue careers. If this is not supported by society at large, millions of women will simply "opt out":

> In a society [that doesn't respect these rights,] they do not provide sufficient day care. Society does not provide an environment where women can bring up their children. So this is revenge from women. They are saying they cannot give birth to children in a society like this. It can be seen as women rising in revolt.
>
> The cost for delivery is also expensive now. It costs several hundred thousands of yen [$4,500 to $5,400] per delivery. They pay for it by themselves and get reimbursed about 300,000 yen [approximately $2,700] afterwards. Still, it costs them 300,000 yen to deliver. Thus the women think if it costs that much, they will not bother. And the monthly checkup costs about 10,000 to 20,000 yen [approximately $90 to $180]. They wouldn't want to spend that much money.

But expense is only part of the equation for Kana. She sees the birth dearth as a consequence of a malaise or society-wide depression that is leaving women without the motivation to marry or raise a family. As she sees it: "The environment in which they grew up is not something that has made them feel happy about being born. They are not motivated to have children in the first place, and there are not appropriate conditions for that, either." Kana's lament focuses on the long-term consequences of the economic stagnation that has plagued Japan for more than a decade. But it is also an uneasy recognition that women have more options in the modern world and that having a family is no longer the unqualified, paramount objective.

There is, of course, a relationship between the growth of the accordion family and the low fertility rates of the native born: the longer young people stay in their parents' home, the longer they delay marriage and childbirth. Thirty-five-year-old newlyweds immediately confront the biological alarm clock: if they have children at all, they might be able to have only one.

The United States would resemble Japan more closely in its overall fertility rate if we did not have a significant population of newcomers who have comparatively large families. In the next fifty years, the populations of the United Kingdom, Germany, Italy, Japan, Russia, Bulgaria, Estonia, and the European Union as a whole will all drop anywhere from 5 to 30 percent. In the United States, though, the population will grow by 25 percent. Accordingly, the Census Bureau projects the population will increase 50 percent in the next fifty years and 100 percent in the next hundred years.[7] But where will this population come from and who will contribute to it? New evidence suggests that the native born in this country are less inclined to have children or at least to have them at a young age. More and more American women are either delaying having children or opting out entirely. The trend seems to prevail across all class, education, income, and ethnic groups.[8] Nearly one in five American women in their forties is childless, compared with only one in ten in 1971.[9]

Although politicians riding the anti-immigrant bandwagon in the United States are not likely to admit it, it is the fertility rates of immigrants that will save us from the fate that befalls Japan. Mexican immigrants, in particular, are responsible for keeping our population growth above the replacement level. Newcomers will help the country by creating a larger, younger, and healthier workforce (assuming, of course, that these children of immigrants decide to remain in the United States). In 2006, the U.S. fertility rate hit its highest level since 1971. This means we are producing enough young people to replace and support our aging workers without going beyond the population size that can be supported by current rates of national taxation.[10]

The Pension Problem

State pensions in most countries, the United States included, depend on the contributions of several active taxpaying workers for every retiree drawing support out of the system. While Europe currently has four people of working age for every older citizen, it will have only two workers per older citizen by 2050. Given current policies, the pension and long-term health care costs associated with an aging population will lead to significant increases in public spending in most EU member states over the next fifty years.

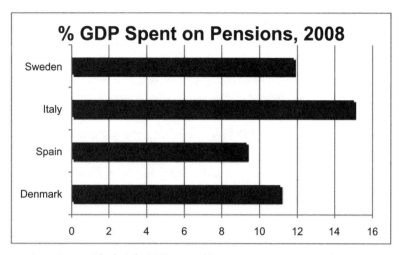

Source: Eurostat, Office for Official Publications of the European Communities, Luxembourg.

When the native-born generations start to "dry up," a trend prompted in part by the growth of accordion families, the base of the pyramid becomes too thin. There are only a few solutions: invite immigrants in to fill the missing space, tax everyone else at much higher rates, or slash the safety net.[11] Of course, what seems demographically plausible can be politically impossible. What would the consequences be if middle-class Americans—of all colors—see a sharp drop in their fertility while poorer families with less education continue to have large families? The answer is clear: we would be at risk for a less productive country unless we quickly invested in public education, enough to insure that future generations were high in human capital. Sadly, particularly in states like California, we seem to be headed in the opposite direction.[12]

Waves of anti-immigrant sentiment—whether bubbling up from below or stoked by politicians from above—seem almost inevitably to follow financial downturns, labor-market competition, or the political battles that attend the cost of the national safety net. Despite the fact that immigrants have helped stoke economic growth in the Southwestern states, Arizona has led the way on this unfortunate front with legislation authorizing the police to stop anyone who might appear to be an illegal immigrant and demand their papers. Calls have been heard to repeal the provisions of the Fourteenth Amendment that grant citizenship to children of illegal immigrants born on American soil. Proponents of the repeal have, among other things, touted it as an anti-terror measure, necessary to address the threat of so-called "terror babies."

Europeans have experienced waves of agitation along the same lines. When a population ages, an already overtaxed welfare system may just collapse because the active workers needed to fuel it are too few in number. Demands for pension reform often follow because the existing system of benefits is too costly. Yet woe be unto the politician who touches this third rail of social policy. A spate of strikes and riots spread through Greece, Germany, Italy, France, Portugal, Spain, and Austria in 2010 as changes in pension benefits, civil-service wages, and the like were proposed to deal with their debt crises. These reforms are rarely popular.

Weakened labor markets, some reflecting the increasing international competition that comes with globalization, mix with the toxic trail of the Great Recession, to produce deep anxieties about the fate of young adults, working-age parents, public-sector workers absorbing cuts in state budgets, and retirees worried about pension reductions. Students in England marched on Parliament in November 2010 in protest against tuition increases prompted by government spending cuts that were, in turn, a conservative effort to reduce deficit spending; French workers have gone on strike in response to government plans to raise the retirement age; Greeks have been on the picket lines objecting to reductions in public-sector employment. These domestic policy debates are unfolding in the context of widespread economic distress not only in the developed nations but in developing countries sending thousands of migrants over the borders in search of whatever work they can find.

Accordion families are growing in number against this backdrop. They see how the younger generation is faltering in the labor market, and they look around to see who might be to blame. Their instrumental concerns—how will my son finish his education, my daughter find a decent job, my mother afford to retire, my father pay for his medicine?— mix with cultural fears that the country is being overrun by strangers who will change its character.

Laura Fuentes has seen her sons devote many years to piling up educational qualifications. Their friends have gone down the same path. Their university years have been worthwhile in their own right, but have they paid off? Not exactly. Jobs are not plentiful even for the well-educated. The available jobs don't require a high skill level or long incubation in the higher-education system. And so those jobs now tend to go to the foreign born, Laura says, adding:

> I think . . . there are not well-paid jobs in Spain for the people, as [highly] qualified as they are. Many students have gone to the university, they have done many courses, and they end up working [in anything]. Then there is a lack of plumbers and manual workers. There are enough jobs like that, and they are occupied by immigrants. But we have a model of the ideal job, and it is very [hard to accept] that someone with a degree, courses, languages cannot find the kind of jobs they would have found in the past. Supposedly, if you were well-educated, you would get a good job with a little effort. And I think that [the situation now] is scary. I think there is also a problem of integration in the sense that there are many immigrants. For younger people, who are eighteen or twenty, it is becoming more difficult.

Why pursue all these credentials if young Italians or Spaniards cannot get work? This is a question many Europeans are asking themselves, as are the Japanese. It is not a simple matter to downsize expectations and ambitions, particularly when the possibility of upward mobility is of such recent vintage. Legions of farmers and factory workers who wanted something better for their children and grandchildren pushed them to go to university—a path they could never have taken themselves. Confronting the possibility that there is no longer a pot of gold at the end of that rainbow has been a monumental disappointment. A change of this magnitude leads ordinary people to dwell on unfair competition, the diminishing control over the fate of their nations. It does not create a favorable context for immigrant assimilation. Laura's son knows firsthand how these mobility ambitions were fueled and how hard it is to let go of them as the opportunities decline:

> Our parents could not study, [so] they have always obliged us to do so. And so even if you [did not want to], you spent ten years [getting] a degree. You still do it. Whereas before that wouldn't have happened because they couldn't pay for you [and it was financially

impossible]. Either you were really good and made the effort or . . . .
Well, there were also many people who didn't have the means, and
so they couldn't [go any further in school].

Now everybody has to [get] a degree, and of course there are not
enough jobs for everybody. We are also forgetting other things. You
can't be spending ten years [getting] a degree, just because you have
to be a graduate, when perhaps you may like more a different path. I
think there it is [the main cause of the problem with qualified jobs].

When the arc of underemployment intersects the growing presence
of immigrants, the two issues can fuse despite being, in some sense,
distinct. Blocking immigrants will do nothing to change the depth of
frustration among the high-skilled native born. We can send every illegal Mexican back across the border with Arizona, but this will not create new jobs for physicists or English-lit majors.

Laura can see that tensions of this kind are building in Spain, but the
national conversation is often eliptical, focusing more on the tensions
that arise from a clash of cultures than on the economic dynamics that
promote immigration. "There are many Arabs in Fuenlabrada, many
Muslims," she explains, "young people who envy the way you live because there is a big difference in the life standard, in how they live and
how we live." Laura is uncomfortable with the underlying racial tension;
it is not a healthy development for Spain. She counsels her brother, who
"doesn't want anything to do with [Muslim immigrants]," to pursue his
education as a way to "see that everybody is the same." But at the same
time, she is skeptical of her capacity to persuade him.

OUR EUROPEAN AND Japanese counterparts weigh the economic imperative to bring immigrants in against the cultural change that their
presence provokes. They worry about whether their country will be rec-
ognizable if the native born stop having kids and immigrants continue
to have large families. The wealthy countries of the European North
have less historical experience with immigration and a far more generous welfare state to assist the newcomers in their midst. Yet in recent
years, as incidents of political violence (including the assassination of
public officials by Muslim extremists) have increased, Scandinavian citizens have also become more wary of the newcomers.

Conservatives see in the immigrants a permanent foreign presence that will never assimilate and should not be given a chance. Immigration should be shut off, closed down; those already present, sent home. Liberals in the Nordic countries are more tolerant of immigrants, but the appreciation for multiculturalism that is a hallmark of the Left and center in the United States is less conspicuous in Europe, hence the policy emphasis has drifted toward increasing educational opportunities that will speed assimilation: language classes, preschool for immigrant children, and ordinances that forbid particular kinds of dress that marks Muslim women by obscuring their faces. Liberals worry out loud that the generosity of the welfare state has promoted social segregation and the growth of a permanent immigrant underclass.

Henrik, the schoolteacher from Copenhagen, has seen the student body change from predominantly native-born Danes to mostly immigrants:

> In this area, there used to be only Danes, but each time there is a war in Bosnia or Somalia or Iraq or Iran . . . there is an inflow of people. It very much depends on the wars. There are a lot of Palestinians and Bosnians and Afghans, because there are also wars there. People come from all the places where the world is on fire.
>
> In Denmark, [we have taken] a very gentle approach toward immigrants that enter the country; there hasn't been very many demands. You have given them a service, but you haven't gotten anything in return. I think there is more focus on that aspect now. Rather than just giving them some sort of pacifying welfare allowance, they should be given a job as quickly as possible, and [we should] teach them to provide for themselves and give them some responsibilities rather than just making them passive. There are a lot of immigrants in this area, and people are afraid it will turn into a ghetto. There has been made [an] attempt to start some activities, but then maybe 300,000 [Danish kroner are] spent [on] some sort of project; this doesn't change anything. It is a long process.

Hans, the MP for the moderate party in Sweden, also made a connection between immigrant assimilation and unemployment by pointing out the relationship between the structural location of immigrants in the economy and the culture they develop. He laments the way in which a "combination of under-the-table work and social welfare becomes accepted. This has even more serious consequences if you're born abroad. A child who grows up with virtually no one in their surroundings with a normally paid job eventually gets a totally screwed up idea of how things should be."

Pym Fortuyn, a Dutch politician who trained as a sociologist, articulated these fears in an attack on Islam as a "backward culture" and advocated closing Dutch borders to Muslim immigrants. Fortuyn was assassinated during the 2002 Dutch national election,[13] but his campaign clearly had its effect. In his country, the People's Party for Freedom and Democracy, staunch opponents of immigration, pushed through legislation that restricts asylum admissions, welfare payments, and citizenship and residency permits for reasons of family unification. Those under twenty-five who marry foreigners no longer have the right to bring their spouses into the country.[14]

This reaction isn't fully explained by tensions in the labor market, for the Netherlands has weathered the challenges of globalization relatively well, as when compared to Spain or Italy. There is virtually no evidence of accordion families in their midst precisely because their youth can still find a place in the labor market and have ample state support for residential independence. Instead, as is the case elsewhere in Scandinavia, they are witnessing a profoundly reactionary rejection of multiculturalism. In a country where, as the Swedish sociologist Åke Daun puts it, "people like being like each other," there is evidence of extreme exhaustion with immigration.

Journalist Christopher Caldwell writes:

Swedes tell pollsters they want no more asylum-seekers. (A common complaint is that prospective arrivals have figured out how to "game" the rules of asylum applications and that the best way to render one's story unchallengeable under the law is to destroy one's identity papers.) A very low rate of mixed marriage is an indication that Swedes may not have been crazy about this immigration in the first place.[15]

Assimilation or Expulsion?

Given the problems in labor markets outside the Nordic sphere, the anti-immigrant movement can be understood as a reaction to economic crisis. The right wing in Italy has pounced on these woes to stir up racial tension over the African migrants landing on their shores. The Northern League launched "Operation White Christmas" in November 2009 to scrutinize the papers of the entirety of one community's foreign population. Those whose residence permits had expired six or more months before and could not prove that they had attempted to renew them were kicked out of the town (and, presumably, the country). The Northern League member and councilor in charge of security for the town (which is an hour's drive from Milan), Claudio Abiendi, commented on the timing of the policy to *La Repubblica* newspaper: "For me Christmas isn't the holiday of hospitality, but rather that of the Christian tradition and of our identity."[16]

Even in the more prosperous countries of Western Europe, the problems attending assimilation are sparking unnerving levels of ethnocentrism and cultural conflict. In November 2010, a prominent member of the German central bank, Thilo Sarrazin, published a book proclaiming the inferiority of Muslim migrants and stoking fears that the country will be overrun by an alien population. The *New York Times*'s coverage of this story reminded many readers of the last time Germans focused their ire on a despised ethnic group with the headline "With Words on Muslims, Opening a Door Long Shut":

> Mr. Sarrazin's latest blunt assessment came in the form of his book, "Germany Does Away With Itself," which was released in August and provoked a heated national debate that has still not cooled. . . .
>
> In a population of about 82 million, there are about four million Muslims (a number he said he calculated partly by looking at census figures for families with lots of children. Big families must be Muslim, he concluded). Within 80 years, he said, Muslims will make up a majority in Germany.
>
> Second, Mr. Sarrazin believes that intelligence is inherited, not nurtured, and since Muslims are less intelligent (his conclusion)

than ethnic Germans, the population will be dumbed down (his conclusion).

Third, to solve a growing demographic problem, Germany will require immigrants, but he says that bringing more Muslims into the country will only make matters worse. He says that after examining three indicators—success in education and employment, and welfare dependency—he concluded that Islam is by its nature a drag on individual success.[17]

Sarrazin's book has sold more than a million copies.

The Nordic countries have long prided themselves on tolerance and egalitarianism. They were the haven for Jews attempting to escape the Nazi maw during World War II and have opened their doors to migrants from North Africa and Indonesia who are, on average, less educated and certainly less wealthy than the average Dane or Swede. But these countries, too, seem to be questioning the wisdom of this generosity and the advisability of multiculturalism. The change has been so swift and on such a scale that even a country like Sweden is showing signs of strain. Caldwell writes:

> Sweden has suddenly become as heavily populated by minorities as any country in Europe. Of 9 million Swedes, roughly 1,080,000 are foreign-born. There are between 800,000 and 900,000 children of immigrants, between 60,000 and 100,000 illegal immigrants, and 40,000 more asylum-seekers awaiting clearance. The percentage of foreign-born is roughly equivalent to the highest percentage of immigrants the United States ever had in its history (on the eve of World War I). But there are two big differences. First is that, given the age distribution of the native and foreign populations, the percentage of immigrants' offspring will skyrocket in the next generation, even if not a single new immigrant arrives, and even if immigrant fertility rates fall to native-born levels. But second, when America had the same percentage of foreign-born, many had arrived decades before, and were largely assimilated.[18]

Mauricio Rojas has emerged as an important voice in Sweden's small, free-market Liberal People's Party. A professor of economic history at the University of Lund, Rojas has raised some issues unsettling to those long accustomed to Sweden's laissez faire culture. In 2004, he completed a nationwide study that showed 136 areas where labor-market participation was under 60 percent—and he wants to remove certain of the subsidies that make such conditions possible. "No one is going to live here without working," he said. "I told immigrant groups, 'If we come to power, seven o'clock Monday morning, it's off to work.' His Liberal party also urged Swedish-language tests for foreigners."[19]Rojas's sentiments are shared, increasingly, throughout the Nordic countries. But they still come as a shock to those accustomed to the old Scandinavia, where legislatures rarely imposed rules on inhabitants that would be regarded as intrusive or harsh. The temperature of the debate is alarming to some, including those who openly acknowledge the need for immigrants even as they also recognize the difficulty of integrating them.

Greta, the Danish woman we met in chapter 4, says: "We have to be careful not to throw people out [of the country] 'cause we need them, too. I don't think we should receive more immigrants, but we have to treat the ones we have well. I think you should treat all people kind. If all this violence carries on, then in a few years it will become extremely awful to live here [in Denmark]."

Greta believes that Danes should provide for immigrants, but she remains wary of them. When violent crime intrudes into her world, they are the first people she thinks about: "It may be the people who come to Denmark. It isn't that we should blame the dark; we shouldn't. But two-thirds of the criminals are immigrants; but we [Danes] aren't free of blame either."

Unlike Americans, who tend to see the integration of immigrants into American culture as the job of immigrants themselves, the Scandinavians understand it primarily as the role of the government. Greta sees it as a state obligation to provide for immigrants while they are in Denmark and to arrange for them to depart. "When they live [in Denmark], they don't have the capacity to save money," she says. "So the state has to give them money so then [they] can manage when they go back."

Sven is sixty-two years old and has been divorced for fifteen years. He is a senior lecturer in Italian studies at the university in Göteborg and has lived there for about nine years. Sven very much dedicates himself to his work; when he is not lecturing, he works as a translator and has his own translation company. Like Greta, Sven does not blame immigrants for the failure to integrate, nor does he think it is entirely their job to do so. All roads lead to the state:

> There are obviously very many immigrants here in Sweden, for bet-ter or for worse, and the sad thing is that the authorities have not managed to see to it that most immigrants get jobs and get an edu-cation, et cetera, et cetera. I argue that the Swedish authorities have failed at integrating immigrants and making sure their children get a proper education and schooling, too, for that matter. And that means then that there is a large group of immigrants in Sweden, both immigrants and their children, which simply have not adapted to Swedish conditions.
>
> I have seen, living here in Göteborg, how gangs are formed, juvenile gangs with immigrant boys and maybe immigrant girls. And I remember from my time in Malmö and Lund and such [that] Swedes don't behave that way.
>
> This whole giant, complex issue, it is a big problem that has not been solved, and it needs to be solved in the future in order not to continue to cause conflicts, racial conflicts.
>
> We have close to 15 percent of the population now immigrants or children of immigrants, and I think no European country has such a high percentage. I believe England has about 10 percent, for example.

In recent years, as incidents of political violence have increased, Scandinavian citizens have become more wary of the newcomers in their midst. It's not that they are opposed to immigration per se. What they want to end is the enclave phenomenon: the segregation of immi-grants into their own neighborhoods, the failure of second-generation children to learn Swedish or Danish, and the lapsing into the arms of the welfare state that seems to be the fate of many immigrants barred from the formal labor market.

The cultural distance between the socially liberal societies of the Nordic countries and the conservative, traditional communities from which so many Muslim immigrants in Europe come does not make the integration task a simple matter, even in a tolerant state.[20]

Camitta Kiersted grew up in a small town south of Aarhus, and she and her boyfriend now live together in a nearby suburb. She has a university degree in anthropology and European studies, and is currently unemployed. When asked what she thinks the biggest social problem is in Denmark today, she points to immigration, partly because of the conservative attitudes of the newcomers, but even more so because of what their presence brings out in her fellow Danes. According to her, it's not a pretty picture:

> The public debate about immigrants [is a real problem]. I think [the] debate might go completely off track as it did . . . in Paris. There are forces inside the Muslim world that are really anti-democratic, I mean crazy. And that shouldn't happen without notice being taken, there must be done something about this.
>
> On the other side in this debate, Denmark is totally way out. Instead of asking people what they would like to do, [the authorities] put up demands that should be met. This is a very mild example. I mean [they are] giving [immigrants so little that] they can hardly live.

Having experienced bouts of unemployment, Camitta is familiar with what it feels like to be on the receiving end of welfare services in Denmark. As the country has become more conservative, wary of the long-term unemployed, the native born have felt that sharper end of the stick. Yet this is mild by comparison to what immigrants experience when they line up for welfare benefits.[21] Camitta shares:

> What happens to me is nothing compared to what immigrants go through. The way the unemployment service [responds in] their letters is very threatening, telling you what will happen if you don't show up to your appointments. The threats are lurking under the surface all the time.
>
> Only it is worse [for immigrants who are under] suspicion all the time. The [unemployment insurance] is almost impossible to

survive on. And at the same time, you have to be available for the labor market. This is people at the bottom of society; these people have to take all kinds of hard jobs at late hours. Nobody asks the person what the person would like to do.

I remember a few years ago when there was a lack of doctors in Odense. A meeting was held where everybody [among the immigrant population] who was a doctor was asked to come and get help so that they could be integrated in the Danish medical force. People were surprised how many doctors showed up. It just surprises me that you don't register the skills of people when they enter the country. You just place everyone in the same lowest-level language class and leave them on their own to become taxi drivers, even though they might be doctors or engineers. It is a complete wrong way to go about things.

Katja, twenty-five, lives in an Aarhus apartment with seven other students. She has recently finished four years of training at a teachers college and has lined up her first teaching job. Katja is also a musician and plays in her own band. She shares with Camitta the sense that the immigration debate is having a corrosive impact on Danish society:

At the moment, immigrants are very much classified as being ethnically different from us. I think this prevents people to look upon other people as human beings. We just look at people and say, you are an Arab; we can't use you for anything. We still have the problem [in Denmark] that you can't get a job if your name is Muhammad.

Social conflict runs in both directions. The native born eye the immigrants with suspicion and, in Katja's view, the second generation—the children of immigrants—can feel the loathing and respond in kind:

It has very much been discussed how we can integrate them into the labor market. They started liking [Danish] society and want to participate and be good citizens and be a part of society. If you don't take part in society and are spit on in the face, then of course you don't desire to contribute to society and you just think that other people are assholes.

Incendiary attitudes of this kind led to a long-simmering spate of riots in the *banlieu*—the Parisian suburbs—as segregated youth of North African descent lashed out throughout France, burning cars, trashing shops, and marauding in the streets and subways. Banished to the outskirts of the city, lacking any means of fitting in, whether in school or the work world, the children of Algerian and Moroccan immigrants let it be known that they had had enough. In Katja's view, Aarhus may not be far behind. Denmark is growing its own segregated, malcontent second generation, as well as an ugly form of Danish nationalism that has no space for diversity.

Katja is a schoolteacher, and she sees that new generation up close. She cannot escape the sense that they are growing up in a different world than the one in which she did. Their home life is, she thinks, disorderly and rough, which means they start out with too many handicaps to be able to blend seamlessly into the Danish world:

> In the elementary school, there [have also] been problems. Here in Aarhus, [in immigrant ghetto schools,] they have relied on the educational strategy they used to practice in the past, where focus was constantly directed at the things the pupils can't do. "You don't know how to spell, learn how to." And these [immigrant] kids don't have a lot of skills, and they really have a lot of trouble, they aren't [properly] fed. They really get crappy food [at home], so they can't concentrate. They have thirteen siblings and parents that are mentally unbalanced and have post-traumatic stress syndrome.
>
> And this is where something should be done, there should be more money given to these schools to make sure that [the kids] get fed properly and so they can stay awake, so that they don't fall asleep or get hyper. A lot of kids get hyper because they get too much sugar. The methods of teaching should be rethought. How could the schools raise the self-esteem of the pupils so the pupils won't end up hating Danes and authorities? So they don't become angry young people that go out and get into trouble like all other people with low self-esteem do.
>
> [I]n general, in this process of globalization, we have to look upon people with other cultures in a more sophisticated manner. That they have other beliefs. We have relics from the age of colo-

nization, about how other races are inferior. It said in the books of history that they were monkeys, the other [races].

These sentiments about the lack of immigrant integration are echoed by some in the Southern European countries as well. Stefano Astore, twenty-six, would agree with Camitta that the biggest problem with immigrants has little to do with their behavior and everything to do with how fellow Italians react to the presence of anyone who is a little different. Stefano lives near Milan with his parents and sister. He did not go to university, but he has worked steadily since he left school at the age of sixteen. Even so, he cannot afford to live on his own. In some settings, that might lead him to blame immigrants for his economic difficulties. Instead, he blames his fellow countrymen for their ignorance: "Immigration is another problem because people become intolerant toward other people, and there's a lot of racism, especially among those people that don't have enough culture to understand that the melting pot is a richness for society."

The dominant tone of the debate in Spain seems to belong to those who believe that the immigrants are a permanent foreign presence that will never assimilate and should not be given a chance. Take Elena, the married mother of three, whose twenty-five-year-old son lives at home with her in Madrid. Elena thinks of herself as a liberal. After all, one of her daughters is a social worker employed by the Refugee Department of the Red Cross. Still, Elena believes that "too many people are coming in, and it is a problem [politicians] have to tackle because it is going beyond their control." Others are less harsh in their views but still express fear of immigrants and are not sure exactly where to place the blame for what they perceive as their bad behavior. Some blame the immigrants themselves, while others blame the state. Most seem to blame a combination of the two.

Conclusion

Migration has long been a feature of the Mediterranean world, but the emergence of the European Union accelerated the trends. As long as the economies were growing and the progression of native-born youth into the labor market was smooth, the absorption of hundreds of thousands of culturally distinctive families was a minor matter. The eruption of budget deficits, rising unemployment, and housing shortages (relative to the demand), created tensions that exacerbated underlying distrust of the newcomers and fueled the ascendance of far-right political parties that had long simmered on the sidelines.

These tensions have emerged in countries with a pronounced trend toward accordion families (like Spain and Italy) and in societies where youth independence remains the norm. Japan is so antagonistic toward the idea of immigration that it has almost none and hence is a rapidly aging society, in which birth rates have declined sharply, and no one is there to fill in the gaps as immigrants have in the United States or Western Europe. Japan escapes the rising anger directed at "the other," only to turn the same kind of frustration toward its own youth. In all of these instances, globalization has set off problems of intergenerational downward mobility, stagnation in labor markets, and fiscal pressures that threaten the safety net. Where immigrants are available to shoulder some of the blame, they find themselves the target of reactionary politics or cultural frustration. There is no direct line between the accordion family and immigration, but the dismay that follows blocked opportunity and disappointment lands on the outsider, whether defined as a Japanese freeter or a Moroccan youth unwelcome in Denmark.

The Messy Politics
of the Accordion Family

GLOBALIZATION IS HERE TO STAY. Increasingly, we see competitive pressures building across the lines of nation-states, forces compromising the options of the generation of young people in the developed world in their twenties and thirties. They have seen labor markets close their doors to their ambitions or open just enough to generate insecure, part-time jobs at modest wages. The maelstrom of globalization is also provoking major changes in the social structure of advanced nations. Everywhere, competition is bearing down on all but the wealthiest citizens. Everywhere, governments are faced with declining tax receipts and ever-greater costs, especially in aging societies. Pension expenditures are rising, medical costs are burgeoning, and the demographic decline in countries like Japan and Italy shows no sign of reversal, threatening productivity. Yet the common conditions provoked by global competition have not produced uniform responses. Accordion families are sprouting in large numbers in some places and have barely emerged in others.

In the United States, the cost of higher education, an essential gateway to middle-class professions, has escalated well beyond inflation and, more significantly, beyond the means of most American families. This alone has contributed to an increase in the proportion of students who live at home rather than go away to college. Our European cousins may be in for a similar shock, as the austerity measures imposed in the wake of the financial crisis of 2008 may well require increasing tuition beyond anything previously seen. British students have already had a taste of this medicine as the newly empowered Conservative government has announced savage cuts to higher education budgets. Faced with shutting down entirely or raising tuition, those universities that believe they can exact fees similar to American private universities are rapidly moving in that direction. Those that cannot command tuition at that level are unlikely to survive. Either way, a university education is about to become more costly for British students. Since similar austerity measures are on the way throughout the European Union, it is probably just a matter of time before millions of households come face-to-face with additional financial pressures of the kind that have already accelerated the growth of accordion families.

Social-service budgets and public employees of every stripe are also on the chopping block. These are organized, unionized sectors in Europe, and they have responded by sending their members to the barricades. Pitched battles have broken out on the streets of several European capitals. Fifty thousand students marched on London in November 2010. French workers, outraged at the idea that the retirement age would be shifted from sixty to sixty-two in order to cut pension costs, brought the roads and bridges to a total standstill the same month. Riots wracked Athens and violent protests escalated into letter bombs sent to politicians proposing budget cuts. And this is at just the beginning of a restructuring aimed at reducing deficits.

In this climate, we can expect a boom time for the accordion family. As labor markets become more strained, wages fall, and higher education and job training become less accessible, the pathways to adulthood become that much harder to pilot. Where are today's twenty- and thirty-somethings going to take refuge? In the weak welfare states of countries like Spain, Italy, and Japan, it is a safe bet that they will continue to live with their parents. The trend has been growing in the United States as well, and we can expect it to continue as long as the underlying economic conditions contributing to it gather force. Our young people will have few other options.

For the middle class, the accordion family represents both a haven in the heartless world of market pressures and a springboard to a more prestigious future. Young people can take shelter and save money, earn an advanced degree, or snap up an internship that pays nothing but adds to the credentials necessary for professional success in the future. For working-class and poor people, the accordion family is less valuable as a launch pad. Instead, survival requires holding onto every wage earner and, where possible, lowering costs by avoiding multiple rents or mortgages. Pooling the resources of extended families—a time-honored strategy familiar to survivors of the Great Depression—is newly relevant to those enduring the Great Recession. The most ambitious and eager millennials in the working class may find their parents insisting that they need to stay, even when they want (and can afford) to leave. These conversations will be particularly stormy in families where retiree health care becomes inaccessible, Medicare is a long way off, and Medicaid inaccessible.

In the weak welfare states of Japan, Italy, and Spain, multigenerational households have become a critical bulwark against intergenerational downward mobility, providing a private safety net underneath a generation (or two) that cannot provide for itself. Governments have done relatively little to cushion the blows of displacement in the labor market for young people, and as the situation has persisted for nearly thirty years (roughly since the mid-1980s), the victims are no longer so young. Instead, they have followed an aberrant pathway toward independence, with long periods of in-house adulthood. Parents adapt to the return or the unbroken presence of their adult children and make the best of it. They often celebrate the intimacy and warmth that they feel when they hold the younger generation close, especially when they think back to the colder, more austere relations they had with their own parents. Enjoying time with their boomerang children without many of the supervisory responsibilities of their teenage years has many benefits, including the sense that they are needed as sources of advice and respected more as equals than as authority figures.

Yet these joys are tempered with an underlying anxiety about the future. One can adapt to a twenty-two-year-old living at home. As age thirty approaches, nervous parents begin to wonder whether in-house adulthood has an expiration date. The more they reckon with the limitations of their budgets and the looming costs of retirement, the less sanguine they can afford to be about the persistent financial dependence of the millennial generation, now many years past what boomer parents have regarded as the normative age of autonomous adulthood. Can the millennials be forever on the parental payroll? In Japan, the wave of freeters created by the labor market restructuring of the 1980s is pushing forty and starting to lean on the pension benefits of their elders. That is a frightening scenario.

At the other end of the spectrum lie the social democracies of Northern Europe. Heavy government investment in the independence of youth has long been the norm in the Nordic countries. Housing subsidies, generous education benefits, unemployment compensation (even for people who have not been in the labor force), universal medical care, training schemes and apprenticeships, and vast tracts of public and rental housing—all of these investments have made it possible for Scandinavian families to avoid the fate that has overtaken their cousins in Southern Europe. We see no signs of the accordion family in the Nordic nations because there is no need for the family to act as a *private* safety net. A very effective *public* safety net is there to cushion the blows of globalization, which are as real for countries like Sweden and Denmark as they are for Portugal or Spain, which do almost nothing to rescue young people from the pressures reducing their life choices. In recent years, the social democracies have become somewhat more conservative, invoking "flexicurity" policies that condition receipt of generous benefits on job training. But compared to the Western European model, the Scandinavian countries remain incredibly generous, with extraordinary levels of redistribution guaranteeing a level of income equality unknown in the rest of the developed world. And they show no signs of developing accordion families. Young people continue to leave home before the age of twenty and are not reliant on their families for support or shelter. If they are unable to make it independently, they have a wide variety of government programs to meet their needs.

To be sure, the Nordic countries have their own social problems. They join their Southern European neighbors in being uneasy about immigration and unsure how to assimilate the newcomers who differ in appearance and religious affiliation from the homogeneous community that once defined nations like Sweden. Moreover, despite the enviable generosity of the European social democracies—largesse that obviates the need for the safety net of the accordion family—disquiet seems to have emerged among Swedes and Danes, at least, unsure whether the emotional bonds that link the generations are strong enough. Yet when it comes to basic economic security and the ability of young Nordics to strike out in new and independent directions, there is little question that the Scandinavian countries are in a league of their own.

The United States is poised—awkwardly—between these two extremes. Our public safety net is stronger than the version we see
in Spain or Japan. We provide more security to the aged and greater
investment in higher education for young people than the weakest welfare states. For all the faults in our housing system, it provides far more
abundant opportunities for rentals and more flexible mortgage practices (even after the tightening brought about by the foreclosure crisis)
than is typically true of countries like Italy. Yet we are a long, long way
from the Nordic model, and hence the economic insecurity that afflicts
our twenty- and thirtysomethings contributes to the growth of the accordion family. Higher education is increasingly expensive, and governments, particularly at the state level, have been withdrawing steadily
from its financial support. While Scandinavian families do not need
to give much thought to covering the costs of a university education
for their children, American parents have to worry about high levels
of debt to make it possible. A recent article pointed out, "Student loan
debt recently surpassed credit card debt. . . . Americans are now sad-
dled with $830 billion in private and federal student loans, compared
with $827 billion in credit card debt."[1] Winning this contest is nothing
to celebrate. While higher education clearly advantages those who can
afford to pursue it, the price tag is climbing so high so fast that it is no
longer clear that it makes sense for millions of young Americans unable
to pay back loans of this magnitude. They may earn more than those
who stop studying after high school but not enough to make it worth
the cost. And if they are on the fence about the matter, the best fence
to sit on is at home.

With unemployment running north of 9 percent in 2009–2010, the
prospects for upward mobility among American youth, while not as
constrained as might be expected in Italy or Spain, is dimmer than it
has been for many years. Parents and adult children are worried about
what the future holds, about whether the millennial generation will
equal, much less surpass, the occupational status and income of the
boomers. To the extent that such a future can be imagined, the accordion family plays an increasingly important role in making a positive
outcome more likely. By banding together under one roof, the price
structure of this kind of extended household enables investments

in credentials and experiences that might be unaffordable if added to the price of independent housing. Accepting young adults back into the fold enables at least middle-class families to support the aspirations of the millennial generation in ways that leave room for the big-ticket item, like a master's degree.

The choice of the "accordion solution" is political, even if it doesn't feel like it. Americans could choose to go the way of the social democracies, placing the burden of youth independence on the state and hence on all taxpaying shoulders. Or we can slice deep, right to the fiscal bone, and cut the deficit by taking away those supports that enable whatever independence or transitional time we provide for young adults. That is the choice, and how we make it will determine whether we end up marching down the path that countries like Spain or Japan have taken or move closer to the Nordic model. In the former direction lies the growth of accordion families; in the latter, continued prospects for adult children to create an independent life.

Thus far, Americans have charted a path that is uneasily in the middle. We have been able to do so, in part, because of another set of political choices. Although hotly contested at times, particularly in a climate of economic uncertainty, our immigration and labor-market policies have saved us from the demographic downturn that is afflicting Japan. Middle-class Americans of all colors and national origins have seen fertility decline sharply, an outcome, although not caused by accordion families, that is certainly accompanied by delayed marriage and prolonged residence in the natal home. But because we do take in millions of immigrants, both legally and illegally, we are able to replenish the national population. We are an aging society as well, but we are nowhere near as "gray" as Japan or Spain. Our productivity is at very high levels (for all kinds of reasons). Yet the increasing reliance on poorly educated immigrants does pose problems for our economic future, especially if we strip our public schools of the capacity to assimilate them through quality education. The workforce of the future will not experience success if we do not invest in it.

The weak welfare states like Italy and Japan will need to find ways to convince their people to work many more years than they are used to or invent ways of becoming massively more productive with an aging workforce. If they are unable to reach those goals, then the need to open the gates to more immigrants will become increasingly urgent. So, too, will the Scandinavian countries need to find a way to smooth the pathway to assimilation, to open their labor markets—which tend to be restricted—and let in the immigrants. This is the way to survive without pockets of hypersegregation and growing unrest among the native born and immigrants alike. As long as they maintain a strong welfare state, the Scandinavian countries will not see the growth of accordion families but will reap the consequences of social distance and an increasingly large population of second-generation migrants who are socially isolated.

Across the board, no matter which direction we turn, the problem of managing an aging society presents itself as a matter of great urgency. The accordion family helps smooth the way for working-age adults and their not-too-old parents. When those parents do indeed become "old old" or the resources they have to help the millennials are hoarded to care for themselves in their declining years, this solution will no longer work. Vladimir Belova, a financial consultant from Russia who settled in Newton twenty-one years ago, is all too aware of what this kind of bind will mean. He says he is caught in between, caring for both his mother and his adult children:

My mother is ninety-two, and I still have to take care of her, and I take care of my children. It also gives me idea[s] of what I should do for myself to make sure that my children will not face the same situation. People forty-five and older should start to think about how they are going to age gracefully and not create a problem for their children. But the children should understand what they should do to make sure that they are helping parents to make the right decision at a certain age, too.

So people didn't live as long before, and people would die. People could live twenty-five or thirty years over time. But people didn't think about it; they [thought] that somebody is going to take care of them. But nobody is going to take care of them, and that is one of the problems we are facing today.

And that is one of the problems young people are facing today. They are [accustomed] to living comfortably, and at some point, all of a sudden, they have to take care of their parents because their parents did not think about the fact that sooner or later they would need some help. And someone has to help them. So I believe that there [are] future consequences for their families if they don't do certain things.

Those "future consequences" are not so easily resolved, particularly if we leave families to their own devices. On their own, they can only support so many generations on the stable salary of the middle generation, and that solution—the accordion family—is only temporarily workable.

The messy politics of the accordion family remain unresolved, both here and abroad. They are enmeshed in the same inequalities that beset the advanced economies of the Western world. Those at the top of the economic heap can afford to purchase a high-quality education for their children, support them as they experiment with internships and international travel, connect them to occupational opportunities, and shelter them from the storm of globalization. Those in the middle can follow suit but at considerable cost to the future retirement security of the boomer generation. And for the millennials, the jury is out. What becomes of them is as much a matter of what the economy provides in the way of opportunity and what we decide we owe them as citizens, future parents, and providers. These are not simply natural outcomes. They are expressions of social solidarity, given shape in the governments we elect and the policies they enact. We know this by looking at the range of variation visible from Japan or Spain on one end to Sweden on the other. These polar opposites represent options decided in a deliberate fashion. Straddling the middle ground, the United States can look to the weak welfare states and see the liabilities that emerge when families are left to fend largely for themselves or we can shift our attention toward the strong welfare states of Northern Europe to see what can be done, and at what cost, to insure the orderly transition of the generations.

GATHERING THE ETHNOGRAPHIC INTERVIEWS for a book of this scope was no small task. Altogether, three hundred people in six countries were interviewed for it, roughly half parents and half adult children. The project began in the summer of 2006 in Italy, Spain, and Japan, three countries with the most pronounced growth of accordion families. It expanded to include Sweden and Denmark during the same time period because these two advanced, post-industrial economies show virtually no evidence of this household configuration. Finally, the United States was added a year later, largely because it lies in the middle of this continuum. It strings a stronger safety net underneath its citizens than Italy or Japan but falls very far short of the social democracies of the Nordic countries.

A project of this magnitude required the dedicated help of colleagues who are native speakers of the appropriate languages, who had the capacity to dig into the lives of people they didn't know personally and insure that we learned about some of the most intimate problems they contend with inside their families. I was fortunate to recruit several members of my research team at the European University Institute in Fiesole (Italy), a graduate institution of social science and historical research that serves the European Union. Through the EUI, I found Emanuela Zilio (Italy), Maria Gomez Garrido (Spain), and Katarina Andersson (Sweden), recent doctorates willing to join me in this exploration. Denmark is not well represented at the EUI, so I turned to my colleague the political scientist Christoffer Green-Pedersen at Aarhus University, who put me in touch with Marie Kappel (Denmark), who was studying under him at the time. Noriko Matsumoto, PhD candidate in the Department of Sociology at the City University of New York, is a native of Japan who had not been home in seven years at the time I asked her to help me with the Japanese interviews.

The U.S. interviews were all conducted in Newton, Massachusetts, by Princeton doctoral student Michael Schlossman. I selected this state because, unique among the fifty states, it requires an annual household census that lists the ages and names of all residents of every household. This makes it possible to deduce accordion families by looking for households with parents in their fifties and sixties and children with the same last name aged twenty-two to thirty-two years old. We were able to find parent-child pairs for most of the American interviews.

These six scholars devoted nearly a year locating our interview participants, speaking with them at length, translating the interviews, and corresponding with me to develop many of the ideas represented here. The interviews they conducted were drawn as a "convenience sample." I instructed my team to select, wherever possible, parents and adult children in the same families so that we would learn something about the dynamics of accordion families. This was not always possible, but it worked well in Spain, Italy, and the United States. It was a complete failure in Japan. Japanese parents and adult children have very private and sometimes raw feelings about their circumstances. They were not comfortable with the idea that interviews would be conducted from within families, even if we insured (as we always did) that they would be private and confidential. We had to respect this constraint; hence, the interviews from our Japanese informants are almost never drawn from parent-and-child dyads. Sweden and Denmark fell somewhere between these extremes. We do have many sets of interviews from multiple generations within the same families, especially in Denmark, but not as much as we did in Italy, where these are uniformly pairs. My team fanned out all around their respective countries as they were asked not to rely exclusively on the capital cities but to get a feeling for the rural regions, families along the class spectrum, and the divergent arrangements of households. In Italy, Spain, and Japan, more than two-thirds of our interviews were with people living in accordion families, while one-third were not. The reverse is the case in Denmark and Sweden. Most of the American interviews were done with parents and in-house adults rather than autonomous youth.

The fieldwork generated more than a thousand pages of interview transcripts and many other data sources drawn from popular culture sources ranging from magazines to TV programs to websites. Analyzing a massive corpus of this kind required the intense devotion of my postdoctoral scholar, Hella Winston, over a period of eighteen months. This book would not exist were it not for Hella's contributions. Many of the ideas here came from conversations we shared in weekly meetings throughout that period. I am entirely in her debt.

I AM EXTREMELY grateful to my research team for the devotion they gave to this project and for sharing my enthusiasm for exploring the ideas developed here. They are and remain committed to the proposition that there is a great deal to learn from comparative work of this kind and that the sensitivity that comes from reliance on homegrown native speakers is well worth the effort.

Scholars are dependent on a like-minded community for thoughtful criticism. A number of them stepped up at the last minute to give me their reactions and made it a stronger piece of work. I am especially grateful to my new colleague at Johns Hopkins University, Andrew Cherlin, and our fellow sociologists in the department. As one of the nation's premier demographers and sociologists of the family, Andy gave me extremely helpful feedback. Jill Suitor, professor of sociology at Purdue University, first invited me to give a public talk based on this research and followed up by reading the book from end to end. Many valuable ideas that began with Jill ended up on these pages. Arlene Skolnick, a well-recognized authority on the family, helped me think through some of the more vexing conceptual issues in *The Accordion Family*. Caitlin Cross-Barnet, who took her PhD in sociology at Johns Hopkins, has worked with me steadily since my arrival at the university and did a good deal of the research presented in the footnotes. I snapped up her ideas on gender differences in the accordion family just as soon as she mentioned them. She has my thanks for seeing me across the finish line.

This book was supported by funds from Princeton University's Woodrow Wilson School of Public and International Affairs in the form of the faculty research account I had during my tenure there (2004–2010). I am grateful to all of my former colleagues in the school and in the Department of Sociology for everything they did to make my years at Princeton such a joy. Special mention should go to the staff and faculty I worked with during my years as the director of the Princeton Institute for International and Regional Studies, which was my home during my final years at Princeton, the period when I did most of the work represented here.

My agent, Lisa Adams, and my editor, Gayatri Patnaik, gave me extremely helpful feedback, not to mention their moral and organizational support for this book. To my friends at Beacon Press, my thanks for giving my work a home. And to all of my new colleagues at Johns Hopkins, particularly my vice deans, Judy Babbitts, Greg Ball, Steven David, Kellee Tsai, and Ben Vinson; colleagues Fred Puddester, Sylvia Eggleston Weir, Ilene McCoy, Alicia Haley, and Dick Kilburg; and the university's leadership, Provost Lloyd Minor and President Ron Daniels, I offer my thanks for the welcome I have received and the toleration every one of them has shown for my desire to remain an active scholar, mainly late at night.

As always, I remain grateful and fulfilled by the support of my husband, fellow sociologist Paul Attewell, and our children, Steven (age twenty-eight) and David (age twenty-two), who started their lives tangled around my ankles when I tried to get my writing done and now as young adults count as among my most insightful readers and critics.

This book is dedicated to one of my most treasured friends, Kathleen McDermott. We met in graduate school at the University of California, Berkeley, where she was the spark that lit the fire for so many of our mutual friends. We came together many years later at Columbia University, where she remained a beloved colleague among faculty and administrators, long after I left for other places. I can safely say that I have never known anyone to touch so many lives, to extend such a caring hand when she had more than enough to contend with in her own life. To Kathleen, I express my thanks and the gratitude of hundreds of faculty, students, and friends for everything that she has done for us.

INTRODUCTION

1. Richard Owen, "Saying Ciao to Mamma," *Sunday Times* (UK), February 3, 2003, http://women.timesonline.co.uk/tol/life_and_style/women/families/article862310 .ece.

2. Nick Pisa, "'Ban Over-18s from Living with Mum and Dad,' Proposes Italian Cabinet Minister . . . Who Lived at Home until He Was 30," *Daily Mail Online* (UK), January 18, 2010, http://current.com/1ibj44c.

3. See J. Cox and M. Schilling, "Lifetime Jobs: End of an Era? High Unemployment, Sour Economy Jeopardize Japanese Workers," *USA Today*, June 9, 1995.

4. See Hiroko Toda, "Lifetime Employment System Over?" *Daily Yomiuri* (Japan), September 7, 2001, http://article.wn.com/view/2001/09/07/Lifetime_employment _system_over/.

5. M. Memmott, "Japanese, in Slowdown, Start Layoffs," *USA Today*, August 20, 1992.

6. "4,000 Layoffs at Nissan," *Gazette* (Montreal), August 29, 1992.

7. "Fujitsu to Cut Staff by 6,000," *Financial Post* (Toronto), July 16, 1993.

8. Paul Wiseman and Naoko Nishiwaki, "Japan Offers a Lifetime Job, If Hired Right out of School," *USA Today*, March 6, 2009, http://www.usatoday.com/community/ tags/reporter.aspx?id=949: "During the sluggish '90s, Japanese companies, seeking ways to cut costs and regain their competitive edge, started turning to part-timers, contract employees and workers dispatched from temporary agencies. Non-regular employees now make up more than 34% of the Japanese workforce, an all-time high and up from less than 17% in 1985, according to the Ministry of Internal Affairs and Communications."

9. Jeff Israely, "In Italy, a Mamma Accused of Doting Too Much," *Time*, October 21, 2009, http://www.time.com/time/world/article/0,8599,1931216,00.html.

CHAPTER 1: THE SLIPPERY STATE OF ADULTHOOD

1. There are coming-of-age rituals in other industrialized nations, but many have a religious connection, and the ritual occurs in early-to-mid-adolescence, long before what would now be considered the onset of adulthood. Examples include the Jewish bar or bat mitzvah, usually conducted at age thirteen, and Catholic confirmation, usually conducted at age fourteen. Other coming-of-age rituals include the *quinceanera*, a Latin American celebration for girls that is increasingly popular in the United States, and secular confirmations that replaced religious ones in Nordic countries; both of these types occur at age fifteen.

2. Karin L. Brewster and Ronald R. Rindfuss, "Fertility and Women's Employment in Industrialized Nations," *Annual Review of Sociology* 26 (2000): 271–96, http://www.jstor.org/pss/223445; "Japan Total Fertility Rate," IndexMundi, http://www.indexmundi.com/japan/total_fertility_rate.html. Japanese women have increasingly been avoiding or postponing marriage and childbearing, in part because of the limits marriage places on their life options. Women in Japan show an M-shaped pattern in their work participation: rates peak for women in their early twenties and late forties, with a long dip in between. Women in Japan take more time out of the labor force for child rearing than do women in most other industrialized nations. The average number of children per woman has decreased from 2.1 children in the 1960s to 1.2 in 2010.

3. Barbara Reskin and Patricia Roos, *Job Queues and Gender Queues: Explaining Women's Inroads into Male Occupations* (Philadelphia: Temple University Press, 1990); "Statistics and Data: Quick Stats on Women Workers, 2009," U.S. Department of Labor Women's Bureau, http://www.dol.gov/wb/stats/main.htm; "Fast Facts," National Center for Education Statistics, http://nces.ed.gov/fastfacts/display.asp?id=72. In 1890, in the United States, women in the paid workforce were almost all young and unmarried. Only 5 percent of married women worked in occupations. As modern technology decreased the labor intensiveness of housekeeping, married women more frequently sought paid work, and by 2009, 59 percent of women sixteen and over were in the labor force. Women represent more than half of workers in higher-paying management and professional positions and are expected to account for more than half of overall labor-force growth in the coming decade.

4. See Richard Settersten Jr. and Barbara Ray, "What's Going On with Young People Today? The Long and Twisting Path to Adulthood," *Future of Children* 20 (2010): 19–41; cited in the *New York Times*, June 11, 2010: "National surveys reveal that an overwhelming majority of Americans, including younger adults, agree that between 20 and 22, people should be finished with school, working and living on their own. But in practice many people in their 20s and early 30s have not yet reached these traditional milestones. Marriage and parenthood—once seen as prerequisites for adulthood—are now viewed more as lifestyle choices, according to a new report released by Princeton University and the Brookings Institution. The stretched-out walk to independence is rooted in social and economic shifts that started in the 1970s, including a change from a manufacturing to a service-based economy that sent many more people to college, and the women's movement, which opened up educational and professional opportunities."

5. See ibid. Other countries are exhibiting similar patterns to the United States, where markers of adulthood commonly include leaving home, finishing school, getting a full-time job, becoming financially independent from one's parents, being able to support a family, marrying, and becoming a parent. In the American post–World War II era, marriage and parenthood were essential markers of adulthood, but in the 2002 General Social Survey, more than 95 percent of respondents said the most important markers were completing school, establishing an independent household, and becoming employed full time. Marriage and parenthood now culminate, rather than initiate, adulthood. In addition, the survey found distinct class differ-

ences, with wealthier respondents more tolerant of later ages for reaching adult markers. Notably, while more than a third of lower-income respondents believed that young adults should marry and have children by age twenty-five, approximately the same number of wealthier adults said marriage and childbearing should be accomplished in one's thirties.

6. Katherine S. Newman and Sofya Aptekar, "Sticking Around: Delayed Departure from the Parental Nest in Western Europe and Japan," in S. Danziger and C. Rouse, eds., *The Price of Independence: The Economics of the Transition to Adulthood* (New York: Russell Sage Foundation Press, 2007).

7. Ibid.

8. Sylvia Nasar, "More College Graduates Taking Low-Wage Jobs," *New York Times,* August 7, 1992, http://www.nytimes.com/1992/08/07/business/more-college -graduates-taking-low-wage-jobs.html; Olivia Crosby and Roger Moncarz, "The 2004–2014 Job Outlook for College Graduates," *Occupational Outlook Quarterly,* Bureau of Labor Statistics, 2006, http://www.bls.gov/opub/ooq/2006/fall/art03.pdf; "Educational Attainment in the United States," U.S. Census Bureau, http://www .census.gov/hhes/socdemo/education/; Lisa Kahn, "The Long-Term Labor Market Consequences of Graduating from College in a Bad Economy," *Labour Econom- ics* 17(2) (April 2010): 303–16 http://mba.yale.edu/faculty/pdf/kahn_longtermlabor .pdf. In the 1960s, only 10 percent of college graduates held jobs that did not re- quire a degree. By the end of the 1980s, that had risen to 25 percent. While college graduates fare better economically than those who do not hold the BA degree, there is increasing competition for the best-paying jobs. In 2006, 28 percent of those twenty-five and older held a bachelor's degree (in the 1950s, fewer than 10 percent did). Employers increasingly wish to hire college graduates for jobs that do not require a college degree. The highest-paying jobs now require advanced degrees, and even lower-paying professional work, such as teaching, may now require post- college education. Graduating in a weak economy can impact career trajectories for decades. Those who graduate from college when economic opportunities are poor are more likely to return to school, but even with the increases in education levels, negative wage effects can persist twenty years later.

9. Reskin and Roos, *Job Queues and Gender Queues;* "Statistics and Data: Quick Stats on Women Workers, 2009," U.S. Department of Labor, http://www.dol.gov/wb/ stats/main.htm. The work world had a sex-segregation index that remained be- tween 65 and 69 percent through 1970 (meaning two-thirds of working men or women would have had to change occupations for the sex ratio to be balanced). Beginning in the 1970s, bolstered by legal protections and cultural shifts, and mo- tivated by feminism and inflation, women began entering a broader range of occu- pations. While professional occupations for women had previously been limited to that of a teacher, librarian, social worker, or nurse, by 2009, more than half of work- ers in higher-paying management and professional positions were female. This cat- egory includes doctors, lawyers, engineers, pharmacists, management analysts, and computer programmers. In 2007–2008, women earned 62 percent of associate's de- grees, 58 percent of bachelor's degrees, 61 percent of master's degrees, and half of first-professional and doctoral degrees. Better-educated women are the most likely

to be employed: among women with a bachelor's degree or more, 73 percent are in the paid workforce.

10. Spengler, "The Day the Slacker Died," *Asia Times* online, June 10, 2008, http://www .atimes.com/atimes/Front_Page/JF10Aa02.html.

11. See J. Arnett, "Adolescent Storm and Stress Reconsidered," *American Psychologist* 54 (1999): 317–26; Michael J. Rosenfeld, *The Age of Independence: Interracial Unions, Same-Sex Unions, and the Changing American Family* (Cambridge, MA: Harvard University Press, 2007); R. Schoeni and K. Ross, "Material Assistance Received from Families During the Transition to Adulthood," in R. A. Settersten Jr. et al., eds., *On the Frontier of Adulthood: Theory, Research, and Public Policy* (Chicago: University of Chicago Press, 2005). The idea of adolescence as a distinct life stage was first developed by G. Stanley Hall in the early 1900s. He characterized this time as one of "storm and stress." Though he believed the tendency toward these was universal and biological, he acknowledged that time, place, and culture impacted expression, with teens in conservative societies less likely to act out than those in the United States. Adolescence is now accepted as a distinct life stage throughout the Western world, with its own psychological and social markers. College attendance has become far more common, further lengthening youth and the period during which young people are expected to be dependent on their parents as a matter of course. As people live longer, another life stage is acknowledged as occurring between adolescence and full adulthood, now frequently referred to as "young adulthood." Young adults have more independence than adolescents and are not marked by the same external "storm and stress" directed at parents, yet they are also not expected to function as full adults, as in previous markers of adulthood such as having stable employment and being married.

12. See "Parents Unaware of How to Help Today's First-Time Buyers," Easier.com, October 13, 2010, http://www.easier.com/78769-parents-first-time-buyers.html. Parental contributions toward—or even outright purchases of—homes for their children are so common that entire websites are devoted to discussing how to obtain financing when parents provide a down payment and how parents can make their contributions toward their children's home purchases tax-deductible. Websites directed toward the younger generation encourage asking for parents' financial assistance with a first home purchase. One European study shows that about a third of parents are willing and able to help finance a child's home purchase. Parents who have the financial resources to offer such help may use home purchases to nudge their children further on the path to adulthood.

13. See Kathryn Edin and Maria Kefalas, *Promises I Can Keep: Why Poor Women Put Motherhood before Marriage* (Berkeley: University of California Press, 2005). There are substantial class-based differences in beliefs about achieving adulthood and in goals young people have toward reaching that status. Edin and Kefalas document the role childbearing plays for young, poor women in Philadelphia. Though these young women have often not finished school, established employment, nor moved out on their own, they are eager to take on the adult role by becoming mothers. Many of these young mothers hope parenthood will push their male partners to "grow up" as well, though most face disappointment in this realm. Among these

young women, childbearing is something to be achieved early rather than post-poned. Interestingly, among these young mothers, marriage is to be postponed until financial stability has been achieved, acting as the culmination of adulthood, much as parenthood seems to function for the middle class.

14. Katherine S. Newman, *No Shame in My Game: The Working Poor in the Inner City* (New York: Knopf, 1999).

15. Read: his wife and children.

16. The 2007 Flash Eurobarometer Youth Survey finds that about 3 percent of young Europeans live at home in order to help support their parents (versus the much larger proportion who live at home in order to be supported by them).

17. In most other countries, family support is the second most common means of in-come. In Italy, family support is the most common form of "income" for twenty- to twenty-nine-year-olds.

18. Although interviewees associate caring about others and the outside world as a mark of adulthood, developmental psychologists indicate that this process begins in early childhood and should be well-formed during adolescence. In Piaget's devel-opmental stages, children begin to lose egocentrism at age two and are fully able to use abstract reasoning in order to express empathy and see beyond the self starting at age twelve. Erik Erikson indicates that developing a strong identity that allows one to see beyond the self is a task for adolescence (identity versus role confusion), while those ages eighteen to thirty-five should be seeking out a life companion and having children (intimacy and solidarity versus isolation). Interestingly, those in the "new" young-adult life stage are often developing intimacy and solidarity but with parents and friends rather than a spouse.

19. Literally "silly soup." The term was used in the old times to refer to the soup given by religious orders to the poor. It was later used to refer to someone who does nothing and is just receiving sustenance from someone else.

20. See E. Almer et al., "A Cross Cultural Analysis of Student Perceptions of Gender Diversity, Family Status and Hiring Practices in Spain and the United States," *Global Perspective on Accounting Education* 2 (2005): 37–51. After the death of Franco, the 1978 Spanish Constitution granted women legal equality, and divorce became legal in Spain in 1981. While this dramatic shift still creates some social tensions, the gov-ernment continues to promote policies to advance the equality of women.

21. A. J. Cherlin, "The Deinstitutionalization of American Marriage," *Journal of Mar-riage and Family* 66 (2004): 848–61; M. Dominguez et al., "European Latecomers: Cohabitation in Italy and Spain," conference presentation, Population Association of America Annual Meeting, New York, March 2007, http://paa2007.princeton.edu/download.aspx?submissionId=71389; Eric D. Widmer et al., "Attitudes toward Non-marital Sex in 24 Countries," *Journal of Sex Research* 35 (1998): 349. Although pre-marital sex is widely accepted in Spain, rates of premarital cohabitation remain much lower than in many other Western countries. In the late 1990s, 63 percent of Spaniards said that premarital sex was "not wrong at all," versus 89 percent in Swe-den but just 44 percent in the United States. Cohabitation, however, is still an avant-garde phenomenon in Spain, while it is commonly accepted as a testing ground for marriage in the United States (where the majority of marriages are now preceded

by cohabitation) and is almost indistinguishable from marriage in Sweden. Unlike in other countries, in Spain (and in Italy) cohabitation has not compensated for the age delay for first marriage, and women in Spain enter their first unions—marriage or cohabitation—at a later age than women in any other European country (with Italy close behind).

22. The death of Franco in November 1975 ushered in a period of transition to democracy that ended in November 1982 with the democratic transfer of power to the Spanish Socialist Workers' Party. In November 1975, Juan Carlos I was proclaimed king and appointed Adolfo Saurez prime minister in 1986. Almost immediately, Suarez rushed through a political reform bill that introduced universal suffrage and a two-chamber parliament, which was endorsed by 94.2 percent of the electorate by referendum. Political parties were legalized and elections held in June 1977. Working with other parties, Suarez and his party managed the transition process, which included drafting and endorsing the 1978 Constitution.

23. It was very common that a family would rent rooms in their house, sometimes with the right to meals.

24. See S. de Sanjose et al., "Age at Sexual Initiation and Number of Sexual Partners in the Female Spanish Population: Results from the AFRODITA Survey," *European Jounal of Obstetrics, Gynecology, and Reproductive Biology* 140 (2005): 234–40; "Average Age at First Sex by Country," ChartsBin.com, http://chartsbin.com/view/xxj. In current times, the average age at first marriage in Spain is twenty-nine, but the average age for first sexual intercourse is nineteen. The majority of Spaniards agree that there is nothing wrong with engaging in premarital sex. In comparison to Spanish women over age fifty-six, Spanish women under age twenty-five were thirty-nine times more likely to have had their first intercourse before age eighteen and—despite being at least thirty years younger—were four times more likely to have had two or more sexual partners.

25. See Almer et al., "A Cross Cultural Analysis." Until 1975 and the death of Franco, the Spanish Civil Code enforced *permiso marital* under Article 57. *Permiso marital* meant that women could not hold a job or open a bank account without the permission of a husband or father.

26. See Widmer et al., "Attitudes toward Nonmarital Sex"; Anastasia Toufexis, Ulla Plon, and Hiroko Tashiro; "Sex Has Many Accents," *Time*, May 24, 1993, http://www.time.com/time/magazine/article/0,9171,978575,00.html. In matters of sex, as in other matters, Japanese parents have shown ambivalence about the increasing freedom of the young. As European parents became more open, Japanese parents remained reserved, even as their tolerance for premarital sexual activity increased. In a cross-national study of attitudes toward sex outside of marriage, answers about the acceptability of premarital sex were generally concentrated in the poles—"always wrong" or "not wrong at all." The Japanese were more than twice as likely than those in any other nation to say that premarital sex was wrong "only sometimes."

27. See M. Brinton, "Social Capital in the Japanese Youth Labor Market: Labor Market Policy, Schools, and Norms," *Policy Sciences* 33 (2000): 289–306. Institutional social

capital in Japan functions in conjunction with personal social capital. Schools have ties with employers who hire directly from the pool of the school's graduates. This creates a structure in which vocational schools feed the lowest tiers of the labor market.

28. See Jim Cullen, *The American Dream: A Short History of an Idea That Shaped a Nation* (New York: Oxford University Press, 2003); Katherine S. Newman, *Declining Fortunes: The Withering of the American Dream* (New York: Basic Books, 1993). In his 1931 book *The Epic of America*, James Truslow Adams characterized the American Dream as a "better, richer, and happier life for all our citizens of every rank." For many years, society seemed to focus on "richer" as the fulfillment of the dream. However, economic changes have made financial advancement harder to obtain, leading to the inability of young people to achieve even their parents' level of success, much less surpass it. An increased emphasis on personal happiness in all aspects of life may be replacing the emphasis on wealth with the dream of personal fulfillment.

29. See Amy Chua, *Battle Hymn of the Tiger Mother* (New York: Penguin, 2011). When an excerpt from Yale law professor Chua's book appeared in the *Wall Street Journal* under the headline "Why Chinese Mothers Are Superior," it set off a firestorm of debate. Chua, who was raised by Chinese immigrant parents, details her own child-rearing methods, which included not allowing sleepovers or playdates, forcing one of her daughters in elementary school to do two thousand math problems per night until she surpassed her Korean competitor, and refusing the gift of her four-year-old's handmade birthday card that she deemed inadequate in effort. Interestingly, the long subtitle of Chua's book is "This is a story about a mother, two daughters, and two dogs. This was *supposed* to be a story of how Chinese parents are better at raising kids than Western ones. But instead, it's about a bitter clash of cultures, a fleeting taste of glory, and how I was humbled by a thirteen-year-old." Certainly Chua's version of events lends credence to Teddy's assessment of Asian immigrant parents and to the culture clash that such parental expectations can engender for children raised in Western society.

30. Richard Alba and Victor Nee, *Remaking the American Mainstream: Assimilation and the New Immigration* (Cambridge, MA: Harvard University Press, 2003); H. J. Gans, "Comment: Ethnic Invention and Acculturation: A Bumpy-Line Approach," *Journal of American Ethnic History* 11 (1992): 42–52; Milton M. Gordon, *Assimilation in American Life: The Role of Race, Religion, and National Origins* (New York: Oxford University Press, 1964); A. Portes and M. Zhou, "The New Second Generation: Segmented Assimilation and Its Variants," *Annals of the American Academy of Political and Social Science* 530 (1993): 74–96. There are many theories of assimilation, and patterns outlined may better apply to some immigrant groups than others. Straight-line assimilation theory, long the predominant theory in immigration literature, assumes that over generations of living in the United States, everyone will eventually assume the same norms and values (see Gordon), but contemporary theorists have questioned this model. Alba and Nee propose that assimilation is a two-way street, with immigrants, native residents, and insti-

tutions gradually adapting to one another. Gans posits that assimilation can take a long time and that immigrants might assimilate in some areas long before others, a process he terms "bumpy assimilation." Portes and Zhou propose that some immigrants will not assimilate to the dominant values of the overall society but to the dominant norms of the neighborhoods in which they settle. Some immigrants might thus experience downward assimilation, a process Portes and Zhou posit will affect non-white immigrants in particular. Of course, the fact that there are large pockets throughout the United States filled with people who have not assimilated to dominant values and norms also indicates that straight-line assimilation has not occurred consistently and that alternate norms and values have long prevailed among subgroups.

31. See "Young Europeans: Survey among Young People Aged between 15–30 in the European Union," Flash Eurobarometer (2007), http://ec.europa.eu/public_opin ion/flash/fl_202_sum_en.pdf. While the majority of European youth either support themselves through full-time work or are primarily supported by their parents or partners, Scandinavian youth frequently cite educational grants as their primary source of income.

CHAPTER 2: WHY ARE ACCORDION FAMILIES SPREADING?

1. Marilyn Gardner, "Adult Children Back in the Nest," *Christian Science Monitor,* February 24, 2009), http://www.csmonitor.com/The-Culture/Family/2009/0224/ p17s01-lifp.html.

2. P. England, "Emerging Theories of Care Work," *Annual Review of Sociology* 31 (2005): 381–99; Nancy Folbre, *The Invisible Heart: Economics and Family Values* (New York: New Press, 2001); *The Global Gender Gap Report 2010,* World Economic Forum, http://www3.weforum.org/docs/WEF_GenderGap_Report_2010 .pdf. While care work is done in the marketplace as well as the home, this work is almost always poorly paid, and work done in the home for family members is rarely compensated directly. Theories abound about the low economic value placed on caregiving work. Folbre asserts that care work produces public goods and that markets consistently rely on altruistic labor to produce such goods. Others say that over time, caregivers become "prisoners of love" who become attached to their charges and continue their labor even when it is not in their economic best interests. The devaluation theory posits that care work is undervalued precisely because it is performed by women, also undervalued. As such, limiting women to caregiving roles was a way to perpetuate patriarchal control. It is noteworthy that, in Nordic countries, the state provides a substantial portion of care work by subsidizing education, housing, health care, and elder care, and also compensating families for a portion of care work, for instance by offering extended, paid parental leave. Changes in the 1990s made a certain portion of parental leave available only to fathers. These policies have been instrumental in generating high levels of gender equity in the Nordic countries, but the research in this book indicates that such policies have also created an overall undervaluation of care at the individual and family levels, a "care gap" that runs inversely to the gender gap.

3.   A. Nishi et al., "Mothers and Daughters-in-Law: A Prospective Study of Informal
     Care-Giving Arrangements and Survival in Japan," *BMC Geriatrics* 29 (2010): 61.
     Daughters-in-law in Japan are second only to spouses as elder-care providers. Stud-
     ies of the health of family-care providers indicate that such caregiving increases
     stress and mortality. In Japan in particular, women living in multigenerational
     households had two to three times the rate of coronary heart disease of similar
     women living with a spouse only. Living arrangements did not change heart dis-
     ease rates for men. The care work performed by daughters-in-law may also take a
     toll on mothers-in-law. Survival analysis indicates that women cared for by their
     daughters-in-law die sooner than women cared for by a biological daughter or
     spouse. Men, however, live longer when cared for by a daughter-in-law than by
     a spouse.

4.   J. Madrick and D. Papanikolaou, "The Stagnation of Male Wages," *Policynote* (May
     2008): 1–9.

5.   Sharon R. Cohany and Emy Sok, "Trends in Labor Force Participation of Married
     Mothers of Infants," *Monthly Labor Review* 130, no. 2 (February 2007), http://www
     .bls.gov/opub/mlr/2007/02/art2full.pdf.

6.   See Martha Holstein and Thomas R. Cole, "The Evolution of Long-Term Care in
     America," in R. H. Binstock et al., eds., *The Future of Long-Term Care: Social and
     Policy Issues* (Baltimore: Johns Hopkins University Press, 1996), 19–47. The devel-
     opment of long-term care and the modern nursing home followed a haphazard
     trajectory in the United States. During the colonial period, elder care was almost
     always provided by family members, with help from the community at large. As im-
     migration increased after the Revolutionary War, community care began to break
     down in order to keep "outsiders" at bay, and new economic opportunities led to
     less sympathy for the needy. Poorhouses were developed with the intent of pun-
     ishing as well as housing the poor, and elders without family members to care for
     them generally had no alternative but to go to these institutions. The Victorian era,
     after 1850, ushered in moral condemnation of those who did not "age well," align-
     ing illness and frailty with moral failure. As social programs emerged for those
     orphaned, able-bodied poor, physically disabled, or mentally ill, the poorhouses be-
     came de facto nursing homes for the elderly indigent. Social Security was intended
     to eliminate almshouses for the elderly, but the lack of universal health insurance
     and the persistence of poverty stymied this intent. The social needs (to work, care
     for children, etc.) of families prevented them from reliably filling the gap, and with
     the need to free hospital beds for the short-term sick, rather than the chronically ill,
     nursing homes began emerging to fill the gap. However, resources for long-term el-
     der care were woefully inadequate. When Medicare and Medicaid offered financial
     resources for nursing-home care, nursing homes became further regulated, which
     in turn led to larger, more bureaucratized facilities. A cycle of increasing regulation
     and bureaucracy emerged, and the uneven quality of nursing-home care remains a
     chronic problem.

7.   *Why Population Aging Matters: A Global Perspective* (Washington, DC: National
     Institute on Aging, National Institutes of Health, U.S. Department of Health and
     Human Services, U.S. Department of State, March 2007), 17. In 1960, close to 90

percent of the population sixty-five and over in Japan lived with a married child or other relative; in 2000, that number had decreased to about 50 percent. In 1960, about 2 percent of the elderly population lived in an institution or with non-relatives. By 2000, that number had approximately tripled to about 6 percent.

8. *The Return of the Multi-Generational Household,* Social & Demographic Trends, Pew Research Center, March 18, 2010, http://pewsocialtrends.org/pubs/752/the-return-of-the-multi-generational-family-household. In 1940, about 25 percent of the U.S. population lived in multigenerational family households. By 1970, that percentage had fallen to about 14 percent. By 1980, it was at about 13 percent; in 1990, 15 percent; in 2000, 15.1 percent; and in 2009, 16.1 percent.

9. The custom in the past was for Japanese women to join the household of their in-laws, but this practice began to disappear some time ago.

10. Israely, "In Italy, a Mamma Accused" (see intro., n. 9).

11. G. Keeley, "Young People Offered Cash to Fly the Nest," *Times of London,* September 20, 2007, 42.

12. F. Govan, "Rising Prices Trap Spanish Young at Home," *Daily Telegraph* (UK), July 28, 2006, July 28.

13. Keeley, "Young People Offered Cash to Fly the Nest."

14. "Share of Single Young Adults Living with Parents, 2005," Network on Transitions to Adulthood, University of Pennsylvania, 2006, http://www.transad.pop.upenn.edu/trends/index.html.

15. Wendy Wang and Rich Morin, "Home for the Holidays . . . and Every Other Day: Recession Brings Many Young People Back to the Nest," *Social & Demographic Trends,* Pew Research Center, November 24, 2009, http://pewresearch.org/pubs/1423/home-for-the-holidays-boomeranged-parents.

16. See *AARP Bulletin,* March 2009. The *Bulletin's* Multigenerational Housing Survey was conducted by International Communications Research Inc. in January 2009. A short telephone survey among a nationally representative sample of adults eighteen and older was conducted to learn more about housing patterns and how respondents' housing situations might change in the next year. The total sample consisted of 1,002 adults.

17. Rosenfeld, *Age of Independence* (see ch. 1, n. 11). Rosenfeld posits that we have entered an "age of independence" in the United States in part because so many young adults are living on their own rather than with a spouse or with their parents. While the number of people in their twenties who do not live with their parents has risen dramatically during the same period that the accordion family has expanded, both trends are bolstered by a precipitous decline in young adults who live with a spouse. The median age at first marriage was at its lowest from 1950 to 1970: at under twenty-one for women and under twenty-three for men. These years also posted the lowest number of men and women in their twenties either living with their parents or as singles on their own. Though a rise in independent living has coincided with the rise in accordion families, there is considerable crossover between the two groups, as young adults take short-term opportunities that lead them to live apart from their parents, then move back home.

18. See Newman, *Declining Fortunes.*

19.   Unemployment rates for persons ages 20–24 (in percent)

	United States	Japan	Italy	Sweden
1970	8.2	2	9	2.2
1975	13.6	2.9	10.6	2.8
1980	11.5	3.3	12.9	3.7
1985	11.1	4.2	18.5	6.4
1990	8.8	3.7	19	3.4
1995	9.1	5.7	28.9	19.9
2000	7.2	8.7	27.1	9.6
2005	8.8	8.4	21.4	17.6
2009	14.7	8.7	23	20

20. The long-term unemployment rate was 21.4 percent in 2000 and 30.7 in 1980.

21. Thomas D. Cook and Frank F. Furstenberg Jr., "Explaining Aspects of the Transition to Adulthood in Italy, Sweden, Germany, and the United States: A Cross-Disciplinary, Case Synthesis Approach," *Annals of American Academy of Political and Social Science* 580 (2002): 257–87, http://ann.sagepub.com/cgi/content/abstract/580/1/257.

22. C. Young, "The Non-Pecuniary Costs of Unemployment" (PhD dissertation, Princeton University, 2010), 17.

23. According to the U.S. Bureau of Labor Statistics, unemployment rates for blacks ages twenty to twenty-four grew from about 19 percent in January 2007 to 25 percent in January 2009. Rates for their white counterparts were about 7 percent in January 2007 and climbed to about 12 percent in January 2009.

24. I dwell on jobless youth here, but they are not alone in having trouble covering their bills. *Under*employed workers—those who hold part-time or seasonal jobs, though they would like to find full-time jobs—are also in trouble. Predictably, the same kind of young workers sidelined completely from the labor market—the low-skilled, poorly educated minorities—are also at greater risk for inadequate employment.

25. Karen Robson, "Predictors and Outcomes of Becoming NEET in Europe," in Paul Attewell and Katherine S. Newman, eds., *Growing Gaps: Education and Inequality around the World* (New York: Oxford University Press, 2010).

26. According to the Organisation for Economic Co-operation and Development (France), in 1950, there were between five and six working-age adults (ages twenty to sixty-four) for every one adult of retirement age (over sixty-four). By 2010, the ratio was between three and five working-age adults for every one of retirement age, and by 2030, the ratio is expected to fall to about 2:1.

27. Y. Genda and M. E. Rebick, "Japanese Labour in the 1990s: Stability and Stagnation," *Oxford Review of Economic Policy* 16 (2000): 85–102.

28. Japanese Institute for Labour Policy and Training, "Freeters: The Outlook and Behaviour of Today's Young People Concerning the Working Life," 2002.

29. Ibid.

30. Genda and Rebick, "Japanese Labour in the 1990s"; R. Kosugi, "Young People in Transitional Crisis: Interview Survey for Young Jobless and Freeters," *JILPT Research Report* 6 (2004), http://www.jil.go.jp/english/reports/documents/jilpt-research/no6.pdf.

31. Mary C. Brinton, *Lost in Transition: Youth, Work, and Instability in Postindustrial Japan* (New York: Cambridge University Press, 2010).

32. See " Freeters, Temporary Workers and Foreign Workers in Japan," Facts and Details, http://factsanddetails.com/japan.php?itemid=907&catid=24&subcatid=156.

33. Martin Fackler, "In Japan, Young Face Generational Roadblocks," *New York Times*, January 27, 2011, http://www.nytimes.com/2011/01/28/world/asia/28generation.html.

34. David Pilling, "Japan's Wageless Recovery," *ZNet*, January 28, 2005, http://www.zcommunications.org/japans-wageless-recovery-by-david-pilling.

35. Genda and Rebick, "Japanese Labour in the 1990s."

36. Youth Affairs Administration, Japan, 1994. Y. Honda, " 'Freeters': Young Atypical Workers in Japan," Japanese Institute for Labour Policy and Training, http://www.jil.go.jp/english/JLR/documents/2005/JLR07_honda.pdf; Kosugi, "Young People in Transitional Crisis"; Pilling, "Japan's Wageless Recovery." Perhaps young people are more likely to change jobs because so many of them are fixed-term and/or part-time workers—2 million in 2002. Freeters are disproportionately young with low levels of education. They have low wages, low probability of a pay raise, and often no Social Security or insurance coverage.

37. Genda and Rebick, "Japanese Labour in the 1990s."

38. K. Golsch, "Employment Flexibility in Spain and Its Impact on Transitions to Adulthood," *Work, Employment and Society* 17 (2003): 691–718.

39. Ibid.

40. Teresa Jurado Guerrero, *Youth in Transition: Housing, Employment, Social Policies and Families in France and Spain* (Aldershot, UK: Ashgate Publishing, 2001).

41. P. Boelhouwer and H. van der Heijden, "Housing Policy in Seven European Countries: The Role of Politics in Housing," *Netherlands Journal of Housing and the Built Environment* 8 (1993): 383–404.

42. "Young Europeans: Survey among Young People Aged between 15–30 in the European Union," Flash Eurobarometer, Gallup Organization, February 2007. C. H. Mulder and P. Hooimeijer, "Leaving Home in the Netherlands: Timing and First Housing," *Journal of Housing and the Built Environment* 17 (2002): 237–68; Tony Fahey et al., *Quality of Life in Europe: First Results of a New Pan-European Survey* (Luxembourg: Office for Official Publications of the European Communities, 2004). Curiously, the data runs in virtually the opposite direction from what we would expect *a priori,* based on government provision of public housing subsidies that go to young people (Mulder and Hooimeijer). Young people in the Nordic

countries and the Netherlands are the most likely to feel that lack of suitable housing impedes their departure from the parental home. Yet these are precisely the countries where the government is generous in providing social housing (Fahey et al.). Boelhouwer and van der Heijden, "Housing Policy"; Fahey et al., *Quality of Life;* Mulder and Hooimeijer, "Leaving Home"; F. G. Castles and M. Ferrera, "Home Ownership and the Welfare State: Is Southern Europe Different?" *South European Society & Politics* 1 (1996): 163–85; C. Holdsworth and M. I. Solda, "First Housing Moves in Spain: An Analysis of Leaving Home and First Housing Acquisition," *European Journal of Population* 1 (2002): 1–19; Guerrero, *Youth in Transition.* Housing affordability and availability differ dramatically from one country to another, and it is particularly complicated in Southern European countries such as Italy, where up to half of housing is illegal. In the Netherlands, where the government explicitly aims to make it easy for young people to live apart from their families, 42 percent of the total housing stock is in the public sector, with housing built specifically for young people, whether they are students or workers. Austria and the United Kingdom also have a great deal of municipal housing—26 percent each. Denmark saw a construction boom in the 1980s, much of it in the public rental sector. Seventy-three percent of rented dwellings in the United Kingdom are public, compared to only 37 percent in France and a meager 8 percent in Spain.

43. J. Ermisch, "Prices, Parents, and Young People's Household Formation," *Journal of Urban Economics* 45 (1999): 47–71.

44. Guerrero, *Youth in Transition.*

45. Clare Holdsworth, "Leaving Home in Britain and Spain," *European Sociological Review* 16 (2000): 201–22.

46. Ibid.

47. Guerrero, *Youth in Transition.*

48. Francesco Saraceno, "Wage Regimes, Accumulation and Finance Constraints: Keynesian Unemployment Revisited," Documents de Travail de l'OFCE 2004-01, Observatoire Francais des Conjonctures Economiques, http://ideas.repec.org/p/wpa/wuwpma/0311007.html.

49. The GI Bill provided veterans with free tuition for college or vocational education and one year of unemployment compensation.

50. Scott Williams, "The GI Bill: The Post-War Boom in Housing & College Enrollment," *Sunflower Journeys* transcript, KTWU-TV, http://ktwu.washburn.edu/journeys/scripts/1306b.html.

51. See *The 2011 Statistical Abstract,* U.S. Census Bureau, http://www.census.gov/compendia/statab/cats/construction_housing/homeownership_and_housing_costs.html.

52. Richard Breen and Marlis Buchmann, "Institutional Variation and the Position of Young People: A Comparative Perspective," *Annals of the American Academy of Political and Social Science* 580 (2002): 288–305. Breen and Buchmann note that liberal and Southern European states have the lowest rates of school enrollment at age seventeen. Unemployment rates are lower in the liberal states, where young people can leave home at younger ages, than in Southern Europe, where unemployment is high and unemployment insurance is minimal.

53. L. Lippman, "Cross-National Variation in Educational Preparation for Adulthood: From Early Adolescence to Young Adulthood," *Annals of the American Academy of Political and Social Science* 580 (2002): 70–102; Cook and Furstenberg, "Explaining Aspects"; Guerrero, *Youth in Transition*. Tertiary education ranges from short three- to four-year programs in liberal regimes like the United Kingdom to seven-year first-degree programs in Italy (comparable to master's programs in the United States) (Cook and Furstenberg). Long first-degree programs are also the norm in the Netherlands, Germany, France, and Sweden. French students can decide at almost any point whether to continue their studies or to leave with a lower-level certificate (Guerrero). While Sweden has short programs as well as long programs, only half graduate by age twenty-five because most people take time off before university (Lippman). Completion of higher education varies greatly in Germany, where there is a tradition of attending several universities before graduation (Cook and Furstenberg). Additional education makes it more likely that a young person in the United States, the Netherlands, and Germany will leave the parental home. Lippman, "Cross-National Variation."
54. Holdsworth, "Leaving Home."
55. Guerrero, *Youth in Transition*.
56. K. Nilsson and M. Strandh, "Nest Leaving in Sweden: The Importance of Early Educational and Labor Market Careers," *Journal of Marriage and the Family* 61 (1999): 1068–79; Cook and Furstenberg, "Explaining Aspects." For more, see "Family Roles—Role Expectations And Demands," *Marriage and Family Encyclopedia*, http://family.jrank.org/pages/580/Family-Roles-Role-Expectations-Demands.html#ixzz18U8Yir54.
57. Cook and Furstenberg, "Explaining Aspects"; Mulder and Hooimeijer, "Leaving Home."
58. Cook and Furstenberg, "Explaining Aspects"; Guerrero, *Youth in Transition*.
59. Cook and Furstenberg, "Explaining Aspects."
60. Guerrero, *Youth in Transition*.
61. Nilsson and Strandh, "Nest Leaving."
62. According to the College Board's *Trends in College Pricing 2009,* for every decade from 1979 to 2009, average tuition and fees at private and public colleges has risen beyond increases in the consumer price index. The average rise for 1979 to 1989 was 4.7 percent for private four-year colleges and 3 percent for public; for 1989 to 1999, it was 2.9 percent for private and 4 percent for public; and for 1999 to 2009, it was 2.6 percent for private and 4.9 percent for public; http://advocacy.collegeboard.org/sites/default/files/2009_Trends_College_Pricing_report.pdf.
63. Jessica Dickler, "Boomerang Kids: 88% of College Grads Move Home," CNNMoney.com, November 15, 2010, http://money.cnn.com/2010/10/14/pf/boomerang_kids_move_home/index.htm.
64. Arnstein Aasve et al., "Does Leaving Home Make You Poor? Evidence from 13 European Countries," *European Journal of Population* 23 (2007): 315–38; Alessandro Cavalli, "Prolonging Youth in Italy: 'Being in No Hurry,'" in A. Cavalli and O. Galland, eds., *Youth in Europe* (New York: St. Martin's Press, 2005); Gianpiero Dalla Zuanna, "The Banquet of Aeolus: A Familistic Interpretation of Italy's Lowest Low Fertility,"

Demographic Research 4 (2001): 133–62; Cook and Furstenberg, "Explaining Aspects"; Mulder and Hooimeijer, "Leaving Home." Aasve and colleagues found that higher household income delays home-leaving in Italy and Spain. Similarly, Cavalli found that young Italians of lower socioeconomic status were likely to leave home earlier. While it is difficult to study actual transfers of economic and especially non-economic resources between the parents and the children, Zuanna, like Cook and Furstenberg, finds that young Southern Europeans tend to contribute little to their parental households even while employed. On the other hand, Holdsworth finds that higher parental education actually speeds up home-leaving in Spain, and Aasve et al. do not find an effect for parental income in Greece or Portugal. In the Netherlands, a higher socioeconomic status of the father speeds up home-leaving of children moving out to live alone but not those entering partnerships, perhaps because assistance to single children is more acceptable (Mulder and Hooimeijer). The French with higher socioeconomic status are also more likely to part with their parents in order to live without partners; see Olivier Galland, "Youth in France: A New Age in Life," in Cavalli and Galland, eds., *Youth in Europe.*

65. "Young Europeans 2001," Eurobarometer, European Commission.

66. Ibid. The percentage of eighteen- to twenty-four-year-olds supported solely by their parents or family in Denmark went from just under 2 percent in 1990 to about 1 percent in 2001. That number increased in Sweden, climbing from 6 percent in 1997 to 8 percent in 2001.

67. Ibid. In 1990, the percentage of eighteen- to twenty-four-year-olds supported solely by their parents or family in Spain was under 30 percent. In Greece, that figure rose from 40 percent in 1990 to close to 55 percent in 2001. Portugal also saw an increase from a little more than 20 percent in 1990 to about 31 percent in 2001. The trend toward increased dependency continued from 1997 to 2001 in some countries (Ireland, Great Britain, and Sweden) but tapered off elsewhere. The European Commission report cited similar results in ages fifteen to twenty-four in 1997 and 2001, focusing on respondents supported by parents or family exclusively or in combination with other sources (not differentiated as in our analysis). See also Francesco C. Billari, "Becoming an Adult in Europe: A Macro(/Micro)-Demographic Perspective," *Demographic Research* Special Collection 3, Article 2 (April 17, 2004): 15–44, www .demographic-research.org/special/3/2/. Also, *Young Europeans: Survey among Young People Aged between 15–30 in the European Union*, Flash Eurobarometer, no. 202, February 2007, Gallup Organization. The survey indicates that the primary source of income is a regular job for only 43 percent of young Europeans, while for 31 percent it is a partner or relatives. Primary source of income varies among countries. In Denmark, 57 percent cite a regular job as their primary source of income; in Italy, 50 percent cite a partner or relatives. An education or training grant is the second-to-most common source of income in Scandinavian countries, after a regular job. Also, see Arnstein Aasve et al., "The Impact of Income and Employment Status on Leaving Home: Evidence from the Italian ECHP Sample," *LABOUR* 15 (2001): 501–29; J. Ermisch and S. P. Jenkins, "Retirement and Housing Adjustment in Later Life: Evidence from the British Household Panel Survey," *Labour Economics* 6 (1999): 311–33; Guerrero, *Youth in Transition;* Mulder and Hooimeijer, "Leaving Home";

Nilsson and Strandh, "Nest Leaving." While parental resources and income were found for the most part to delay departure from the home in Southern Europe, the North moves in the opposite direction. Parental income and resources speed up departure from the nest in Germany and the Netherlands: a father's higher socio-economic status increases the likelihood of home-leaving in the Netherlands, and parental resources speed up men's residential independence in Sweden. The difference between the two regions is perhaps due to the fact that Northern European parents continue to help their children once they move out, whereas adult children in the South are on their own when not residing with their parents. French parents, for instance, support their children in a separate household more often than Spanish parents because in Spain, residential independence is synonymous with financial independence. The United Kingdom differs from Germany and the Netherlands in that higher parental income has been found to delay home-leaving, as in Southern Europe. Parental education among the British affects the destination after home-leaving: parents with more education are less likely to have adult children who leave to start a union. American youth with more education, however, are more likely to move out to marry, while Europeans with more education are less likely to leave in order to form a union and more likely to transition to living without a partner.

68. Zhu Xiao Di et al., "Young American Adults Living in Parental Homes," Joint Center for Housing Studies, Harvard University, May 2002, especially 9–10; http://www.jchs.harvard.edu/publications/markets/di_W02-3.pdf. The research on the effect of parental resources on young adults' living arrangements in the United States seems to be inconclusive. Di et al. cite a longitudinal study drawing on the 1968–1988 *Panel Study of Income Dynamics* data, which found that parental income had a negative effect on children becoming independent until about age eighteen for girls and nineteen for boys. At that point, higher parental income increases the probability that the child will become independent. However, Di and colleague's work suggests that personal income may be more relevant than parental income. They found that while parental wealth and income are influential in home-leaving behavior, they are not statistically significant when other factors such as personal income are considered.

The following is excerpted from "Young American Adults Living in Parental Homes":

Studies investigating the effect of parental resources on young adults' living arrangement generated inconsistent findings. Hill (1977), using the PSID data, found that parental income has no effect on children leaving home. Ten years later, Bianchi (1987), using the CPS fertility data, found that higher parental income significantly reduced children's living away from home. Using Australian data, Young (1987) also found that family economic resources raised the likelihood of co-residence. Later on, however, Goldscheider and DaVanzo (1989) used the National Longitudinal Study of the High School Class of 1972 and found that greater parental resources significantly increased the likelihood that young adults would leave home both before and at marriage. Rosenzweig and Wolpin (1990, cited in Schoeni 1993) also found that a rise in parental income by

$5,000 increased the probability that the adult child would receive a monetary transfer while living outside the home by 2.2 percent and decreased the probability of co-residence by 2.5 percent.

More recently, Avery et al. (1992) used 1984 PSID data and found that, overall, parental income had no significant effect on children's nest leaving, but the effects of parental income differ sharply by the age of the young adult. Higher parental income decreases nest leaving significantly in the early stages of the nest leaving process whereas it accelerates it significantly in the waning stages. He also found that parental income has no effect on leaving for premarital residential independence, but that the higher the parental income, the less likely the young adult is to leave home due to marriage. Each increment of $10,000 reduces the odds of leaving home due to marriage by 0.87.

Similarly, a longitudinal study using the 1968–1988 PSID data by Whittington and Peters (1996) found that parental income has a negative effect on children becoming independent until about age 18 for girls and age 19 for boys. After that point, higher parental income increases the probability that the child will become independent. They speculated that parents of young children might prefer that their children remain dependent, but parents of older children might either be neutral or prefer their children to be on their own. Parents with higher income have more power over their children and would be better able to elicit the desired behavior.

Finally, White (1994) argues that, regardless of what statistical significance parental income may have on children's leaving home to have independent lives, a two-tier structure may exist in terms of parental financial assistance to their adult children.

Residential independence of children is possible for better-off parents while a relatively large amount of resources flow from parents to children. For those from lower income parents, however, co-residence may be necessary if children are to have access to parents' resources.

69. D. S. Reher, "Family Ties in Western Europe: Persistent Contrasts," *Population and Development Review* 24 (1998): 203–34.
70. Aasve et al., "The Impact of Income and Employment"; S. Spilerman, "The Impact of Parental Wealth on Early Living Standards in Israel," *American Journal of Sociology* 110 (2004): 92–122. Spilerman has shown that the same expectation governs the Israeli system, in which parents finance the purchase of a home for their children.
71. C. Saraceno, "Patterns of Family Living in Europe," in J. Alber et al., eds., *Handbook of Quality of Life in the Enlarged European Union* (Oxford, UK: Routledge, 2008), 47–72. Saraceno points to a clash between ingrained traditions pertaining to family responsibilities and both evolving gender roles and rapid aging of the population to explain how Southern Europe can have significantly lower fertility rates than the countries of Northern Europe with traditionally "weak" families (less marriage, more divorce, more cohabitation, more single parenthood, etc.).
72. D. J. van de Kaa, "Europe's Second Demographic Transition," *Population Bulletin* 42 (1987): 1–59.

73. Viviana A. Zelizer, *Pricing the Priceless Child: The Changing Social Value of Children* (Princeton, NJ: Princeton University Press, 1994).
74. Makoto Atoh and Mayuko Akachi, "Low Fertility and Family Policy in Japan," *Journal of Population and Social Security*, supp. to vol. 1 (2001), http://www.ipss.go.jp/webj-ad/webjournal.files/population/2003_6/1.Atoh.pdf; Genda and Rebick, "Japanese Labour in the 1990s" (see ch. 2, n. 27).
75. Kosugi, "Young People in Transitional Crisis."
76. Eurobarometer data allows us to look at how flexible youth views are on the matter of job quality. Across the four-year period of 1997 to 2001, we see a pronounced unwillingness to lower expectations even in the face of unemployment.

If you were unemployed, which of the following would you most probably do?
(Only one answer possible)

	1990	1997	2001
01. *Accept any job, whatever the conditions*	n/a	14%	12%
02. *Accept any job, provided it was stable*	n/a	17%	16%
03. *Accept any job, provided it was well paid*	n/a	14%	17%
04. *Accept any job, provided it was appropriate to my level of qualification*	n/a	14%	15%
05. *Accept a job only if it was stable, well paid and if it was appropriate to my level of qualification*	n/a	12%	13%
06. *Accept to do social activities without being paid, voluntary work*	n/a	1%	1%
07. *Take advantage of the situation by traveling and visiting different countries*	n/a	4%	4%
08. *Try to establish my own company*	n/a	4%	3%
09. *Work in the "black economy," that is, without declaring my earnings*	n/a	2%	2%
10. *Try to do an apprenticeship/traineeship, or training courses, or I would look for a different career*	n/a	15%	11%

In the 2007 Flash Eurobarometer Youth Survey, one in three young Europeans said that if confronted with unemployment, he or she would accept any job, as long as it met certain conditions like stability and a good salary. One in ten would accept any job without such conditions.

77. C. Pickvance and K. Pickvance, "The Role of Family Help in the Housing Decisions of Young People," *Sociological Review* 42 (1995): 123–49; Zuanna, "The Banquet of Aeolus." Zuanna notes that economic conditions in Italian homes are since the 1980s, coinciding with a decline in how much young adults contribute to the parental household and an increase of employed children living with parents. Zuanna describes this phenomenon as the "Golden Cage": young adults in Italy choose to

stay at home where economic conditions are much better than they could hope for were they to move out and live on their own. British youth may be experiencing a Golden Cage phenomenon as well: a study by Pickvance and Pickvance found that transfers from parents to children affect at most one-third of families in the southeastern United Kingdom, and thus few adult children can count on support once they move out.

78. M. Yamada, *The Age of Parasite Singles* (Japan: Chikuma Shiso, 1999); Genda and Rebick, "Japanese Labour in the 1990s."

79. J. M. Raymo, "Premarital Living Arrangements and the Transition to First Marriage in Japan," *Journal of Marriage and Family* 65 (2003): 302–15.

80. Genda and Rebick, "Japanese Labour in the 1990s."

81. "EurLIFE: Mean Age at First Marriage," Eurofound, 2009, http://www.eurofound .europa.eu/areas/qualityoflife/eurlife/index.php?template=3&radioindic=186&id Domain=5; "Trends in Median Age at First Marriage," National Healthy Marriage Resource Center, http://www.healthymarriageinfo.org/docs/medianagemarriage. pdf; "Average Age at First Marriage: By Gender, EU Comparison, 1961 and 1998," *Social Trends* 32, Office for National Statistics (UK), http://www.statistics.gov.uk/ STATBASE/ssdataset.asp?vlnk=4980&More=Y; "Some Statistics about Marriage, Employment and Family Life in Japan," Zipangu Transcultural Network, 2001, http://www.ezipangu.org/english/contents/news/naname/kekkon_etc/kekkon_etc .html.In the United States, in 1960, the median age at first marriage was 22.8 for men and 20.3 for women; by 2004, it was 27.4 for men and 25.8 for women. In Denmark, in 1961, the average age at first marriage was 25.7 for men and 22.8 for women; by 2003, it was 32 for men and 30 for women. In Sweden, in 1961, the average age at first marriage was 26.6 for men and 23.8 for women; by 2003, it was 33 for men and 31 for women. Those in Italy and Spain have long married later, but the mean age of marriage has risen in those countries as well. In 1961, the mean age of first marriage in Italy was 28.5 for men and 24.7 for women; in 2000, it was 30 for men and 27 for women. In 1961 in Spain, it was 28.8 for men and 26.1 for women; by 2002, it was 30 for men and 28 for women. In Japan, the average age of first marriage for women in 1950 was 23; by 2000, it had risen to 27.

82. Henry Tricks, "A Special Report on Japan: Into the Unknown," *Economist*, November 18, 2010, http://www.economist.com/node/17492860.

83. Fackler, "In Japan, Young Face."

CHAPTER 3: IN-HOUSE ADULTHOOD

1. See A. Schalet, "Sex, Love, and Autonomy in the Teenage Sleepover," *Contexts* 9 (2010): 16–21; Widmer et al., "Attitudes toward Nonmarital Sex" (see ch. 1, n. 21). Though allowing an unmarried child to share a bed with her partner is a radical departure from the morals of previous generations, U.S. parents are still significantly more conservative than many of their European counterparts in matters concerning their children's sexuality. For instance, about two-thirds of Dutch high schoolers, both male and female, report that their parents allow them to have sleepovers with a romantic partner. Interestingly, Dutch parents consider having in-house

sleepovers a way to exercise social control over their teens, much as American parents feel they exert control by laying down rules preventing such sleepovers. U.S. parents' attitudes toward sexual activity tend to relax somewhat once children pass adolescence, though on average, people in the United States remain more conservative than their counterparts in most other Western nations in attitudes toward sex outside of marriage.

2. D. Harding and C. Jencks, "Changing Attitudes toward Premarital Sex," *Public Opinion Quarterly* 67 (2003): 211–26. The introduction of the contraceptive pill in the early 1960s was closely followed by a series of court cases that allowed legal access to contraception and abortion. These cases included Griswold v. Connecticut, 381 U.S. 479 (1965), which allowed married couples to obtain contraception; Eisenstadt v. Baird, 405 U.S. 438 (1972), which granted the same right to unmarried couples; and Roe v. Wade, 410 U.S. 113 (1973), which gave women the legal right to abortion. A shift in attitudes toward premarital sex occurred with shocking speed between 1969 and 1973, with the percentage of adults in the Gallup poll saying that premarital sex was "not wrong" nearly doubling from 24 to 47 percent. The number of people in Gallup's General Social Survey who identified premarital sex as wrong "only sometimes" or "not wrong at all" changed gradually from 1972 to 1982, from 52 percent to 62 percent, and there has been little change since.

3. G. Greenwood and N. Guneer, "Social Change: The Sexual Revolution," *International Economic Review* 51, no. 4 (November 2010): 893–923; D. Smith and M. Hindus, "Premarital Pregnancy in America, 1640–1971: An Overview and Interpretation," *Journal of Interdisciplinary History* 4 (1975): 537–70; R. Wind, "Premarital Sex Is Nearly Universal," Guttmacher Institute, December 19, 2006, http://www .guttmacher.org/media/nr/2006/12/19/index.html. It has always been the case that some couples have engaged in sex before marriage. Although only 6 percent of teen girls admitted to premarital sex in 1900, rates of premarital pregnancy generally vacillated between 10 and 30 percent from the colonial period through the mid-twentieth century. Reports looking at adults from the 1950s onward indicate that 95 percent or more had sex before marriage, even before the advent of the sexual revolution in the 1960s. A more striking difference is that the delay in age at first marriage leads to contemporary adults having more sexual partners before marrying than those who came of age in the 1950s and 1960s.

4. Jesús Fernández-Villaverde et al., "From Shame to Game in One Hundred Years: An Economic Model of the Rise in Premarital Sex and Its De-Stigmatization," NBER Working Paper No. w15677, Social Science Research Network, January 2010, http:// papers.ssrn.com/sol3/papers.cfm?abstract_id=1540982; C. Goldin and L. Katz, "The Power of the Pill: Oral Contraceptives and Women's Career and Marriage Decisions," *Journal of Political Economy* 110 (2002): 730–70. By reducing the consequences of sex, the Pill helped to destigmatize sex outside of marriage. As availability and use of the Pill spread among younger women in the late 1960s and early 1970s, women increasingly entered professional programs and delayed marriage. The Pill decreased the costs to women of remaining unmarried and investing in education and career. In considering the power of the Pill for women's autonomy,

Japanese women have delayed marriage and decreased fertility from the 1970s onward but have not made the same economic advances as American women; the Pill was not legally available in Japan until 1999.

5. See E. L. Schor and American Academy of Pediatrics Task Force on the Family, "Family Pediatrics: Report of the Task Force on the Family," *Pediatrics 111*, supplement (June 2003): 1541–71. Many psychologists, pediatricians, and others see parents' unconditional love as an essential component of children's health. Growing up in such an environment promotes becoming a psychologically healthy adult who can maintain bonds with parents and form intimate bonds with others.

6. L. Steinberg, "We Know Some Things: Parent-Adolescent Relationships in Retrospect and Prospect," *Journal of Research on Adolescence* 11 (2001): 1–19. Conflict between parents and teens was long seen as a crucial step in establishing adolescents' independence. The norming of "storm and stress" during adolescence was fueled by the generation gap experienced between boomers and their parents. However, the intensity of teen-parent conflict may have been overplayed, especially in more recent times by an overzealous media that feeds on stories of strife. The mildly upsetting conflicts typical in most households may be quite easy to bridge once the younger generation has passed the teen years, especially if family relationships were generally healthy and based on authoritative (rather than authoritarian, neglectful, or overly indulgent) parenting.

7. See Mark Granovetter, "The Strength of Weak Ties," *American Journal of Sociology* 78 (1973): 1360–80. In this classic, Granovetter points out the importance of network connections, even those that appear weak, in diffusing information and opportunities that can lead to professional success. The "parental consulting firm" is a prime example of the advantages of loose but extensive networks.

8. G. Spitze and R. Ward, "Household Labor in Intergenerational Households," *Journal of Marriage and Family* 57 (1995): 355–61. Data from the National Survey of Family Growth indicates that adult children in intergenerational households typically make substantial contributions to housework and do more the older they get. While on average, daughters perform more hours of household labor and are more sensitive to what must be done when, sons also make significant contributions.

9. References to the stigma of living at home are common on dating websites. One site points out that men are especially vulnerable to stigma because living at home brands them as "mamma's boys" who expect to be cared for by women; "Handling the Stigma against Single Men Living at Home," Practical Happiness.com, October 16, 2010, http://www.practicalhappiness.com/handling-stigma-against-single-men-living-at-home/. Another site says that a man living at home won't be considered a "real man," and that girls won't give him "the time of day"; "Why Shouldn't Single Adults Live at Home??," Yahoo Answers, n.d., http://answers.yahoo.com/question/index?qid=20081124231235AAnRtpa. On a question forum, a woman asks about her attraction to some men still living at home; the answers almost universally refer to the men as "losers," "bums," or "brats"; "Men Ages 27-32 Still Living with Their Parents but So Attractive and Charismatic?," Finance Discussion Forum, FinancialCrisis2009.org, n.d., http://www.financialcrisis2009.org/

forum/Personal-Finance/Men-ages-27-32-still-living-with-their-parents-but-so
-attractive-and-charismatic-219033.htm. Even advice that does not automatically
rule out the potential of romance with a man living at home may caution that a
woman should make sure that he has a plan for independence in order to avoid
a "launch-pad failure"; "Tips for What to Do When the Man You're Dating Lives
at Home," AskApril.com, n.d., http://www.askapril.com/dating-tips-dating-tips
-failure-to-launch-94.html. Advice to men suggests that they need a backstory to
justify their living situation if they hope to attract a partner; "The 'Living at Home'
Scenario," eHarmony Advice, January 5, 2011, http://advice.eharmony.com/boards/
dating-advice/dating/48821-living-home-scenario-2.html.

10. Dating-advice forums do not pillory women as much as men for living at home. One
points out that women who live with their parents—at least up to a certain age—
may be assumed to be helping their parents and remaining sexually chaste, while
men are more likely assumed to be taking advantage of an opportunity to freeload;
"Tips for What to Do," AskApril.com. However, once women reach their thirties,
such living arrangements become more questionable, with increasing references
to their relationship with their parents being "not healthy" or "sad"; "Women in
Their 30s and 40s Living with Their Parents," PlentyofFish.com, n.d., http://forums
.plentyoffish.com/datingPosts10552058.aspx.

11. Widmer et al., "Attitudes Toward Nonmarital Sex." Attitudes toward premarital sex
in Italy are not particularly conservative in comparison to those in other Western
nations. While 19 percent say that premarital sex is "always wrong," 59 percent say
it is "not wrong at all." However, a mother's feelings about her daughter's behavior
may differ from her abstract moral judgments.

CHAPTER 4: I'M OK, YOU ARE NOT

1. R. L. Coley and B. L. Medeiros, "Reciprocal Longitudinal Relations Between Non-
resident Father Involvement and Adolescent Delinquency," *Child Development* 78
(2007): 132–47; D. P. Moynihan, "The Negro Family: The Case for National Action,"
Office of Planning and Research, U.S. Department of Labor, March 1965, http://
www.dol.gov/oasam/programs/history/webid-meynihan.htm; L. Pagani, F. Vitaro,
R. E. Tremblay, P. McDuff, C. Japel, and S. Larose, "When Predictions Fail: The Case
of Unexpected Pathways toward High School Dropout," *Journal of Social Issues* 64
(2008): 175–94; A. Thomas and I. Sawhill, "For Love and Money? The Impact of
Family Structure on Family Income," *Future of Children* 15 (2005): 57–74. Moynihan
set off a firestorm when he posited that father absence had left African American
families in a "tangle of pathology," but subsequent studies have continued to explore
the impact of the absent father. Single motherhood has become more common
among all racial and ethnic groups since the release of the Moynihan report, and
father absence (particularly when the family is poor and the mother remains unmarried) has been blamed for a host of ills, including juvenile delinquency, school
dropout, and poverty.

2. See Paula J. Caplan, *The New Don't Blame Mother: Mending the Mother-Daughter*

Relationship (New York: Routledge, 2000). Mothers have consistently been blamed for the ills that face their offspring: autism was thought to be caused by mothers who were cold and distant; and homosexuality, once believed to be a mental illness, was often blamed on defective mothering. Much of the exploration of various personality disorders focused on what mothers did wrong rather than on the confluence of factors that could potentially have led to the emergence of the problems.

3. Tomoko Hamada, "Absent Fathers, Feminized Sons, Selfish Mothers and Disobedient Daughters: Revisiting The Japanese *Ie* Household," Japan Policy Research Institute, working paper no. 33, http://www.jpri.org/publications/workingpapers/wp33.html. In traditional Japanese family relationships, mothers are central and fathers almost invisible. Mothers in Japan have long been expected to make caregiving their primary occupation, with the mother-child relationship superseding all others. The phrases *kodomo-ga-ikigai* ("my child is my raison d'être") and *orkodomo wa jibun no bunshin* ("my child is my alter ego") are common in reference to mothering roles.

4. Terry McCarthy, "Out of Japan: Mother Love Puts a Nation in the Pouch," *Independent* (UK), October 4, 1993, http://www.independent.co.uk/news/world/out-of-japan-mother-love-puts-a-nation-in-the-pouch-1508595.html.

5. Hamada, "Absent Fathers."

6. J. Raymo and M. Iwasawa, "Marriage Market Mismatches in Japan: An Alternative View of the Relationship between Women's Education and Marriage," *American Sociological Review* 70 (2005): 801–22; R. Retherford et al., "Late Marriage and Less Marriage in Japan," *Population and Development Review* 27 (2001): 65–102. Just as in other countries, highly educated women in Japan are the most likely to delay or forgo marriage. This may be because they have the option not to marry, but it may also be because there are fewer appropriate potential spouses. Japan continues to emphasize women's dependence on men after marriage, yet the supply of highly educated, high-earning young men is dissipating at the same time that women's opportunities have increased. The appeal of marriage may also be dissipating for women because premarital sex has become more acceptable, and the rising Japanese divorce rates mean that marriage no longer guarantees women life security.

7. See K. Applbaum, "Marriage with the Proper Stranger: Arranged Marriage in Metropolitan Japan," *Ethnology* 34 (1995): 37–51. Arranged marriage is still fairly common in Japan. In the 1990s, it was estimated that 25 to 30 percent of marriages were arranged by the couple's parents

8. J. Raymo et al., "Cohabitation and Family Formation in Japan," *Demography* 46 (2009): 785–803. Rates of cohabitation in Japan have historically been very low, with rates of premarital cohabitation as low as 1 to 2 percent from 1987 to 2005. However, recent data from the National Survey on Population, Family, and Generations in Japan indicated that 20 percent of women ages twenty-five to thirty-four reported having had a cohabiting union, a rate twice that of women a decade older, even with the shorter exposure time for having such relationships.

9. "Japan Retired Divorce Rate Soars," BBC News online, February 22, 2006, http://news.bbc.co.uk/2/hi/asia-pacific/4741018.stm. Divorce rates per thousand in Japan are similar to those in many European nations:

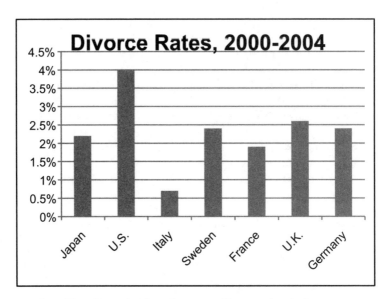

Source: DivorceRate.org, http://www.divorcerate.org/divorce-rate-japan.html.

However, divorce rates in Japan have more than doubled since the mid-1980s. Sonoko's analysis is quite accurate: much of the rise is among couples who have been married for twenty years or more, and is initiated by women.

10. K. S. Lee et al., "Separate Spheres or Increasing Equality? Changing Gender Beliefs in Postwar Japan," *Journal of Marriage and Family* 72 (2010): 184–201. Ideas about gender have changed in response to other social changes, such as delayed marriage and women's increased representation in the professional workforce. Younger cohorts increasingly express more egalitarian beliefs, yet there remains an overall high value on the role of housewife and mother, as well as sanctions against wives' and mothers' employment.

11. Y. Nozaki and K. Matsuura, "The Increasingly High Sex Ratio and Lifelong Unmarried Rate in Japan," *Journal of Population Research* 27, no. 1 (June 2010): 43–57.

12. Sonni Efron, "Me, Find a Husband? Later, Maybe," *Los Angeles Times,* June 26, 2001, http://articles.latimes.com/2001/jun/26/news/mn-14693.

13. Social theorist Anthony Giddens argues that action and structure operate reciprocally. Individual acts, when combined, create a social force that can change social structures, but intentional behavior by individuals is not necessarily rooted in overall social goals. At the same time, structural change can shape individual behavior. The Japanese sentiment relies heavily on agency over structure in considering current social problems, while the analysis in this book investigates the vast structural changes that may affect individual behavior.

14. Anne Hornsby, "Lifetime Employment in Japan: Myths and Misconceptions," ASIANetwork.org, 2004, http://www.asianetwork.org/exchange/2004-winter/anex 2004-winter-hornsby.pdf. Kuniko Ishiguro, "Japanese Employment in Transformation: The Growing Number of Non-Regular Workers," *Electronic Journal of Contem-*

porary Japanese Studies, 2008, http://www.japanesestudies.org.uk/articles/2008/ Ishiguro.html.

15. Fackler, "In Japan, Young Face" (see ch. 2, n. 33).

16. M. Manacorda and E. Moretti, "Mamma's Boys: Why Do Most Italian Young Men Live with Their Parents," *CentrePiece* 10 (2005): 12–13, http://cep.lse.ac.uk/centre piece/.

17. Donald MacLeod, "Italian Mammas Making Offers Their Sons Can't Refuse," *Guardian* (UK), February 3, 2006, http://www.guardian.co.uk/education/2006/ feb/03/highereducation.uk.

18. See Newman and Aptekar, "Sticking Around" (see ch. 1, n. 6). The more ubiquitous a practice (for example, accordion families), the less stigma it carries.

19. See *La Repubblica* (Italy), July 6, 2006.

20. Nancy Scheper-Hughes, *Saints, Scholars, and Schizophrenics: Mental Illness in Rural Ireland* (Berkeley: University of California Press, 2001).

21. Gary Picariello, "In Italy, Living at Home Well into Your 30s Is Perfectly Normal," AssociatedContent.com, July 14, 2006, http://www.associatedcontent.com/ article/43571/in_italy_living_at_home_well_into_your.html.

22. "Young Europeans," Flash Eurobarometer. Italy is one of only four countries in the European Union (the others are Bulgaria, Greece, and Hungary) in which income from relatives or a partner is a more common source of income than a regular job among people ages fifteen to thirty.

23. "Older Mothers—Facts and Figures," Mothers 35 Plus, http://www.mothers35plus .co.uk/intro.htm. Italian mothers are older at the birth of a first child than mothers in any other Western country. Almost 20 percent of children in Italy are born to a mother over age forty.

24. "Demographic Change Is Not on the Political Agenda," interview with Professor Dr. Manuela Naldini, University of Turin, Project IGLOO, October 21, 2008, http:// www.iglooproject.eu/index.php?article_id=114&clang=0&PHPSESSID=h37tgd2ia 0ul28hb3t903rlar6. Italian sociologist Naldini confirms the ubiquity of such attitudes as Carla's about family, residence, and gendered responsibility. Multigenerational households are common, and even when children move out, they seldom live far from their parents. Despite an active women's movement that resulted in laws guaranteeing gender equality in the 1970s, there has been little change in the gendered division of labor in the family. Women, Naldini says, are forced into lifelong caregiving roles because of the lack of social services, particularly for child care and elder care.

25. "Italian Women Shun Mamma Role," BBC News online, March 27, 2006, http:// news.bbc.co.uk/2/hi/europe/4739154.stm. From 2004 to 2006, the Italian government tried interventions to increase fertility, offering one-time bonuses of 1,000 euros to women who had a second child, then later offering bonuses for women having a first child. As sociologist Manuela Naldini points out, these short-term bonuses did little to change the structural difficulties that made Italian young people delay or forgo childbearing. Italian women's representation in the workforce nearly doubled in the decade following 1996, yet there are few provisions for child care. There is no government "family allowance." Italian social spending on children is

far below EU averages. Italian couples say they cannot afford to have children earlier than their mid-thirties, and many Italian women, who now frequently work to make ends meet, are loath to take on the added responsibilities of a second child in a culture in which men do little household labor.

26. See "Living in Spain: Cost of Living," Spain-Info.com, http://www.spain-info.com/Living_in_Spain/Cost%20of%20living.htm. The cost of housing in Spain has risen dramtically, especially in urban centers. Those buying a house today can expect to put half of their household income toward the mortgage.

27. On the brink of bankruptcy, the regime was convinced in 1959 to adopt a free-market economy. The economic liberalization was not accompanied by political reform. Because of the continued repression, mass emigration ensued, both to other European countries and to South America. The reduced population, as well as monetary remittances supplied to the country by the emigrants, helped Spain's economy. During the 1960s, the wealthy in Spain became more so, particularly those who remained politically faithful to the Franco regime. International firms set up factories in Spain because of the low salaries, nearly nonexistent taxes, a prohibition on striking, and the absence of labor, health, or real estate regulations.

28. P. Heuveline and J. Timberlake, "The Role of Cohabitation in Family Formation: The United States in Comparative Perspective," *Journal of Marriage and Family* 66 (2004): 1214–30. Cohabitation is still relatively infrequent in Spain. The incidence of premarital cohabitation is 14.7 percent versus 66.7 percent in Sweden and 83.3 percent in France.

29. J. Mutchler and L. Baker, "The Implications of Grandparent Coresidence for Economic Hardship among Children in Mother-Only Families," *Journal of Family Issues* 30 (2009): 1576–97; T. Tai and J. Treas, "Does Household Composition Explain Welfare Regime Poverty Risks for Older Adults and Other Household Members?" *Journals of Gerontology* 64B (2009): 777–87. Children in mother-only families are much less likely to live in poverty if there is a grandparent present in the home. Mutigenerational households also reduce poverty rates for older adults. Multigenerational households commonly compensate for a weak welfare state.

30. Dickler, "Boomerang Kids" (see ch. 2, n. 63).

CHAPTER 5: WHEN THE NEST DOESN'T EMPTY

1. R. Krech, "Statistics Show More Seniors Are Remaining in the Workforce," AssociatedContent.com, September 22, 2007, http://www.associatedcontent.com/article/388823/statistics_show_more_seniors_are_remaining.html?cat=9.

2. See the United Nations Economic Commission for Europe, http://w3.unece.org/pxweb/dialog/varval.asp?ma=04_GEFHAge1stChild_r&path=../database/STAT/30-GE/02-Families_households/&lang=1&ti=Mean+age+of+women+at+birth+of+first+child. Mean age at first birth has gone up considerably in all countries of interest here, and countries for which data is available after 2005 show that the mean age continues to rise. The mean age at first birth for educated women is even higher.

Women's Mean Age at First Birth

Country	1980	2005
Denmark	24.6	28.4
Italy	25.1	29.6
Spain	25.5	29.3
Sweden	25.3	28.6
U.S.	22.7	25.2

Source: UN Economic Commission for Europe, UNECE Statistical Database, "Mean Age of Women at Birth of First Child," http://w3.unece.org/pxweb/dialog/varval.asp?ma=04_GEFHAge1stChild_r&path=../database/STAT/30-GE/02-Families_households/&lang=1&ti=Mean+age+of+women+at+birth+of+first+child.

3. See "Generation Gap Narrows: Parents, Kids See Eye-to-Eye on More Things," results from the Nickelodeon 2008 Family Study, conducted by Harris Interactive, November 25, 2009, at Marketing Charts.com, http://www.marketingcharts.com/topics/behavioral-marketing/generation-gap-narrows-parents-kids-see-eye-to-eye-on-more-things-11188.

4. M. Lowenthal and D. Chiriboga, "Transition to the Empty Nest: Crisis, Challenge, or Relief?," *Archives of General Psychiatry* 26 (1972): 8–14. During the baby boom, the average woman had four children. Early studies of parents' response to the empty nest indicated that the primary feeling parents had upon the exit of their last child was relief.

5. Sharon Hays, *The Cultural Contradictions of Motherhood* (New Haven, CT: Yale University Press, 1998); Annette Lareau, *Unequal Childhoods: Class, Race, and Family Life* (Berkeley: University of California Press, 2003). Hays refers to this paradox as the cultural contradiction of motherhood. Our society places value on work for income yet is currently demanding a form of intensive mothering seemingly incompatible with full-time employment. Lareau notes that patterns of parenting exhibit a class divide, with middle-class parents practicing "concerted cultivation." This parenting style involves intense scheduling and mediation of children's play and social activities. In contrast, poor and working-class parents are more likely to assume that providing for their children's needs is sufficient and that they will develop appropriately through "natural growth."

6. See Hilary Levey, *Playing for Keeps* (Berkeley: University of California Press, forthcoming).

7. According to Erikson, the mid-thirties through mid-sixties is the stage of "generativity vs. stagnation," when the work of raising young children is over and adults focus on their career development. As those in the previous stage postpone marriage and childbearing, they also postpone their parent's progression to the next stage.

8. See Kathleen Gerson, *The Unfinished Revolution: How a New Generation Is Re-shaping Family, Work, and Gender in America* (New York: Oxford University Press, 2010). Gerson's research "indicates that regardless of the structure of their family growing up, young adults state preferences for egalitarian relationships, with shared parenting and income earning, and progressive attitudes toward child rearing.

9. Jan Hoffman, "Young Obama Backers Twist Parents' Arms," *New York Times,* April 8, 2008, http://www.nytimes.com/2008/04/08/us/politics/08kids.html.

10. See S. Fruh et al., "The Surprising Benefits of the Family Meal," *Journal for Nurse Practitioners* 7 (2011): 18–22. Eating with family members has a positive impact on all involved that includes better nutrition but also other benefits, such as family closeness, a reduction in risky behavior, lowered rates of obesity, and higher job satisfaction.

11. See Michael Kimmel, *Guyland: The Perilous World Where Boys Become Men* (New York: Harper Collins, 2008). Kimmel addresses the difficulty (middle-class, straight, white) young men often have in forming intimate emotional bonds with their male peers. Instead, male bonding is often confused with the sadistic rituals of fraternity hazing or centers around activities that require little emotional investment or communication, such as drinking or playing video games. When the period of young adulthood is over, unlike women, men enter marriages without having developed intimate friendships. The father-son relationship may be one of the only opportunities fathers (and their twentysomething sons) have for genuine male bonding.

12. See Gregory J. Jurkovic et al., "Parentification of Adult Children of Divorce: A Multidimensional Analysis," *Journal of Youth and Adolescence* 30 (2001): 245–57. Children of divorced parents are at risk for what has been termed "parentification" or "adultification." This peer-like or caregiving role that children take on can persist into their actual adulthood.

13. *Return of the Multi-Generational Household* (see ch. 2, n. 8).

14. See R. Jones et al., "Adolescents' Reports of Parental Knowledge of Adolescents' Use of Sexual Health Services and Their Reactions to Mandated Parental Notification for Prescription Contraception," *Journal of the American Medical Association* 293 (2005): 340–48. Given Americans' discomfort with their children's sex lives, there is a high level of communication between American parents and children regarding contraceptive use—even in the children's teens. Sixty percent of young women obtaining prescription contraceptives have told their parents.

15. C. Carpenter and C. Dobkin, "The Effect of Alcohol Consumption on Mortality: Regression Discontinuity Evidence from the Minimum Drinking Age," *American Journal of Applied Economics* 1 (2009): 164–82; R. Hingson et al., "Age of Drinking Onset and Injuries, Motor Vehicle Crashes, and Physical Fights after Drinking and When Not Drinking," *Alcoholism: Clinical and Experimental Research* (2009): 33, 783–90; F. Lucidi et al., "Sleep-Related Car Crashes: Risk Perception and Decision-Making Processes in Young Drivers," *Accident Analysis & Prevention* 38 (2006): 302–9; J. Schwartz, "Gender Differences in Drunk Driving Prevalence Rates and Trends: A 20-Year Assessment Using Multiple Sources of Evidence," *Addictive Behaviors* 33 (2008): 1217–22. People who begin drinking at earlier ages have greater

odds of being in motor-vehicle accidents. Drinking increases substantially at age twenty-one, and there is a 9 percent increase in the mortality rate at that age, primarily due to motor-vehicle accidents. Men in their twenties are significantly more likely than women the same age to drive late at night and to engage in risky driving behavior. Men constitute about 86 percent of drunk drivers but are less likely than women to be arrested when they do drive under the influence.

16. See S. Lipka, "Helicopter Parents Help Students, Study Finds," *Chronicle of Higher Education* 54 (2007): 4. The term *helicopter parent* has been used in particular to derogate parents who continue to attempt to manage their children's academic success once the children are in college. Despite the negative connotations of the term, such parenting actually appears to facilitate college students' success and engagement.

17. See "Surprising Facts about Grandparents," Grandparents.com, http://www.grand parents.com/gp/content/opinions/from-the-editors/article/surprising-facts-about -grandparents.html. The average age to become a grandparent in the United States is forty-eight, but this statistic consists of about 47 percent of adults who have no education beyond high school. As noted elsewhere, there is an increase in age at first birth that comes with higher education—through the generations, that would also translate to older grandparenthood.

18. Kimmel, *Guyland*. Young men, particularly if white and middle class, often spend their late teens and twenties in a limbo that Kimmel refers to as Guyland. In the buddy culture of Guyland, young men drink, play videogames, watch porn and sports, have casual sex, and purchase electronic gadgets, all without taking on responsibilities such as economic independence, family formation, or investment in the future.

19. Heather Boushey, "Are Young Women Earning More Than Their Boyfriends?" *Slate*, September 7, 2010, http://www.slate.com/id/2266148/; Michael S. Rendall et al., "Increasingly Heterogeneous Ages at First Birth by Education in 'Conservative' Southern-European and 'Liberal' Anglo-American Family-Policy Regimes," RAND Working Paper, March 2009, http://www.rand.org/pubs/working_papers/2009/RAND_WR676.pdf. Studies now show that though an overall gender wage gap persists, single, childless, and educated women in their twenties now outearn their male peers in urban areas. Though half of U.S. women with low levels of education have given birth by age twenty, educated women in the United States increasingly postpone childbearing to their mid-thirties and beyond (a trend also evident in Spain and Italy).

20. *The Return of the Multi-Generational Household.*

21. See W. G. Axinn et al., "Gender Double Standards in Parenting Attitudes," *Social Science Research* 40 (2011): 417–32. Financial and sexual independence combine with gender norms in parental attitudes toward children's family formation. Though overall societal attitudes have become more egalitarian, parents, when it comes to their own children, are more likely to accept that a son will date young, have sex at a younger age, and cohabit. On the other hand, they would prefer on average that their daughters marry at a younger age and believe less strongly that

a daughter should work before marrying. Veronica's feelings about her daughter's sexual relationship, lack of interest in marriage, and financial reliance on her parents rather than a spouse may, in part, reflect this gender dichotomy.

22. See Emory Baldwin, "Housing in Response to the Human Life Cycle," in W. C. Mann, ed., *Aging, Disability and Independence: Selected Papers from the 4th International Conference on Aging, Disability and Independence* (Amsterdam: IOS Press, 2008), 1–18. Though household structure is changing, with the accordion family being a prime example, most homes are designed for "the singular needs of a romanticized nuclear family."

23. See "List of National Debt by Country," EconomicsHelp, February 7, 2011, http://www.economicshelp.org. According to the U.S. Government Accountability Office, the annual deficit reached $1.4 trillion in 2009, while the national debt had exceeded $14 trillion by the start of 2011. For the countries addressed in this book, the national debt as of 2008 was an estimated 38.1 percent of Danish GDP, 115 percent of Italian GDP, 192 percent of Japanese GDP, 59.5 percent of Spanish GDP, 43.2 percent of Swedish GDP, and 90.8 percent of U.S. GDP. National debt is already highest in the countries with the weakest welfare states, which also tend to be the countries most focused on cutting government budgets.

24. See Richard Lloyd Parry, "A Nation Lives in Fear of the Neets and Freeters," *Times of London,* November 2, 2006, http://business.timesonline.co.uk/tol/business/markets/japan/article622158.ece. Credit Suisse Group estimates that under-employed young adults could eventually saddle Japan's taxpayers with $67 billion a year in retirement and health-care costs if they do not find full-time, steady employment.

25. As an example of Alonzo's concern, a retirement savings balance of just $1,000 at age twenty will yield $1,100 of monthly retirement income at age sixty-five, taking into account inflation and taxes. The same balance at age forty will yield $385. It would take a starting balance of nearly $50,000 at age forty to have the same yield as $1,000 at age twenty (estimates generated from the Retirement Savings Calculator at the Massachusetts Mutual Life Insurance Co. website, www.massmutual .com).

26. Anthony Faiola, "Sick of Their Husbands in Graying Japan: Stress Disorder Diagnosed in Many Women after Spouses Retire," *Washington Post,* October 17, 2005, http://www.washingtonpost.com/wp-dyn/content/article/2005/10/16/AR2005101601145.html.

CHAPTER 6: TROUBLE IN PARADISE

1. Inequality is often measured through the Gini coefficient. At zero, the Gini coefficient reflects complete equality (all citizens would have equal resources); at one hundred, complete inequality (one person would have all resources). The highest Gini coefficients (in the forty-to-sixty range) are predominantly in the global South (Africa and South America).

   Only Spain and Sweden did not increase their levels of inequality from the previous decade.

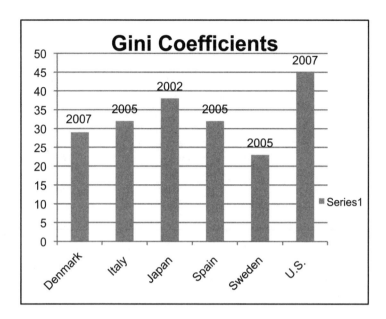

2. See P. Pierson, "Three Worlds of Welfare State Research," *Comparative Political Studies* 33 (2000): 791–821. The nature of the welfare state strongly impacts gender equality, as the division of labor in society is not just between state and market but also includes the household. State policy often determines a woman's degree of dependence on a male breadwinner. The degree to which caregiving is provided by independent families rather than supported by the state is central to women's access to paid employment.

3. P. Hall and K. Thelan, "Institutional Change in Varieties of Capitalism," *Socioeconomic Review* 7 (2009): 7–34. Though Sweden and the United States developed social welfare policies at roughly the same time, the structures of the systems were very different, based in part on institutional structures in other spheres of the political economy. For instance, because Sweden's centralized bargaining system limited wage competition, employers competed for skilled workers through offering competitive pension plans. As the costs of these plans rose, employers were happy to transfer the costs to the state and thus advocated for generous public pensions.

4. More than 4 percent of GDP was spent on family benefits (cash and services) in 2004, in comparison to about 3.5 percent three years later.

5. T. Iversen and D. Soskice, "Distribution and Redistribution: The Shadow of the Nineteenth Century," *World Politics* 61 (2009): 438–86. Redistribution is strongly tied to political systems. Scandinavia's system of proportional representation ini-

tially promoted redistribution and insurance through a center-left alliance of social democrats and independent peasants. In majoritarian systems, left-of-center candidates have to appeal to more centrist and conservative voters, which ultimately makes for lower redistribution.

6. T. Iverson and F. Rosenbluth, "Work and Power: The Connection between Female Labor Force Participation and Female Political Representation," *Annual Review of Political Science* 11 (2008): 479–95. Such policies are particularly important in ensuring adequate political representation for women. Their participation in the labor force both imbues women with the skills they need for holding political office and helps voters see women as having these competencies. In addition, family-friendly policies that apply to both genders place fewer limits on mothers, often hurt politically by career interruptions to have children, particularly in nations that have candidate-centered political systems (rather than proportional-representation systems).

7. See Pierson, "Three Worlds." The welfare state can clearly reveal the impact of political choices. Variations in public benefits make substantial contributions to the cross-national differences evident in areas such as income inequality, women's participation in labor, and degrees of unionization. Despite increasing globalization, the welfare state retains a nation-based character. Pierson writes, "Social democratic welfare states wrestle with fiscal overload, Christian democratic regimes with mounting unemployment, and liberal ones with worsening wage inequality and high poverty rates."

8. Christoffer Green-Pedersen, "Still There, but for How Long? The Counter-Intuitiveness of the Universal Welfare Model and the Development of the Universal Welfare State in Denmark," Ministère du Travail, de l'Emploi, et de la Santé (France), http://www.sante-sports.gouv.fr/IMG/pdf/rfas200304-art04-uk.pdf. Welfare systems in Nordic countries such as Denmark are characterized by "universalism," meaning that the entire population is provided with benefits adequate to meet their needs. Even under a policy of "permanent austerity," instituted in the mid-1990s and designed to control costs of such generous benefits, many of Denmark's benefits have continued to expand. Factions from the right and left in Denmark both support welfare policies. The Left likes that they benefit the poor and sometimes suggests means testing as a cost-saving measure, but the Right values that welfare benefits the rich as well as the poor and feels that Denmark's universalistic policies do not discourage taking jobs or saving for retirement.

9. Most twenty- to twenty-four-year-old Swedish non-students are in steady jobs. To judge by the 8 percent unemployment rate, nearly all the remainder have access to temporary and part-time work that allows them to experiment with what they would like to do on a more permanent basis. Still, it may not be much of a consolation to know that youth employment is better in Sweden than almost anywhere else.

10. Cook and Furstenberg, "Explaining Aspects" (see ch. 2, n. 21).

11. See Thomas Bunk, "Unemployment High among Young People in Sweden," Eurofound, 2009, http://www.eurofound.europa.eu/eiro/2008/11/articles/se0811019i.htm; "Youth Unemployment," Ekinomofacta, http://www.ekonomifakta.se/en/Facts-and-figures/The-Labour-market/Unemployment/Youth-unemployment-/.

12. See "Factsheet on Unemployment in Sweden," Youth Partnership, Council of Europe European Comission, http://youth-partnership-eu.coe.int/youth-partnership/documents/Questionnaires/Employment/Sweden.pdf. In 2006, the share of youth ages twenty to twenty-four with a high school education not in education, employment, or training was 7.2 percent. That same figure for those with low education was 31.1 percent.

13. Peter A. Hall, "Re-forming Capitalism," faculty website, 2009, http://www.people.fas.harvard.edu/~phall/EJS%202009.pdf. In this paper, Peter Hall posits that neoliberal policies initiated by Ronald Reagan and Margaret Thatcher ultimately led to the unbridled competition that resulted in a global recession thirty years later. After heavy reliance on markets, more citizens are now looking for states to regulate and distribute resources.

14. As of mid-1998, child allowances had returned to their nominal high of a few years earlier (only slightly below the real high) and were worth about 7.5 percent of average manufacturing wages. The supplementary benefit for larger families was reinstated, benefit replacement rates had been increased to 80 percent of prior wages, the block grants to municipalities for social services including child care were close to the high level of the earlier 1990s, the budget was in surplus, and the surplus was projected to be even larger for the next year. By 2001, child allowances were above their earlier real high, 950 kroner for each of the first two children and still higher for subsequent children. The benefit was raised again several years later.

15. See "Higher Education and Research in Sweden," Swedish Institute, 2007, http://www.si.se. In the 2004–2005 academic year, 45.6 percent of young Swedes entered a university or college. Study grants and loans are available to everyone, with loans comprising about 72 percent of the total.

16. See the Swedish Institute, http://www.si.se/English/.

17. Folk high schools are adult-education institutions that generally do not grant academic degrees though might offer certain courses that lead to that goal.

18. See "Swedish Student Aid: CSN Information Leaflet 2010," Centrala studiestödsnämnden (CSN) (Sweden), http://service.csn.se/CSNOrder/GemensammaFiler/Blanketter/2130E.pdf.

19. See following web pages of CSN: http://web.archive.org/web/20070928114901/http://csn.se/Avdelningar/Studerande/HogskolaOchUniversitet/Studiemedel/StudiemedlensStorlek/StudiemedlensStorlek.asp?MenyIdnr=507 and http://web.archive.org/web/20070928114855/http://csn.se/English/Students/ThisIsHowMuchStudentAidYouCanReceive/TheTotalAmountIsTheSumOfTheGrantAndLoan.asp?MenyIdnr=1016.

20. Cook and Furstenberg, "Explaining Aspects."

21. See "Housing Allowance [Bostadsbidrag] for Young People without Children [Bostadsbidrag till unga utan barn]," Försäkringskassan, 2008, http://www.forsakringskassan.se/irj/go/km/docs/fk_publishing/Dokument/Publikationer/Faktablad/Andra_sprak/Engelska/bob_unga_eng.pdf. Applications are made on the basis of the income that applicants expect to have during the calendar year. If the income turns out to be higher, applicants may have to reimburse the government. If income turns out to be lower, the recipient may receive more allowance in arrears.

Applicants can receive at most 1,100 kroner per month in housing allowance:they can receive allowance for housing costs that exceed 1,800 kroner per month; they cannot receive allowance for costs exceeding 3,600 kroner per month;they cannot receive allowance for more than 60 square meters; they can receive allowance if their income exceeds 77,000 kroner per year. Spouses and partners cannot receive allowance if their combined income is higher than 94,000 kroner per year.

22. In the mid-1990s, 32 percent of Swedish women and 27 percent of Danish women between the ages of twenty and thirty-nine were living with a partner. In Southern Europe, less than 10 percent of the women in this age group were living with a partner; in Italy, only 2 percent were. Countries in the intermediate category show figures ranging from 8 to 18 percent, with France, the Netherlands, Austria, and Switzerland at the high end, and Belgium, the United Kingdom, and Germany at the low end. Where cohabitation is well established, a person's first union is almost always a cohabiting union. Very few Swedes start their first partnership as a married one.

23. See K. Kiernan, "European Perspectives on Union Formation," in L. J. Waite et al., eds., *The Ties That Bind: Perspectives on Marriage and Cohabitation* (New York: Aldine de Gruyter, 2000), 40–58. Data from the 1992 Swedish Family Survey show that only 2 to 3 percent of forty-three-year-old women and about 5 percent of forty-three-year-old men had never formed a relationship with a partner. Kiernan finds that younger cohorts of cohabiting Swedish women show slower rates of entry into marriage and a higher likelihood of having their first union dissolved after two to five years.

24. See A. Duvander, "Why Do Swedish Cohabitants Marry?" (licentiate thesis, Stockholm University, 1998); M. Bracher and G. Santow, "Economic Independence and Union Formation in Sweden," *Population Studies* 52 (1998): 275–94.

25. S. Jayson, "Out-of-Wedlock Births on the Rise Worldwide," *USA Today*, May 13, 2009.

26. See National Center for Health Statistics, European Commission, http://ec.europa.eu/research/social sciences/projects/310_en.html.

27. See Andrew J. Cherlin, *The Marriage-Go-Round: The State of Marriage and the Family in America Today* (New York: Knopf, 2009).

28. Ibid.

CHAPTER 7: THE BIRTH DEARTH AND THE "IMMIGRANT MENACE"

1. David McNeill and Chie Matsumoto, "Fertility Crisis in Japan: Let the State Find You a Mate," *Independent* (UK), November 10, 2009, http://www.independent.co.uk/news/world/asia/fertility-crisis-in-japan-let-the-state-find-you-a-mate-1817736.html.

2. "Birth Dearth Can Turn Japan into a Nation of Ancients," Buzzle.com, February 3, 2002, http://www.buzzle.com/editorials/2-3-2002-9992.asp.

3. Ibid.

4. In Japan's South and the Islands, which are much poorer and where opportunity for employment is far more limited, migration represented only 2.1 percent of the total population.

5. See "Vital Statistics: Provisional Data, 2008," Instituto Nacional de Estadística (Spain), http://www.ine.es/en/prensa/np552_en.pdf. The total number of births to foreign mothers reached 107,475, with an increase of 15 percent over the previous year. Moroccan women had the most children, representing 23.5 percent of the total births to foreign mothers.

6. See Google.com Public Data (source: World Bank, World Development Indicators, 2011), www.google.com/publicdata?ds=wbwdi&met=sp_dyn_tfrt_in&idim=count ry:ITA&dl=en&hl=en&q=fertility+rates+in+italy. As of 2008, the fertility rate in Spain was 1.461 births per mother. As of 2008, the fertility rate in Italy was 1.41.

7. Minnesotans for Sustainability, http://www.mnforsustain.org/social_security _dependency_ratio_fair.htm.

8. Sarah Geraghty, "The Birth Dearth in the U.S. and the EU: Are Socio-Cultural Steps a Better Remedy than Immigration?" European Institute, http://www.european institute.org/August-September-2010/the-birth-dearth-in-the-us-and-the-eu-are -socio-cultural-steps-a-better-remedy-than-immigration.html.

9. Gretchen Livingston and D'Vera Cohn, "The New Demography of American Motherhood," *Social & Demographic Trends,* August 19, 2010, http://pewresearch .org/pubs/1586/changing-demographic-characteristics-american-mothers.

10. Minnesotans for Sustainability. But for how long will this be the case? The course of the Great Recession of 2008–10 may shift the outcome: immigration to the United States, especially from Mexico, has declined sharply. Yet we need that flow, both to fill the jobs that the native born will not accept and to shore up Social Security. Suzy Khimm, "Could Immigrants Help the U.S. by Having More Babies?" *Mother Jones,* August 12, 2010, http://motherjones.com/mojo/2010/08/immigrant-fertility -birthright-citizenship.

11. There are yet other alternatives. Swedish history offers an interesting example of a country that took a different path. Labor shortages that emerged in the 1960s led the country to look for ways to intensify women's commitment to the labor market and avoid leaning on migration to solve their problems. It did so by bankrolling expensive social policies that made it far more likely that women would fill the jobs for employers going begging. Maternity leave was broadened to include men in the form of parental leave. As a consequence, "female employment shot up from 48% in 1970 to 80% in 1986, effectively consigning the male breadwinner model to history"; see Geraghty. And they did not stop there:

>   By the early 1990s, [Sweden] had already gone further than many countries have even now in relieving the burden of working mothers: children had access to subsidized preschools from 12 months; grandparents were offered state-sponsored elderly care; the parent on leave got almost a full salary for a year before returning to a guaranteed job, and both parents could work six-hour days until children started school.

>   Now new laws—which are arriving on the heels of longer-term social changes in this sector—now require that at least two months of the well-paid, 13-month parental leave be reserved exclusively for fathers. Now eight in ten fathers take a third of the total leave—up four percent from a decade ago. The

figure reflects profound changes in socio-cultural attitudes in Sweden that seem remote in most other countries.

The overarching Swedish goal has long been to provide families with enough support that a U.S.-style "choice" between family and work does not have to be made. And it works: Sweden has a birth rate of around 1.8 children per woman—among the highest in Europe—along with female employment levels (72 per cent) among the highest in the world. (Geraghty)

12. See *Public Education Finances 2008,* U.S. Census Bureau, June 2010, http://www2 .census.gov/govs/school/08f33pub.pdf; "Just the Facts: Immigrants in California," Public Policy Institute of California, ppic.org, June 2008, http://www.ppic.org/ content/pubs/jtf/JTF_ImmigrantsJTF.pdf. In 1978, California voters passed Proposition 13, which limited property tax increases. As a result, fewer funds for public education were available. California absorbs high numbers of immigrants (one in four residents was an immigrant in 2008), and the declining fortunes of the schools, which serve many immigrant students, helped fuel Proposition 187, also known as SOS (Save Our State). The referendum, which passed in 1994, included prohibitions against social services for immigrants, including specific provisions to prevent children who were illegal immigrants from attending school. The law was challenged, and the state stopped its appeals in 1999; however, high antipathy for immigrants remains. In 2008, California was behind the national average in public-school spending.

13. Although widely rumored to be a vicious attack by a Muslim offended by Fortuyn's own intemperate attacks on their community, in fact he was murdered by Volkert van der Graff, a self-described animal rights activist and environmental extremist who claimed he assassinated Fortuyn in order to "protect weaker groups in society."

14. Christopher Caldwell, "A Swedish Dilemma," *Weekly Standard,* February 28, 2005, http://www.weeklystandard.com/Content/Public/Articles/000/000/005/271dgkju .asp?page=4.

15. Ibid.

16. "Italian Town Dreaming of a White Christmas," *Telegraph* (UK), November 19, 2009, http://www.telegraph.co.uk/news/worldnews/europe/italy/6602625/Italian -town-dreaming-of-a-White-Christmas.html.

17. Michael Slackman, "With Words on Muslims, Opening a Door Long Shut," *New York Times,* November 12, 2010, http://www.nytimes.com/2010/11/13/world/ europe/13sarrazin.html.

18. Caldwell, "A Swedish Dilemma."

19. Ibid.

20. See Michèle Lamont, *Money, Morals, and Manners: The Culture of the French and the American Upper-Middle Class* (Chicago: University of Chicago Press, 1992). In her study of the elite in France and the United States, Lamont points out that "subjective, symbolic boundaries . . . frame, channel and limit people's lives." Cultural differences are an essential component of stratification systems, and the upper classes most often value moral, economic, and cultural traits and characteristics typical of those like them. Thus it can be hard to integrate those who come from different cultures, even if those in the host culture purport to be open-minded.

21. See Thomas Liebig, "The Labour Market Integration of Immigrants in Denmark," Organisation for Economic Co-operation and Development, March 5, 2007, http://www.oecd.org/dataoecd/8/28/38195773.pdf. Though Denmark has a low immigrant population in comparison with many other European nations (less than 7 percent of the population), there is still widespread concern over the role of immigrants in Danish society. Both disadvantage and discrimination prevail and persist across generations. Educational attainment of second-generation immigrants is far below that of native Danes, but those immigrants with higher levels of Danish education and training still fare poorly in the labor market. In response to rising immigration, Denmark instituted residency requirements for welfare in 2001. Those who have not resided in the country for seven of the previous eight years receive lower benefits.

CONCLUSION

1. Scott Waldman, "Full Mind, Empty Pockets," *Times Union* (Albany, NY), November 28, 2010, http://www.timesunion.com/local/article/Full-mind-empty-pockets-662274.php.

American youth: benefits of living at
home for, 65–69; case of entitlement
in, 11–12; path to adulthood, 3–5,
9–10, 11; sense of entitlement in, 11;
understanding of adulthood, 5, 9,
12–13
anti-immigration sentiment, 179–89
Arizona, anti-immigrant sentiment in,
179–80
Arnett, Jeffrey Jensen, 23
Asian parents, 33
Asia Times, 11
assimilation, immigrant, 183, 185–86, 187,
201, 213–14n30
Astore, Stefano, 192
asylum-seekers, 184, 186
Athens, riots in (2010), 196
attitudes toward accordion families. *See*
accordion families, attitudes toward
Austria, 51, 180, 240n22
autonomy: balancing closeness to
parent with, 67; impact on parent-
adult relationships, 161–62; of
Italian youth, 6; parent-child, 147–
48; parents not allowing, 73–
74; prioritizing or sacrificing, 44,
122. *See also* independence
Azarian, Kate, 9–10, 21–22

baby-boomer parents: being cared for
by their children, 201–2; compared
with postwar parents, 127; delaying
aging, 129–30, 131–32; delaying
grandparenthood, 129, 130, 139–41;
relationships with their parents,
130–31; retirement savings and,
148–50; social changes experienced
by, 150–51
baby-boom generation: compared with
millennials, 63–64; compared
with postwar parents, 128–29;
cultural connection with millennial
generation, 128; economic
growth during youth of, 44; on
intergenerational differences in

Spain, 23–28; older vs. younger, xx–
xxi; on path to adulthood, 15–16. *See
also* baby-boomer parents
banlieu, 191
bar/bat mitzvah, 207n1
Belgium, 51
Belova, Vladimir, 201–2
Berlusconi, Silvio, x
birth-control pill, 64–65, 226–27n4
birth dearth, 61; causes of, 54–55, 177;
expenses of childrearing and,
176–77; immigrant births and, 176;
in Japan, 175; pension problem and,
178–80. *See also* fertility rates
blue-collar working-class families, xvii–
xviii. *See also* working-class families
"boomerang" adults, xxi, 42, 115
brain development, 23
Bra, Italy, ix
Brunetta, Renato, x
budget cuts, European government, 180,
195–96
Bulgaria, 178

Calatrava, Agata, 25–26
Caldwell, Christopher, 184, 186
Caldwell, Lisa, 3–5
Campos, Julia, 111–12
career: genders converging on
importance of, 4–5
caregiving work, 214n2, 215n3
Cherlin, Andrew, 169–70
child allowances, 154, 158, 239n14
child bearing: average age for first birth,
233; delaying or not choosing, 178;
among immigrants, 176; in Italy, 231–
32n25; out-of-wedlock, 159–60, 170.
See also birth dearth; fertility rates;
parenthood
China, 156; parenting in, 213n29
Clark University, 23
class differences: in entering parenthood,
210–11n13; housing options for youth
and, 52–53; markers of adulthood
and, 208–9n5; self-actualization and,

Helsinki, 40

Henig, Robin, 22–23

Higher-education: globalization and, 40; jobs and people without, 180–81; saving money for, 40; student housing and, 51–52, 158–59; in Sweden, 158; wage effects of, 209n8; of women, 209–10n9

higher-education costs: financial aid for, 158; in Great Britain, 195–96; increase in, 220n62; spending retirement savings on, 148–49; and student loan debt in the U.S., 4, 199; in the U.S., 195

hikkimori (shut-ins), 81, 83

Hillerod, Denmark, 165

Hitachi, xiv

home ownership: in Europe, 50; parents helping with purchase of, 210n12; in the U.S., 50–51

Honda, xiii

household responsibilities, of adult children, 64, 70

housing: family wealth and, 52–53; in Nordic countries, 17, 49, 158–59; reliance on owner-occupied, 106–7; of Swedish students, 158–59; in the U.S., 42, 199. *See also* rental housing; student housing

housing allowances: in European countries, 52; GI Bill, 50; in Nordic countries, 40, 49, 159; in Sweden, 239–40n21

housing costs: as factor for accordion families, 35, 49–51; increase in, growth of accordion families and, 39; in Spain, 27, 49, 106–7, 111, 112; in the U.S., 50–51; for youth in European countries, 49–50

immigrants: African, 185; assimilation of, as role of state, 187–88; birth rates among, 176; as cure for aging population, 61; in Denmark, 243n21; filling in for population loss, 178, 179; in Italy, 176; in Japan, 175; jobs going to, 180–81; needed for labor market, 200–201; in Newton, Massachusetts, xv; parent-child relationships among, 33–34; parents keeping salary of, 115–16; pension problem and, 178–80; relationship between accordion families and, 176; repeal of Fourteenth Amendment and, 179–80; unemployment of, 189–90; U.S. population growth and, 58, 178, 200

immigrants, attitudes toward: education and, 191–92; in Germany, 185–86; in Italy, 185; in Nordic countries, 182–84, 186–92, 198; in Spain, 180–81, 182, 192; in the U.S., 179–80

income. *See* wages

independence, xviii; as deviant in Italy, 98–99; gender differences in, 142–43; of Italian adult children, 101; in Japanese families, 91–92; in Spain, 24–27; structural barriers to, xix–xx; valued over emotional ties, 171; valued over material goods, 44; youth evaluating one another based on, 75. *See also* autonomy; residential independence

India, 45, 156

individualism, 164–65

individuality, in Japan, 3

in-house adulthood: adult romantic relationships and, 75–77; avoiding battles in, 73–74; benefits and pleasures of, 64–71; for middle-class families, 63–64; parents' boundary rules for, 71–75; for working-class families, 63. *See also* adult children living at home

in-migration, 61

Ireland, education in, 51

irregular workers, in Japan, xiv–xv

Islam, attack on, 184

Italian parents: attitudes toward accordion family, 98, 100–102;

working-age adults to retirees in, 60; rental vs. owner-occupied housing in, 106–7; Roman Catholic Church in, 109; short-term jobs, 48; student housing in, 51, 52; students living away from home in, 52; women's mean age at first birth in, 233

Spanish Civil War (1936–39), 108

Spanish parents, xxii; adjustments to accordion families, 143–146; attitude toward delayed departure by, 114, 124; on grandparenthood, 140; on intergenerational differences, 23–28; on transition to adulthood, 16

Spanish Socialist Workers' Party, 212n22

Spanish youth: adulthood defined by, 12, 13; attitudes toward accordion families, 110–14; on living with one's parents, 23–24; political activity of, 107–8, 109–10

Stack, Carol, 63

standard of living: cultural shifts in, 55–56; cultural values and, 44; preferred over independence, xxi, 56

status transitions, 2, 5. *See also* adulthood, markers of

"stem families," 55

Stockholm, 40

"storm and stress" during adolescence, 210n11, 227n6

structural forces: education, 51–52; family income and wealth, 52–53; globalization, 45–49; individual acts changing, 230n13; in Italy, 100; in Japan, 97; preventing residential independence, xix–xxi; relationship between cultural values and, 44–45; in Spain, 113–14. *See also* economy/economics; employment; globalization

student housing: differences in European, 51–52; in Northern Europe, 49; in Sweden, 51, 52, 158; in the U.S., 52

student loan debt, 4, 199

subsidized housing, 49

Supreme Commander of Allied Powers, 86

Suto, Akiro, xii, xv

Sweden: attitude toward immigrants in, 186–87; child bearing in, 159–60; cohabitation in, 211–12n21, 232n28, 240n22; divorce rates in, 230; education in, 220n53; fertility rates in, 58; gender equity in, 155; higher education in, 158; immigration into, 186; impact of globalization on, 153–54; median age of first marriage in, 225n81; money spent on social protection in, 154; national debt in, 236n23; percentage of adults living with parents in, 41; percentage of students in 20–29 age group, 18; ratio of working-age adults to retirees in, 60; unemployment benefits in, 157–58; unemployment in, 157, 217; women's mean age at first birth in, 233. *See also* Nordic countries

Swedish youth: living independently, 36, 40, 51–52; social policy supporting, 154; student housing for, 51, 52, 158–59; understanding of adulthood by, 20–21

Tang, Lucy, 132

Telefónica, Spain, 105, 106

temporary employment, 47, 48

Termina, Alberto, ix, xi, xxi

Termina, Giorgio, x

Termina, Giovanni, ix, xi, xxi, 5–6

Termina, Laura, x

Termina, Maria, ix, xi, xxi

Tessiore, Marina, 176

Tjelden, Mathilda, 164

Tokyo, xi

Tortolli, Angela, 102

tourist industry, American, 38

Toyota, xiii

training/work study programs, 158